Ideas of Power

This groundbreaking book challenges the dominant view of ideology held by both political scientists and political commentators. Rather than viewing ideological constructs like liberalism and conservatism as static concepts with fixed and enduring content, Professor Verlan Lewis explains how the very meanings of liberalism and conservatism frequently change along with the ideologies of the two major parties in American politics. Testing a new theory to help explain why party ideologies evolve the way that they do, this book traces the history of American political parties from the Hamiltonian Federalists and Jeffersonian Republicans of the 1790s to the liberal Democrats and conservative Republicans of today. *Ideas of Power* shows us how changing party control of government institutions, such as Congress, the presidency, and the Supreme Court, influences how party ideologies develop.

Verlan Lewis is a postdoctoral scholar in the Department of Political Science at Stanford University. His research focuses on how political institutions and ideas interact over time, and his work has appeared in a variety of publications, including *Studies in American Political Development*, *Presidential Studies Quarterly*, *The Forum*, and *The Washington Post*.

Ideas of Power

The Politics of American Party Ideology Development

VERLAN LEWIS

Stanford University

CAMBRIDGE
UNIVERSITY PRESS

CAMBRIDGE
UNIVERSITY PRESS

University Printing House, Cambridge CB2 8BS, United Kingdom

One Liberty Plaza, 20th Floor, New York, NY 10006, USA

477 Williamstown Road, Port Melbourne, VIC 3207, Australia

314–321, 3rd Floor, Plot 3, Splendor Forum, Jasola District Centre,
New Delhi – 110025, India

79 Anson Road, #06–04/06, Singapore 079906

Cambridge University Press is part of the University of Cambridge.

It furthers the University's mission by disseminating knowledge in the pursuit of
education, learning, and research at the highest international levels of excellence.

www.cambridge.org
Information on this title: www.cambridge.org/9781108476799
DOI: 10.1017/9781108568852

First published 2019

A catalogue record for this publication is available from the British Library.

Library of Congress Cataloging-in-Publication Data
NAMES: Lewis, Verlan, author.
TITLE: Ideas of power : the politics of American party ideology development /
Verlan Lewis.
DESCRIPTION: Cambridge, United Kingdom ; New York, NY : Cambridge University
Press, 2019. | Includes bibliographical references and index.
IDENTIFIERS: LCCN 2018050806| ISBN 9781108476799 (hardback : alk. paper) |
ISBN 9781108701549 (pbk. : alk. paper)
SUBJECTS: LCSH: Political parties–United States–History. | Ideology–United States. |
United States–Politics and government.
CLASSIFICATION: LCC JK2261 .L49 2019 | DDC 324.273/13–DC23
LC record available at https://lccn.loc.gov/2018050806

ISBN 978-1-108-47679-9 Hardback
ISBN 978-1-108-70154-9 Paperback

For Katherine

Contents

Figures

Tables

Preface

This book tells the story of American party ideologies by chronicling the ideas and rhetoric articulated by the two major parties throughout US history: from the Federalists and Republicans of the late eighteenth century, to the Whigs and Democrats of the mid-nineteenth century, to the Republicans and Democrats of today. Unlike most scholars of American party ideologies, I emphasize how they have changed over time rather than how they have stayed the same. One of the reasons that political scientists tend to overlook party ideology evolution is because the dominant paradigm of their discipline rests on the assumption that political ideologies like "liberalism" and "conservatism" ("left" and "right") have fixed and enduring meanings. Thus, in this mistaken view, as long as one party has always been "liberal" and another party has always been "conservative," we can conclude that the ideologies of the two major parties must have been relatively fixed and static over the course of American history.

The first main contribution of the book is to show why we are mistaken when we conceptualize ideology in this way. Once we recognize that the meaning and content of ideological constructs like "liberalism" and "conservatism" are subject to dramatic change over time, we can recognize that the ideologies espoused by the Democratic and Republican Parties are likewise subject to significant change even if one is always "liberal" and the other is always "conservative." After establishing the fact that party ideologies can, and do, evolve in important ways, we face the question of what explains the ideological transformations we observe. While some political scientists have written about the *economics* or *psychology* or *sociology* of American party ideology development, ironically, few have examined the *politics* of this phenomenon (Gerring 1998, 257–275).

The second main contribution of this book is to show how a political factor – party control of government institutions – also helps explain the evolution of American party ideologies. The influence of changing party control of government institutions is examined across three domains of party ideology: economic policy, foreign policy, and judicial policy. To do this, I use both direct and indirect measures of ideology.

We can measure party ideology *directly* by analyzing the language espoused by partisans. After all, party ideology exists in language: in "thinking, speech, and writing" (Elkins and McKitrick 1993, 13). To directly measure ideology, I read every party platform published in American history, and took note of every sentence dealing with economic policy, foreign policy, and judicial policy. I also examined the speeches and writings of party leaders like presidents, members of Congress, and presidential candidates. To quantify the ideological content of party platforms, I relied on the coding decisions made by researchers contributing to the Manifesto Project Dataset. An analysis of party rhetoric demonstrates that the two parties have changed their ideologies significantly over the course of American history, and that the meanings of "liberalism" and "conservatism" have similarly changed.

We can measure party ideology *indirectly* by analyzing the behavior of partisans that we have reason to believe are influenced by party ideology. To do this, I examined the roll call votes cast by members of Congress, the political decisions made by presidents, and the survey responses given by ordinary party identifiers. To the extent that we believe party ideology influences the roll call votes cast, the political decisions made, and the survey responses given, these can be indirect, or proxy, measures of party ideology. These supplementary measures of party ideology confirm the finding that "liberalism," "conservatism," Democratic Party ideology, and Republican Party ideology have all changed significantly over time.

"IDEAS OF POWER"

The title of this book, "Ideas of Power," has three different meanings. First, it refers to the fact that the two major parties' ideologies are *powerful ideas*. As this book shows, even though they are often in flux, party ideologies are not mere rhetoric. They are mental frameworks and linguistic structures that shape the way Americans think about politics, talk about politics, and act in politics – for better or for worse. Given the force that they have in determining political outcomes, despite their evolutionary character, ideas are some of the most important things for political scientists to study (Goldstein and Keohane 1993, R. Smith 1995, Ceaser 2006, Rodrik 2014).

Second, I use the title "Ideas of Power" because this book focuses on certain kinds of ideas: namely, *ideas about power* and who should or should not wield it. Ideologies are vast and expansive mental frameworks and language structures that hold together many different ideas (e.g., issue positions, ideas about the ends of politics, social attitudes, ideas about the appropriate distribution of economic goods, religious values, ideas about the relationships between groups in society, theories of historical progress, and ideas about justice). While I will, of course, touch on many of these aspects of party ideologies, in the finite space of this book I will focus on describing the two major parties' evolving ideas about how power should be distributed among different government institutions and how much power the US government should exercise in American society and the world. Specifically, the three empirical chapters of this book examine party theories of presidential power and foreign intervention, theories of national government power and economic intervention, and theories of judicial power and judicial intervention.

Third, and finally, "Ideas of Power" refers to one of the important factors determining the content of party ideologies: *exercising power* in government. I argue that changing party control of government helps drive changes in party ideology over time. This theory is tested across three branches of government (the presidency, Congress, and the Supreme Court) and three policy areas (foreign policy, economic policy, and judicial policy). I chose these policy domains both because they are useful tests of the proposed theory about how party ideology develops and because I believe they are of general interest to most people. The two major parties' dominant ideas about economic policy, foreign policy, and judicial policy have enormous consequences for American politics and the world more broadly.

OUTLINE OF THE BOOK

In Chapter 1 I demonstrate the dynamic character of American party ideologies, and I show why this is an important corrective to the static view currently dominant among political scientists. With the evolutionary character of party ideologies established, the rest of the book examines the question that necessarily follows: What causes the changes in party ideologies that we observe?

Chapter 2 proposes a new political institutional theory of when and why party ideologies change. I argue that whichever party controls government is likely to exercise and expand the powers at their disposal. When they do this, they face incentives to change their ideology in ways that justify this behavior. Likewise, whichever party is in opposition faces incentives to change their ideology in ways that criticize this behavior. As a result, changes in control of government institutions can lead to enduring changes in party ideologies.

Chapters 3–5 then test this theory in three different ways. Chapter 3 shows how changes in party control of the presidency have shaped changes in party ideas about executive power and foreign intervention. In this chapter, I look at the ideologies of the two parties in every presidential administration from Theodore Roosevelt to the present. Chapter 4 shows how changes in party control of unified government have shaped changes in party ideas about national government power and economic intervention. This analysis covers every era in American history – from the Hamiltonian Federalists and the Jeffersonian Republicans of the 1790s to the liberal Democrats and conservative Republicans of today. Finally, Chapter 5 shows how changes in party control of the Supreme Court have shaped changes in party ideas about judicial power and judicial intervention. I examine each of the five periods of party control of the Supreme Court in American history: Federalist Party control at the turn of the nineteenth century, Democratic Party control in the mid-nineteenth century, Republican Party control at the turn of the twentieth century, return to Democratic Party control in the mid-twentieth century, and return to Republican Party control at the turn of the twenty-first century.

Chapter 6 concludes by summarizing the findings of the three empirical chapters and reminding us of the two main contributions of the book. I also reflect on the blind spots in the political science discipline that have prevented us from seeing these things before and suggest directions for future research.

Acknowledgments

Many people, too numerous to thank, have played an important role in bringing this book to fruition, but I would like to briefly mention just a few. First, I am grateful to my parents for instilling in me from a young age an interest in ideas and the history of ideas. Second, I am deeply indebted to my academic mentors at Cambridge, Virginia, and Stanford. Anyone familiar with the scholarly work of James Ceaser, Hyrum Lewis, Terry Moe, Sidney Milkis, and John Aldrich will recognize the influence of their ideas on this book. In particular, I would like to thank Jim Ceaser, who gave me every opportunity to succeed during the five years I was his PhD student in Charlottesville and showed me unfailing kindness and generosity. In Palo Alto, Terry Moe and Hyrum Lewis constantly encouraged me to publish this book even when I had my doubts. Third, I am very grateful to the participants at our annual American Political Science Association panels on parties and ideologies in American politics. In particular, I thank Frances Lee, Rogers Smith, Hans Noel, Richard Bensel, and David Karol for believing in my project and offering useful criticisms and feedback. I should also mention the kindness shown to me by Morris Fiorina and Paul Pierson in taking the time to discuss this book project with me. Fourth, I am truly grateful to the various organizations that have given financial support and given me the time to write this book, including the Department of Political Science at Stanford University and the Center for the Study of Government and the Individual at the University of Colorado in Colorado Springs. Fifth, I would like to express great thanks to Cambridge University Press for their editorial support in bringing this book to publication. Finally, I am forever grateful to my wife, Katherine. Without her, this book would have never been started or finished.

The Liberal Conservative Myth and Political Science

I remember once being much amused at seeing two partially intoxicated men engage in a fight with their great-coats on, which fight, after a long, and rather harmless contest, ended in each having fought himself out of his own coat, and into that of the other. If the two leading parties of this day are really identical with the two in the days of Jefferson and Adams, they have performed about the same feat as the two drunken men.

–Abraham Lincoln, April 6, 1859

I INTRODUCTION

On the eve of the American Civil War, a committee of Boston Republicans sent a letter to Abraham Lincoln inviting him to speak at an upcoming celebration in honor of Thomas Jefferson's birthday. In his reply, Lincoln noted the irony of this situation given that Lincoln's newly formed Republican Party supposedly descended from the Federalist Party of John Adams, whose greatest strength had been in Boston and the Northeast, and their Democratic opponents supposedly descended from the Jeffersonian Party, whose greatest strength had been in the South. Lincoln then went on to relate the parable quoted above.

What Lincoln wisely noticed, but what many partisans and ideologues tend to forget, is that party positions and ideologies often switch places over time. Many partisans are embarrassed by party ideology change – perhaps they think it indicates a lack of seriousness, a lack of sincerity, or a lack of integrity – and so they often insist that their party has always held the same correct principles and positions. Furthermore, they insist that their opponents have always espoused the same wrong ideas and issue positions.

In addition to partisanship, our tendency to view the past anachronistically also causes us to forget how parties used to speak and act differently than they do today. For example, in the first half of the GOP's history, the party typically called for higher taxes, more federal spending, and greater government intervention in the economy to regulate large corporations and help those in need.[1] Likewise, in the first half of the Democratic Party's history, it typically called for lower taxes, less federal spending, and free markets (Gerring 1998). Thus, in the 1932 presidential campaign, Franklin Roosevelt criticized the Herbert Hoover administration for being "committed to the idea that we ought to center control of everything in Washington as rapidly as possible … I regard reduction in Federal spending as one of the most important issues of this campaign. In my opinion it is the most direct and effective contribution that Government can make to business" (F. Roosevelt 1932). Because the parties' positions and ideologies with regard to government intervention in the economy switched places in the 1930s, it is tempting to mistakenly think that the Democratic Party has always advocated increased government spending and economic intervention while the Republican Party has always advocated *laissez-faire* economics.

The two parties have not only changed their minds with regard to government spending, but also with regard to foreign policy, taxes (Burns 1997), women's rights (Wolbrecht 2000), racial politics (Carmines and Stimson 1989), abortion (G. Adams 1997), and military spending (Fordham 2007). The two major parties have switched positions – often multiple times – on virtually every significant, enduring public policy issue in American history. Furthermore, the parties have not only changed their issues positions, but they have also changed the systems of ideas they articulate that bundle those issue positions together. In other words, they have changed their ideologies.

In the following sections, this chapter will explain why political scientists, in general, fundamentally misunderstand ideology and overlook party ideology evolution, and I will then suggest a methodological

---

[1] For a description of how the Republican Party founded the welfare state in America, see Skocpol (1992). For a description of how Theodore Roosevelt returned the GOP to being "the radical progressive party of the Nation again," see chapter 10 of Theodore Roosevelt's autobiography (T. Roosevelt 1913) and chapter 6 of *The Politics Presidents Make* (Skowronek 1997).

approach that can improve our understanding of how party ideologies develop. The greatest source of confusion concerning ideology is something I call the "Liberal Conservative Myth," which I explain and illustrate in Sections 2 through 5. In place of this misleading approach, in Section 6, I recommend that political scientists treat ideologies to a historical institutional analysis. Looking at party ideologies this way allows us to see their dynamic character – something Lincoln understood almost two centuries ago.

2 THE LIBERAL CONSERVATIVE MYTH

In addition to partisanship and anachronism, another reason we tend to underestimate how much party ideologies change over time is the Liberal Conservative Myth (LCM). This is the mistaken view held by many people that political history can be meaningfully described as the movement of individuals and groups on an ideological spatial spectrum frozen in time. This spatial spectrum consists of static ideological dimensions that run from "liberal" to "conservative," or "left" to "right," and whose meanings are fixed and unchanging. Thus, if one party has always been "liberal" or on the "left," and another party has always been "conservative" or on the "right," then we can conclude that the two parties' ideologies have been relatively static over long stretches of time. This is a mistaken view of political history because, over time, the very meanings of "liberalism" and "conservatism" ("left" and "right") themselves are evolving and can hide significant party reversals.

For example, what was said in the previous section about changes in Democratic and Republican Party ideologies can also be said of "liberal" and "conservative" political ideologies. In the 1930s, not only did Democratic Party ideology change to accommodate the New Deal, but the very meaning and content of "liberalism" itself changed to accommodate interventionist economic policy. In the nineteenth century, liberalism was defined by free market ideology: limited government, lower taxes, little government spending on social programs, and free trade. During the 1930s and 1940s, liberalism came to be defined by active government intervention in the economy, higher taxes, and increased government spending on social programs (Milkis 1993, 49). There were, of course, traditional free marketers that continued to insist from the 1930s through 1950s that they were the true "liberals," but very few people paid attention to, or believed, them (Forcey 1961, xiii–xiv).

The meaning of "liberalism" in popular discourse radically changed whether the old liberals liked it or not.[2]

Like economic "liberalism" and "conservatism," foreign policy "liberalism" and "conservatism" have seen similar transformations. In the 1930s and 1940s conservatism was defined by isolationism, from the 1960s through the 1980s conservatism meant hawkishness on foreign policy, and in the 1990s it returned to being critical of foreign military adventures before, in the 2000s, it was once again defined by the idea of spreading democracy internationally through military force. During the Obama administration, anti-interventionists became increasingly influential within conservatism – so much so that conservatives nominated Donald Trump, with his isolationist rhetoric, as the GOP nominee in 2016.[3]

Similarly, from the late 1930s to the early 1960s, liberalism was defined by an interventionist foreign policy that sought to involve the United States in conflicts in Europe, Korea, and Vietnam. From the late 1960s through the 1980s, it was defined by a dovish foreign policy that called for America to "come home." In the 1990s it defended military interventions abroad, and in the 2000s it returned to criticizing American imperialism.

The same kind of changes to liberalism and conservatism can be noted about almost every issue area in American politics – whether it is foreign policy, taxes, spending, civil rights, or international trade. No matter how many, or which, ideological dimensions an analyst chooses to use, the meanings of liberalism and conservatism are constantly evolving. As a result, any discussion of a voter, politician, party, or country moving left or right (or up or down or diagonal) on an ideological spatial spectrum must be accompanied by a detailed description of what that dynamic spectrum means at different times. To do this, of course, makes a spatial spectrum cumbersome to use and it soon loses its value as an analytical tool. The value of using ideological spectra to chart historical change is dependent on the assumption that the dimensions of a spectrum have fixed meanings frozen in time. If this assumption were true, then the statement that a person or a group became more or less "conservative" or "liberal" would contain meaningful information. Such a statement

---

[2] These old liberals eventually adopted the term "classical liberal" to distinguish themselves from the "new liberals."

[3] Whether President Trump governs according to the noninterventionist rhetoric on which he campaigned is a separate question (V. Lewis 2017).

would signal a host of inferences that can be drawn about how a particular person or group changed their attitudes about dozens of issues. Unfortunately, this assumption is not true. On nearly every major political issue, conservative and liberal – left and right – have, at some points in time, evolved to mean the opposite of what they meant at other points in time. Thus, statements about individuals or groups becoming more or less liberal or conservative tend to confuse more than they clarify.

3 THE LIBERAL CONSERVATIVE MYTH AND POLITICAL SCIENCE

Although it is a problem in many fields of social science, the Liberal Conservative Myth is particularly problematic for political science because ideology is one of the most prevalent analytical concepts in the discipline. As Frances Lee has documented, almost half of all major political science journal articles, and over 80 percent of articles on Congress, refer to ideology (Lee 2009, 29–30). As Jacob Hacker and Paul Pierson have convincingly shown, the "master theory" of American political science claims that ideology is what drives the voting behavior of ordinary voters in the electorate, members of Congress, presidents, bureaucrats, and judges – and ultimately drives the most significant political outcomes. The Downsian spatial model of "ideological positioning" has formed the basic intellectual framework of "almost a half a century of leading political scientists" (Hacker and Pierson 2014, 643). However, if we fundamentally misunderstand what ideology is, and what it does, then an entire superstructure of political science research built on that mistaken conception of ideology is seriously flawed.

The dominant conception of ideology underpinning contemporary political science claims that the preference points of all political actors can be mapped onto an ideological spatial spectrum, and that each dimension of this space (the number of dimensions varies depending on the model employed) runs from "liberal" to "conservative." In the neo-institutional version of this conceptualization, these potentially evolving ideological preference points, interacting with a potentially evolving institutional environment, determine the important political outcomes we observe over time. The main problem with this approach is that in claiming that the preference points of political actors can become more or less "liberal" or "conservative" over time, scholars do not recognize that the very meanings of "liberal" and "conservative" also change over that same time period. The fact that these ideological constructs are subject to constant transformation renders these spatial models mostly useless for measuring the ideological movement of political actors and groups.

For example, the political phenomena that have captured the American public's imagination over the past few decades have been partisan fighting, polarization, gridlock, and dysfunction. The most common explanation for this political warfare between "red" and "blue" America has been ideology. Journalists and political scientists alike increasingly point to how the two major parties have become more ideologically homogenous and extreme. Liberals have sorted themselves into the Democratic Party and conservatives have sorted themselves into the Republican Party (Layman and Carsey 2002, Carsey and Layman 2006, Levendusky 2009, Fiorina 2013). At the same time, the Democratic Party has moved to the "left" on the liberal-conservative spectrum, and the Republican Party has moved, even farther, to the "right" (Hacker and Pierson 2005, McCarty, Poole, and Rosenthal 2006, Pierson and Skocpol 2007, Poole and Rosenthal 2007, Abramowitz 2010, Mann and Ornstein 2012, Hare and Poole 2014). Studies of these changes in the ideological positioning of the two parties have filled the pages of political science journals and books in recent years.[4] The first claim, "party sorting," is straightforward and compelling. However, the second claim, "ideological polarization," is deeply problematic.

If the meaning and content of the ideological poles of a spatial spectrum ("left" and "right") are evolving, then claims of polarization become confusing. Such claims may help us recognize increasing ideological homogeneity within the two major parties (as DW-NOMINATE scores may indicate), but they tell us nothing about the content of that ideological homogeneity: nothing about the actual ideas and policy positions articulated by the two major parties. We may learn the content of the two parties' ideologies from analyzing the ideas that partisans articulate in everyday discourse – and many of the works I just cited do a good job of documenting this – but we do not learn the content of the two parties' ideologies by observing that they are "liberal" or "conservative" because the meanings of "liberalism" and "conservatism" are in constant flux.

For the past eight decades or so, virtually whatever the Democratic Party does is termed "liberal" and whatever the Republican Party does is

---

[4] The focus on party polarization has become so great that it was a central object of study in a recent American Political Science Association Task Force (Barber and McCarty 2013).

termed "conservative."[5] Thus, changes in the parties themselves are helping to drive changes in the meanings of the ideological poles of "liberalism" and "conservatism." In this situation, claims about party polarization simply become tautological.

For example, if the Republican Party moves toward free trade principles, as it did in the 1960s and 1970s, then we are told that this is evidence of a move toward "right-wing" libertarianism. If, on the other hand, the Republican Party moves away from free trade, as it has recently, then we are told that this is evidence of a move toward "right-wing" nationalism. If the Democratic Party moves toward free trade, then we are told that this is evidence of a move toward "left-wing" internationalism. If, on the other hand, the Democratic Party moves away from free trade, then we are told that this is evidence of a move toward "left-wing" laborism.

If the Republican Party moves toward an interventionist foreign policy, as it did during the Bush administration, then we are told that this is evidence of a move toward "right-wing" hawkishness. Conversely, if the Republican Party moves away from an interventionist foreign policy, as it did during the Clinton and Obama administrations, we are told that this is evidence of a move toward "right-wing" isolationism. If the Democratic Party moves toward an interventionist foreign policy, as it during the Clinton administration, then we are told that this is evidence of a move toward "left-wing" internationalism. If, however, the Democratic Party moves away from interventionist foreign policy, as it did during the Bush administration, we are told that this is evidence of a move toward "left-wing" dovishness.

If the Republican Party moves toward embracing tax cuts, as it did in the 1970s and 1980s, we are told that this is evidence of a move toward "right-wing" libertarianism. If, on the other hand, the Republican Party moves away from tax cuts, as it did during the Kennedy administration, we are told that this is evidence of a move toward "right-wing" budget hawkishness.[6] If the Democratic Party moves toward embracing tax cuts, as it did in the 1960s, we are told that this is evidence of a move toward "left-wing" Keynesianism. Conversely, if the Democratic Party moves away from tax cuts, as it did during the 1980s, we are told that this is evidence of a move toward "left-wing" liberalism.

---

[5] Democrats who vote with, or support, Republicans are called "conservative Democrats" and Republicans who vote with, or support, Democrats are called "liberal Republicans."

[6] "Mr. Conservative" Barry Goldwater, for example, argued that the Kennedy tax cuts were "dangerously inflationary" (Donovan 1964, 112).

Whatever the Republican Party does (even if it is the opposite of what Republicans did previously) is described as "conservative," and whatever the Democratic Party does (even if it is the opposite of what Democrats did previously) is described as "liberal." Thus, claims that the Democratic Party moved to the "left," or that the Republican Party moved to the "right" are not helpful because they are tautological. In reality, what is happening is that the Democratic and Republican parties (in particular, their leaders in the White House) are constantly redefining what "liberalism" and "conservatism" mean. Thus, claims about ideological movement to the "left" or the "right" over long stretches of time are nonsensical. This is just one of the ways that the Liberal Conservative Myth infects our political science scholarship.

4 WHY DW-NOMINATE CANNOT MEASURE PARTY IDEOLOGY DEVELOPMENT

To illustrate this point in more detail, this section will focus on the problems that party voting approaches face in trying to measure party ideology development. This is the most common way in which scholars rely upon the Liberal Conservative Myth. Political scientists typically try to measure party ideology by using Congressional roll call scaling applications, which posit that ideological positions on a liberal-conservative spectrum (consisting of however many dimensions) determine the roll call voting behavior of a party's legislators. While the following critique applies to any measure of party ideology that proceeds in this way, the most widely used measure is the DW-NOMINATE scaling application (Carroll et al. 2015), and so I will focus on this well-known example in order to illustrate the conceptual problems we face.

In deriving their index of scores, the authors of DW-NOMINATE code millions of roll call votes cast by thousands of MCs over hundreds of years. Given the mountain of data they collect, they cannot take the time to describe the content of these millions of votes. They concede that they are merely using the term "ideology" as "shorthand" to describe the tendency in voting behavior of MCs, but using this "shorthand" is problematic for several reasons.

First of all, it inevitably leads those who use the scores – political scientists and journalists alike – to explain the voting behavior of MCs in terms of "liberalism" and "conservatism" (i.e., in terms of "ideology"), even though ideology is not always what determines voting behavior.[7] Sophisticated analysts do point out that ideology is only one of multiple factors that determine a legislator's preference point and vote choice (Lee 2009, Barber and McCarty 2013). Nonetheless, even if we recognize that vote choices are only partially determined by ideology, we still cannot coherently talk about the preference points of politicians or parties moving through n-dimensional space over time if those preference points are based, even if only partially, on ideologies that are assumed to be static but are in reality dynamic.[8] For example, several critics have pointed out that NOMINATE is unclear about how much the scores represent partisanship and how much they represent ideology, and Poole and Rosenthal, themselves, admit that their DW-NOMINATE scores measure both "loyalty to a political party and loyalty to an ideology" (Lee 2016).[9] However, these criticisms and admissions overlook the endogeneity problem associated with conceptualizing NOMINATE scores as partly a measure of partisanship and partly a measure of ideology. Not only are NOMINATE scores an unclear mix of both ideology and loyalty to a party, but (as this book will show) it is also true that loyalty to a party *causes change in* the meaning and content of ideologies like liberalism and conservatism.

Secondly, and more importantly, roll call scaling applications like DW-NOMINATE are problematic because they are based on the Liberal Conservative Myth. Given the dynamic character of ideology, when analyzing the roll call scores produced by DW-NOMINATE, it remains unclear what ideas, bound together in what structure, are constraining MC voting behavior in the form of ideology at different times. It is unclear what it means to say, for example, that a politician or party in one decade and a politician or party in another decade had the same DW-NOMINATE score and, thus, the same ideological

---

[7] Poole and Rosenthal themselves talk this way (2007, 3).

[8] In addition to the problems that arise from the fact that ideology is dynamic, the problem is likely compounded by whatever other factors we might posit as determining ideal spatial preference points because these other factors – like partisanship or constituent interests – are *also dynamic*. That is, the preference content of things like partisanship (the pressures that the Democratic and Republican parties place on party members in Congress) and constituent interests (the pressures that constituents place on their representatives) change over time, just like the preference content of "liberalism" and "conservatism."

[9] See also Noel (2016).

constraint. A closer analysis of political history reveals that identical ideological scores are often given to MCs and parties with opposite issue positions.

For example, on the liberal side of the spectrum, twentieth-century senators "Cotton" Ed Smith (D-SC, 1909–1944), Henry "Scoop" Jackson (D-WA, 1953–1983), and Ron Wyden (D-OR, 1996–present) all had, according to DW-NOMINATE, the same liberal ideal preference point (–0.3), but the ideological worldview of each was significantly different. Smith was a racist demagogue who opposed the New Deal, Jackson was a "neoconservative" who supported both the Great Society and the Vietnam War, and Wyden is a "progressive liberal" who opposes racism, has sought to reform entitlement spending, and opposes militarism.[10] As we can see, what it meant to be a "liberal" MC in the 1930s was very different from what it meant to be a "liberal" MC in the 1970s, and both are very different from what it means to be a "liberal" MC today. Thus, it makes no sense to say that the Democratic Party has become more "liberal" since the 1940s (or the 1970s or the 1990s) because it is unclear what the party is moving "more" toward? More toward Senator Smith (more racist and more demagogic)? More toward Senator Jackson (more hawkish and more in favor of the welfare state)? More toward Senator Wyden (more committed to entitlement reform and more opposed to militarism)? We may know what we mean when we say "more liberal" from studying other sources (by reading party platforms, candidate speeches, or survey results), but we do not learn this information from DW-NOMINATE.

The foregoing illustration of the problem with DW-NOMINATE is not solved by disaggregating the scores of those senators onto multiple dimensions. The problem does not go away because the ideological content of each dimension – regardless of how many are used – are all subject to change over time.[11] For example, the meanings of "liberal

---

[10] Smith's inclusion as a "liberal" is not surprising. In the first half of the twentieth century, the most "liberal" members of Congress, according to DW-NOMINATE, tended to be Southerners opposed to federal government intervention in the economy.

[11] For example, Miller and Schofield (2003) insightfully point out that intraparty tensions on different ideological dimensions – economic policy and social policy – help drive changes in the demographic and ideological content of political parties over time. However, to the extent that Miller and Schofield believe that the meanings of liberal and conservative economic policy, and liberal and conservative social policy, are static, they cannot meaningfully measure party ideology change through their static, two-dimensional, ideological space.

economic policy," "liberal foreign policy," and "liberal social policy" have all changed over time – just like "liberalism" itself has changed.

On the conservative side of the NOMINATE spectrum, there are also many MCs with the same ideological scores but divergent ideological worldviews. For example, twentieth-century senators Henry Cabot Lodge (R-MA, 1893–1924), Barry Goldwater (R-AZ, 1953–1965), and Jesse Helms (R-NC, 1973–2003) all had the same DW-NOMINATE ideal preference point: 0.6 (Carroll et al. 2015). About the only thing that the New England "progressive," the Western "libertarian," and the Southern "traditionalist" had in common was a party label. It would be hard to find any political issue on which all three of those politicians agreed – even though they presumably shared the same "conservative" ideological space. What it meant to be a "conservative" MC in the 1920s was very different from what it meant to be a "conservative" MC in the 1950s, and both were very different from what it meant to be a "conservative" MC in the 1990s.

Similarly, President George W. Bush and Congressman Howard Buffett (father of Warren Buffett and representative of Nebraska's Second Congressional District in the 1940s and 1950s) had the same DW-NOMINATE score (0.7) but the opposite political positions. Bush's version of conservatism represented increases in federal debt through tax cuts and increased spending on the military, education, and Medicare. His administration expanded executive power and US military power overseas. The conservatism of Rep. Buffett, on the other hand, advocated the exact opposite: balanced budgets, federal government austerity, decreased spending on the military, limited executive power, isolationist foreign policy, and cutting back on the kind of social programs that Bush expanded. Buffett was a member of the "Old Right" that took libertarian positions on foreign intervention, federal spending, and federal debt, while Bush was a member of the very different "New Right." On those issues that remained constant over time (spending, taxes, and foreign policy), the two politicians had exactly opposite political views but the same DW-NOMINATE scores.

Thus, it makes no sense to say that the Republican Party has become more "conservative" since the 1960s (or the 1970s or the 1990s) because it is unclear what they are moving "more" toward. More toward the "conservatism" of Senator Lodge (more in favor of government intervention in the economy)? More toward the "conservatism" of Senator Goldwater (more critical of the Religious Right)? More toward the "conservatism" of Senator Helms (more in favor of using military force to spread democracy abroad)? We may know what we mean when we say "more conservative" from studying other sources, but we do not learn this information from DW-NOMINATE.

Going forward into the future, according to DW-NOMINATE, whatever Republican MCs vote for will tautologically be defined as "conservative" and whatever Democratic MCs vote for will tautologically be defined as "liberal." If, in future sessions of Congress, Republican MCs vote for free trade policy, and Democratic MCs vote against it, support for free trade will be defined as "conservative" and opposition to it will be defined as "liberal." If, on the other hand, Republican MCs vote for protectionist trade policy, and Democratic MCs vote against it, support for protectionism will be defined as "conservative" and opposition to it will be defined as "liberal." The same is true for every possible public policy issue. Such a tautology is worthless in terms of measuring ideology, which is what roll call scaling applications like DW-NOMINATE claim to do.

While roll call scaling scores can be very useful in telling us who votes with who at any given time, they are not useful in telling us about the structures of attitudes and ideas that shape and constrain the rhetoric and behavior of political actors (i.e., ideology). This limitation causes problems when these scores are used, as they frequently are, to try to measure party ideology change over time. Given the dynamism of ideology, a "conservative" score might be assigned to an MC calling for more government intervention in the economy, or less; higher taxes, or lower; and more spending, or less. Similarly, a "liberal" score might be assigned to an MC calling for more racial equality, or less; more hawkish foreign policy, or more dovish foreign policy; and more social welfare programs, or fewer. There is no way to know what these scores mean without detailed historical context: the roll call scores are devoid of information without that context. When paired with a merely surface-level understanding of American history, they can become sources of misinformation.

Despite this fundamental problem, many political scientists attempt to measure party ideology evolution by tracking the average roll call scaling scores of party members in Congress over time (McCarty et al. 2006, Hare and Poole 2014). Even though political scientists make claims about party ideology development based on these spatial moves, these roll call scores actually contain no substantive information about ideology. While these scores may tell us how often co-partisans vote together, they do not tell us what these votes mean in terms of ideology.

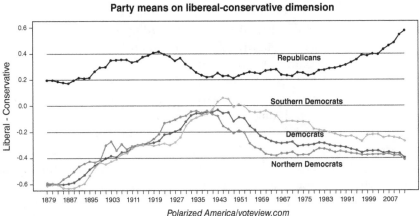

FIGURE I.I Party ideology development since 1879 using DW-NOMINATE scores[12]

What, exactly, does it mean for a party to have an average score of 0.6 conservative or –0.3 liberal? That depends *entirely* on context, which is always changing.

While Poole and Rosenthal recognize and admit that "how policy issues map onto liberal-conservative preferences may have changed," (McCarty, Poole and Rosenthal 2006, 8), the authors of DW-NOMINATE conclude that the liberal-conservative ideology continuum they identify in American politics has had "remarkable stability since the Civil War" (Poole and Rosenthal 2007, 7). This claim becomes problematic, however, when we recognize that even though the positions and ideologies of the parties have changed dramatically, the average NOMINATE scores of the Democratic and Republican Parties never switch positions in ideological space throughout American history.

Figure I.I tracks each party's average DW-NOMINATE scores in the Senate since Reconstruction. According to this index of ideology scores, the Democratic Party's high-water mark for liberalism was in the 1880s and early 1890s during the Bourbon Democratic administrations of Grover Cleveland, but in reality the Democratic Party during this time advocated relatively *laissez-faire* economic policies. They did not advocate more welfare spending, taxes, infrastructure spending, income

---

[12] This figure is from Jeffrey Lewis, Keith T. Poole, and Howard Rosenthal, voteview.com.

redistribution, regulation, or trade restrictions than the Republican Party – on the contrary. Nonetheless, they are somehow coded as significantly more "liberal" than the GOP. According to this measure, the Democratic Party of Woodrow Wilson, Franklin D. Roosevelt, Lyndon B. Johnson and Barack Obama is much more conservative than the Democratic Party of Cleveland. These scores suggest, confusingly, that the Democratic Party moved rightward, toward less government intervention in the economy, during the late 1890s (when the party merged with the Populist Party), the 1910s (during the Wilsonian Progressive Era), and the 1930s–1940s (during the New Deal) – almost reaching the political center by the end of FDR's administration. This characterization of the movement of Democratic Party ideology contradicts our normal thinking about "left" and "right." The scaling application's description of Republican Party history since Reconstruction is equally puzzling.

Mistakenly assuming that the meanings of liberalism and conservatism have remained static can lead us to erroneously conclude that the two major parties have had relatively fixed ideologies throughout American history. If we assume the Liberal Conservative Myth, and if one of the two major parties has always been identified as "liberal" and the other has always been identified as "conservative," then we must falsely conclude that the two parties have held relatively consistent stances on all of the major enduring issues over time. However, if we move beyond the Liberal Conservative Myth, we can clearly see that the two major parties are constantly switching positions on political issues – even when they stick with the same ideological labels over time.

5 PREVIOUS HISTORIES OF AMERICAN PARTY IDEOLOGY DEVELOPMENT

Having established how problematic the Liberal Conservative Myth is for roll call scaling applications, I will now focus on how the LCM has led scholars of American political development to overlook dramatic and important changes to the ideologies of the two major parties. Historians of American party ideologies typically analyze the language used by parties in the past, specifically searching for some single theme that has characterized and differentiated the two parties. When they find this one critical factor, they then conclude that this characteristic is essential to the nature of the parties: Not only is it found in all past eras, but we can expect it to characterize the parties in all future eras. I call this approach the "continuous party battle" literature. What usually happens, however, in the decades following this post-hoc analysis, is that the parties evolve in some way that invalidates the generalization. Later scholars must try again to find a different unifying and essential theme.

For example, Croly (1909) argued that the two parties are fundamentally divided between a theory of national power and union (characterizing the Federalists, Whigs, and Republicans) and a theory of democracy and individual liberty (characterizing the Jeffersonian Republicans and Democrats).[13] After party ideology changes in the 1910s falsified this claim, Beard (1928) argued that the two major parties are essentially divided over government support of agriculture (the Jeffersonian Republicans and Democrats) or industry (the Hamiltonian Federalists, Whigs, and Republicans).[14] When FDR's Democratic New Deal coalition falsified this claim, Hartz (1955) argued that the two major parties have always been divided, within liberalism, between relatively "whiggish" aristocracy (Federalists, Whigs, and Republicans) and relatively radical democracy (Jeffersonian Republicans and Democrats). When Nixon and Reagan's populist, New Right coalition falsified this claim, Gerring (1998) argued that "through all periods of American history one party [the Federalists, Whigs, or Republicans] has adhered to the interests of business and the advance of a capitalist economy, whereas the other [the Jeffersonian Republicans or Democrats] has often been more critical of this advance" (1998, 20). Ironically, in this formulation, the Democrats are the "conservatives" resisting capitalist transformation, and the Whigs and Republicans are the "progressives" pushing change and "advance." Donald Trump's Republican Party is now in the process of further falsifying that claim through its own critique of the "advance of a capitalist economy." The party now seeks to hold back the advances of globalization, post-industrialization, and a new knowledge economy

---

[13] The subsequent history of the twentieth century would prove this generalization to be false: Almost every Democratic administration from Wilson to the present, including FDR's New Deal and LBJ's Great Society, would employ a theory of national government power. Likewise, the Republican Party since the New Deal has largely embraced the Jeffersonian rhetoric of limited government and individual liberty.

[14] The subsequent history of the twentieth century would prove this generalization to be false, as well: FDR's New Deal coalition famously brought together urban labor and rural farmers, and since 1933 Democrats have often promoted government policies aimed at aiding industrial labor. At the time of Beard's writing, the two parties were divided between a Republican industrial North and a Democratic agrarian South. In the intervening nine decades, the two parties have switched with Democrats now stronger in the industrial Northeast, upper Midwest, and West Coast, and Republicans dominant in the rural South, lower Midwest, and Mountain West.

through calls for protectionist trade policy, decreasing immigration, and supporting older, rust belt, manufacturing industries. These failed attempts to find some essential difference between the two parties demonstrate the futility of this approach.[15]

The most recent historians have concluded that the core of GOP ideology is free market economics, traditional Christian morality, and interventionist foreign policy (Nash 2006). Shortly after drawing this conclusion, however, Trump became the spokesman for the party, and Trumpism has violated these principles in important ways. No doubt, in the aftermath of Trump, someone will try again to cobble together a post-hoc rationalization for the "essential core" of "conservatism" and "Republicanism," but the historical record suggests that these descriptions will soon fail, as well.

Political scientists with a nuanced understanding of American history have admitted that American party history has been characterized by significant discontinuities, but they generally still try to find some overarching theme that ties it all together (Gerring 1998, Brewer and Stonecash 2009). According to Brewer and Stonecash, "For much of American history ... the Democratic Party's concern for the have-nots has persisted. Republicans, on the other hand, have largely defended free markets and represented those who have fared relatively well ... Partisan conflict in the United States has always reflected this cleavage to some degree" (2009, 4). As we will see in Chapter 4, Democrats have, in fact, for much of American history, "defended free markets," and they have often defended those who have fared relatively well.[16] Likewise, the Republican Party's commitment to free markets has only characterized a third of American history, and they often express concern for the have-nots – even if they use a different ideological discourse than Democrats (H. Lewis 2017).

---

[15] It is worth noting here that I find these previous theories falsified *not* because they could not explain all eras of American history. A theory that can explain most cases and most variation, but not all, is still useful. Instead, I find these theories to be falsified because they are committed to the untenable position that party ideologies are fundamentally static, and that one, continuous, overarching theme divides the two major parties in all time periods. In reality, of course, party ideologies are social and political constructs that are always subject to change. Thus, once the ideas and cleavages dividing the two major parties change, those ideological differences are proven to be historically contingent and temporary – not essential and universal as claimed by the authors of those theories.

[16] Brewer and Stonecash's definition, in any event, is itself a partisan definition (H. Lewis 2017).

To overcome the problem of each new post-hoc theory being successively falsified, adherents to the "continuous party battle" school of thought have begun taking a new approach. Rather than posit relatively concrete (and thus relatively falsifiable) theories – like national power vs. individual liberty, agriculture vs. industry, aristocracy vs. democracy, or haves vs. have-nots – scholars now claim that the enduring ideological cleavage is characterized by concepts so amorphous and vague that the theory is not falsifiable. For example, in James Reichley's history of American political parties (2000), he argues that there is an enduring ideological divide between a "liberal" party (Jeffersonian Republicans and Democrats) and a "republican" party (Hamiltonian Federalists, Whigs, and Republicans). More recently, and more widely cited, Keith Poole and Howard Rosenthal (2007) claim that American party history in Congress is characterized by a "liberal" party (Jeffersonian Republicans and Democrats) and a "conservative" party (Hamiltonian Federalists, Whigs, and Republicans). In this strange way of thinking, Democratic members of Congress were acting on "liberal" political ideology both when they opposed a national bank in the 1830s and supported it in the 1910s, when they opposed Republican Reconstruction in the 1860s–1870s and supported desegregation in the 1960s–1970s, when they opposed progressive economic legislation in the 1880s–1900s and supported it in the 1930s–1960s, when they opposed anti-lynching bills in the 1900s–1930s and supported civil rights legislation in the 1960s, when they pursued tax cuts in the 1950s–1960s and opposed them in the 1980s–2010s, and when they promoted the Vietnam War in the early 1960s and opposed it in the late 1960s. In this approach, terms like "liberal," "conservative," and "republican" are so ambiguous that they are useless in telling us anything about the ideological content of party conflict at any given time.

In addition to this "continuous party battle" literature, in the second half of the twentieth century, a "party realignment" literature emerged among historically minded scholars of American political parties. Realignment theorists noticed that, over the course of American history, the two major parties had periodically changed their respective shares of the American electorate. One version of the theory claimed that party realignments at "critical elections" were characterized by intraparty ideological "polarization."[17] However, this particular version of the

---

[17] As Mayhew (2002) convincingly shows, these intraparty "polarizations" – in 1844, 1848, 1860, 1896, 1912, 1924, 1948, 1968, and 1972 – were not correlated with the supposed "critical elections": A few occurred in those years, but many did not.

realignment literature was beset by the same false assumptions as the scholars that preceded them (Croly, Beard, and Hartz) and followed them (Reichley, Gerring, Nash, Poole and Rosenthal, and Brewer and Stonecash). All of these scholars wrongly assumed that there is some static, enduring ideological divide that characterizes all of American party history. In reality, the ideological content of these intraparty and interparty battles changes dramatically over time. Thus, the "intraparty polarizations" focused on by the realignment theorists involved a constantly changing variety of ideological dimensions: Party factions divided over slavery in 1860, monetary policy in 1896, progressivism in 1912, the KKK in 1924, civil rights in 1948, the Vietnam War in 1968, the "culture war" in 1992, and immigration policy and foreign policy in 2016. There is no static content to the ideological "poles" to which parties and intraparty factions constantly "polarize" and "depolarize."

Thankfully, there have been some students of American party ideologies whose scholarship is not beset by the Liberal Conservative Myth. In a brief overview of American party ideology development, James Ceaser (2006) insightfully showed how the "foundational ideas" of party ideologies frequently change.[18] Dan DiSalvo (2012) noted that every party ideology is the product of intraparty conflict between various factions, and that this conflict results in constant party ideology change. Hans Noel (2013) showed how political parties adopt different political ideologies and focused on the role of "academic scribblers" in diffusing ideas from elites to the masses. While these studies improved our understanding of *how* party ideologies change over time, they did not offer a theory to explain *why* they change the way they do, which is what this book attempts.

In addition to these important books on party ideology development, an "issue evolution" literature has emerged in recent decades. These articles and books demonstrate how, in response to changes in society, the two parties constantly change which issues they emphasize – and

---

[18] For example, Jackson's Democratic Party ideology was founded on the idea ("Manifest Destiny") that history has an inevitable direction. Lincoln's Republican Party ideology was founded on the idea that individuals are equally endowed with certain natural rights. Theodore Roosevelt's Progressive Party ideology was also founded on the Jacksonian idea that history has a known direction. Since that time, various factions of the Republican and Democratic parties have had foundational ideas that could be categorized as reaching for ultimate justifications in nature, history, or religion (Ceaser 2006).

what positions they take on these issues – over the course of party battle. Notably, David Karol (2009) helpfully pointed out that the two major parties frequently change positions on issues like international trade, civil rights, defense spending, fiscal policy, abortion, and gun control as a result of the pressures of coalition management. In this way, it contributes to the society-centered scholarship that argues that party dynamics are the product of political entrepreneurs responding to changes in society (Sundquist 1973, Carmines and Stimson 1989, Adams 1997, Wolbrecht 2000, Ware 2006, Stonecash 2010, Skocpol and Williamson 2012). While this literature is useful in showing the society-centered factors that influence party ideology change, the book you are reading will add to these studies by showing how a polity-centered factor (party control of government institutions) also influences party ideology change.

6 IMPROVING OUR UNDERSTANDING OF PARTY IDEOLOGY DEVELOPMENT

The foregoing critique does not mean that political scientists and historians should abandon using ideology as an analytical concept. Ideology exists in the political world, and we need to come up with ways to effectively describe, measure, analyze, and explain it. In his seminal study of political ideology, Philip Converse explained that the neglect of ideology as a subject of study by political scientists prior to 1964 was a primary exhibit "for the doctrine that what is important to study cannot be measured and what can be measured is not important to study" (1964, 206). Despite his important work on the nature of belief systems in mass publics, ideology remained relatively unexamined by political scientists after Converse until the invention of roll call scaling applications. Once scholars had a numerical value they could assign to a person or party, then the use of ideology in scholarship became ubiquitous. This may be an example of the measurement tools available to scholars (despite their flaws) driving the substantive issues political scientists address rather than the other way around. We should continue to try to understand ideology because it plays such a significant role in explaining important political phenomena, but we need to do so more coherently and accurately. The foregoing critique simply points out that we cannot use unstable analytical concepts, like liberalism or conservatism, to measure change in party ideology. Trying to use ideologies that are always in flux as standards of reference to measure change in something else over time is incoherent.

Furthermore, this critique does not mean we should abandon using dynamic analytical concepts. It might be useful to talk about a person or party's liberalism or conservatism at a given point and place in time, but this must be accompanied with a description of what that concept meant at that specific time and place. If we want to measure party ideology evolution, we should use more stable analytical concepts as standards of reference. For example, we could measure changes in a party's advocacy for welfare spending, entitlement spending, tax rates, regulation levels, trade barriers, foreign military intervention, racial desegregation, etc. We could speak coherently about a party developing in such a way that it calls for more or less spending on social programs, a higher or lower minimum wage, and a more restrictive or permissive abortion law even if we cannot talk coherently about a party becoming more or less liberal or conservative over time.

To improve our understanding of how American party ideologies evolve, we would benefit from returning to Lincoln's story about the fighting men in their "great-coats." In this metaphor, the combatants, of course, represent the political parties. In particular, the drunken men under their coats represent the sometimes-unwieldy coalition of groups in each party that agree to work together to fight their opponents in hopes of achieving some objective. The coats, on the other hand, represent the ideologies worn by the parties. These great-coats, when worn during battle, are structures that limit and constrain the way the men fight. The coats constrain how high the fighters can raise their arms and in what direction they throw their punches. Similarly, party ideologies structure and constrain the attitudes expressed and the issue positions taken by party members. The coats, of course, are not the only factors that affect the behavior we observe, but they are important. Furthermore, the nature of their constraint is not entirely fixed – they are great-coats and not straight-jackets. Over the course of party battle, the form and shape of the coats/ideologies change. This analogy represents a better approach to understanding what ideology is, what party ideologies do, and how party ideologies evolve. Ideologies are political structures (ideas of power) that shape the behavior of political actors, and whose structural shape is subject to change by those same actors. In other words, to better understand the development of ideologies over time, we should treat them to historical institutional analysis.

In adopting Lincoln's metaphor, we can apply the methodological insights of neo-institutionalism to the problem of political ideology. Ideologies are endogenous political structures that both constrain the behavior of political actors and are subject to transformation by those same actors over time. Thus, just as previous scholarship has examined the politics of party *organization* choice and development (Aldrich 2011) and the politics of party *policy* choice and development (Anzia and Moe 2016), this book examines the politics of party *ideology* choice and development.

In calling for social scientists to treat ideologies as endogenous political structures, this book builds upon previous scholars who have paved the way for this kind of analysis. First, early influential behavioral scholarship on belief systems in the mass public recognized that ideology is a "structure of attitudes" (Campbell et al. 1960, 192). An ideology's idea-elements are structured, or "bound together, by some form of constraint or functional interdependence" (Converse 1964, 207). This constraint largely arises from the way that ideology is diffused from elites to "consumers" in society as a "package" of ideas and issue positions (Converse 1964, Noel 2013).[19]

This scholarship not only recognizes that ideology is a political structure that constrains the attitudes and behavior of individuals, but it also recognizes that ideologies are created and transformed by individuals. "Ideological structures represent ... social constructions of reality because they do not descend from the heavens and are not randomly generated – they are created and elaborated by certain groups" (Gillman 1993, 16). Where Gillman emphasizes the role that groups have in changing the content of ideologies, Converse and Noel emphasize the role of elites: "the shaping of belief systems of any range into apparently logical wholes that are credible to large numbers of people is an act of creative synthesis characteristic of only a miniscule proportion of any

---

[19] From the standpoint of sociological institutionalism, ideology can be seen as a constraint in the sense that it provides a script to follow, or role to play, for those who identify with the ideology. Those within the ideological group think within the ideational framework provided by the ideology by habit. From the standpoint of rational choice institutionalism, ideology can be seen as a constraint in the sense that it is a structured equilibrium that the ideological participants have agreed to, and will continue to agree to, until it benefits them to alter the institution (the status quo equilibrium), which the following chapters demonstrate is more often than is commonly thought.

population" (1964, 211).[20] This book will show that both elite individuals and social groups are important in the creation and transformation of ideologies.

Second, by recognizing that ideology does not simply exist inside the head of an individual, but that it exists in groups through language, theoretically oriented political scientists have pointed out another way that ideology is a political structure: Ideology shapes and constrains individual behavior and action because language, in general, shapes the behavior of individuals who think within and use that language. In this way, ideology is a mental framework that not only gives coherence to disparate attitudes and ideas, but also structures the way people think and talk. Ideologies structure how political actors conceive of political events by providing "the languages, the concepts, categories, imagery of thought, and the systems of representation" that political actors use to engage with the world around them (S. Hall 1986, 25–26). As a system of ideas that exists in the form of linguistic discourse, ideology constrains political debate both within and between members of ideological groups (Hinich and Munger 1994, 62).

Third, given that ideologies are narratives and systems of ideas in language discourse, historically oriented political scientists have pointed out that they are socially constructed.

Political positions that seemed to rest on natural affinities in fact were established slowly over decades during which otherwise disparate elements were hitched together through associative chains. The principal task of [ideological] analysis, as we understand it, is to denaturalize the prevailing associations by recouping the acts of cultural suturing that linked social and linguistic fragments into seemingly coherent political positions.

(Hattam and Lowndes 2007, 204)

As social contructs, ideologies are created and transformed by individuals in the relevant language community. This book traces how the ideas and theories that make up a party ideology at any given time were brought together, transformed, and discarded. I find that political office-seekers and office-holders are some of the most important political actors in changing party ideologies.

Fourth and finally, the methodological approach of this book has benefited from scholars that have pointed out the institutional character

---

[20] For example, Democratic Party ideology constrained the thinking, speaking, and acting of both elite Democratic politicians and ordinary self-identifying Democratic voters in the 1932 campaign and election, but FDR did more than anyone else to transform the meaning and content of Democratic Party ideology over the course of his presidency.

of ideology. Rogers Smith, for example, identified "political ideologies" as one among "a very broad range of structures" that "shape the conduct of political actors" (1997, 510). He has insisted that, when thinking about institutions and ideas, "a sharp dichotomy doesn't work" (R. Smith 1995, 139). Richard Bensel identified "ideational communities" as an example of "institutions" whose transformations are studied in the subfield of "American political development" (APD) (2014, 104–105). James Ceaser argued that political scientists should study political ideas, including "foundational ideas," and how they change over time (2006).

Unfortunately, in most APD scholarship, "the relationship between ideation and behavior usually focuses on the role of ideology as motivation or frame for political action and usually neglects the fact that ideology is as much a product of political action as its cause." We need to go another step further "to unpack the relationship so that it can be restructured as a dialectically transformative process for both ideation and behavior" (Bensel 2014, 104–105). As Byron Shafer pointed out, "if central policy preferences can be argued to *drive* the interaction of the elements of political structure, they are just as much a *product* of that interaction" (Shafer 1991, 44).

By treating ideologies as institutions that both shape the behavior of political actors and are transformed by political entrepreneurs, this book seeks to take up the challenge to examine how "ideology [is] significantly affected by politics" (March and Olsen 1984). Ideologies are not formal organizational institutions like legislatures and political parties, but they are informal structures: prescriptions, mental frameworks, and norms that "constrain and shape human beliefs, values, [and] interests" (Katznelson and Weingast 2005, 14). Thinking of ideologies as endogenous political structures helps us avoid the Liberal Conservative Myth. This more accurate conception of ideologies will shape the discussion of party ideology development in this book.

7 SOCIETY AND POLITY-CENTERED VIEWS OF AMERICAN PARTY IDEOLOGIES

The first chapter of this book has argued that ideologies are subject to dramatic change over time. This insight has enormous consequences for the currently dominant "master theory" of political science, which frequently assumes the Liberal Conservative Myth (Hacker and Pierson 2014). This first chapter has also made the methodological case for treating ideologies as endogenous political structures. Our next task is to face the question that naturally follows: What explains the changes we observe in party ideologies over the course of American history?

To the extent that scholars have recognized the evolutionary character of American party ideologies, they have focused almost exclusively on non-political factors. Political economists and political sociologists have pointed out how changes in the economy and society drive changes in the parties. However, these explanations are incomplete by ignoring the impact of autonomous political actors and institutions. The subsequent chapters of this book, instead, follow the recommendation of institutional scholars that "political party behavior is best understood by observing the strategic imperatives of political leaders and institutional arrangements, rather than by focusing on the demands of a mass constituency" (Mettler 1996, 339). Specifically, this book focuses on the changing incentives of party leaders as parties change control of government institutions.

In 1998, John Gerring ended his study of American party ideology history by concluding that there is "no general factor at work that might explain the development of American party ideologies" (1998, 274). He faulted the previous "society-centered" attempts at explaining American party ideology development as misconceiving the role that the mass public has in shaping party ideologies, and as being unable to account for many of the changes observed in American party history. More recent scholars have taken up this challenge to show how polity-centered factors have influenced party ideology evolution (James 2000). This book also takes up Gerring's challenge to see if a "polity-centered" approach can improve our understanding of change in party ideologies.

It is important to understand how party ideologies evolve because the particular meaning and content of the two major parties' ideologies have a tremendous impact on American social and political life. To a large extent, party ideology "is the basis for choice in large, mass electorates" (Hinich and Munger 1994, 95). The ideologies that the two major parties present to the electorate shape the way Americans think about politics, the issues they debate, and the policies they pursue – for better or for worse.

2

A Political Theory of American Party Ideology Development

What is government itself, but the greatest of all reflections on human nature? If men were angels, no government would be necessary. If angels were to govern men, neither external nor internal controls on government would be necessary. In framing a government which is to be administered by men over men, the great difficulty lies in this: you must first enable the government to control the governed; and in the next place oblige it to control itself.

–James Madison (1787)

I INTRODUCTION

In addition to pointing out the severe problems caused by the Liberal Conservative Myth, and its implications for the currently dominant "master theory" of political science, Chapter 1 also established the fact that American party ideologies are constantly subject to dramatic change. Chapter 2 will now address the question that naturally arises from this conclusion: "What explains the developments we observe?" In tackling this question, I do not want to dismiss the important work done by political scientists showing that ideas, including ideologies, are powerful catalysts for important changes to institutional arrangements and political outcomes. I agree that ideas matter, and that they are powerful sources of political change (Leighton and Lopez 2013). The ideas that are dominant in a given community help determine how people conceive of their interests and how they choose and shape their political institutions. However, this book shows that the reverse is also true:

Institutional arrangements and the interests of individuals help determine how communities choose and shape their ideologies or "public philosophy" (Lowi 1969, Beer 1978).

This chapter outlines a political institutional theory of American party ideology development focusing on party control of government institutions. The subsequent empirical chapters demonstrate that alternating party control of government institutions has a significant influence on how party ideologies evolve.[1] Before articulating this theory, it will be useful here to define the terms "political party," "ideology," and "party ideology" as they are used throughout the rest of the book.

2 DEFINING POLITICAL PARTIES, POLITICAL IDEOLOGIES, AND PARTY IDEOLOGIES

The conceptual definitions of parties and ideologies used in this book draw upon a long line of social science scholarship. A political party is a team of individuals "seeking to control the governing apparatus by gaining office in a duly constituted election" (Downs 1957).[2] Parties are not only a team of individuals, but they are also organizations. They are political institutions created and transformed by politicians, partisan activists, and ambitious office seekers and officeholders (Aldrich 1995).[3] Parties are not only teams of individuals and organizations, but they are also diverse "coalitions of groups with intense preferences on issues managed by politicians" (Karol 2009). These politicians aggregate and articulate the preferences, attitudes, and ideas of the groups in their coalition (Key 1964, 22). Thus, parties are constituted in government,

---

[1] Of course, party control of government is not the only factor. The most significant driver of party ideology change is public ideology development, which is the product of innumerable historical contingencies and factors including major events (like wars and economic depressions) and major secular developments (like industrialization, immigration, urbanization, the development of the welfare state, the development of the national security state, and racial, class, religious, and ethnic conflicts). The parties change their positions and ideologies as the larger public changes its positions and ideologies. The study of American political culture, "traditions," and thought, which bears on public ideology change, has rightfully received a great deal of attention by historians and political scientists (Croly 1909, Hartz 1955, R. Smith 1993, Sandel 1996).

[2] These individuals may seek to control governing institutions because they want to implement certain principles, because they simply want to enjoy the benefits of holding office, or both.

[3] These party actors who construct and change parties are often theoretically minded politicians like Hamilton, Jefferson, Madison, Van Buren, TR, Wilson, and FDR (Ceaser 1979, Milkis 1993, Skowronek 1997).

in party organizations, and in the electorate.[4] Parties are characterized by caucuses of politicians who seek to control government institutions; by formal organizations with officers and resources like the Democratic National Convention, the California Republican Party, or a city political machine; and by interests and ideologies that shape the way party members talk and act in dealing with each other and with the public.

It is important to distinguish between political parties and political ideologies. Even though they have similar functions – organizing coalitions of individuals – they do so in different ways (Noel 2013, 2, 8, Hinich and Munger 1994). A political ideology is a "verbal image of the good society and the chief means of constructing such a society" (Downs 1957). Because an ideology has a broad idea about what the good society looks like, and what society now looks like, it includes a variety of specific means of achieving the desired ends. Thus, an ideology includes several different issue positions that are linked together through this "verbal image." Ideology is a "configuration of ideas and attitudes in which the elements are bound together by some form of constraint or functional interdependence" (Converse 1964, 207). This configuration of political ideas, attitudes, and issue positions are linked together by, and constrained by, the verbal image of the good society. In this conceptualization, ideology is "a shared body of reference – a configuration of more or less abstract ideas" (Elkins and McKitrick 1993, 13).

An ideology is a mental framework that not only gives coherence to disparate attitudes and ideas, but also structures the way people think and talk.[5] While ideologies of course exist inside the heads of individuals, like languages, they also exist in communities as shared ways of speaking, thinking, and writing. Thus, an ideology is the "more or less coherent body of assumptions, values, and ideas that [bind people] together as it shape[s] their common understanding of society and politics and len[ds] a common meaning to events" (Banning 1978, 15).

Groups, including political parties, articulate ideologies partly because they are "economizing device[s]" that simplify decision-making for individuals who identify with, or subscribe, to the ideology (North 1981, 49). As Downs explained, "when voters can expertly judge every detail of

---

[4] This book will focus on parties at the national level. Specifically, in analyzing party ideology, this book follows Gerring (1998) in focusing on the "presidential wing" of the party – that is, the national messages that parties articulate through presidents and presidential candidates.

[5] An ideology need not be coherent to the outside observer in order for it to do the work of structuring disparate attitudes and ideas.

every stand taken and relate it directly to their own views of the good society, they are interested only in issues, not in philosophies. Therefore parties never need to form *weltanschauungen* at all, but can merely take *ad hoc* stands on practical problems as they arise" (Downs 1957, 98). However, given the information costs involved, party ideology is a useful heuristic that parties use to appeal to individuals' more general belief systems and worldviews – which are also tied up in their sense of group attachments.[6] As "norms of cultural appropriateness," ideology helps party members "cope with the cognitive constraints on their information-processing" (Teles and Dagan 2015). Parties use ideology for the same reason that they use patronage jobs or policy programs: to attract people to their party. Just as the spoils of office can attract office-seekers to work for a party's victory at the polls, and just as policies aimed at certain constituencies or interest groups can attract groups into a party's coalition, so, too, can a party ideology attract individuals and groups to support a party.

A party ideology is a system of ideas shared by party members that shapes the way they think, talk, and act. As political structures, party ideologies are belief systems that shape and constrain the thinking, attitudes, decision-making, and behavior of party members. Like party organizations (Aldrich 1995), though, party ideologies are also created and transformed by political actors, and it is often elites who play a decisive role in determining the meaning and content of a party's ideology at any given time (Converse 1964, Noel 2013). Party ideologies "provide the language in which groups debate and disagree" (Hinich and Munger 1994, 5).

Although they are related, it is important here to distinguish between party ideology and the behavior of party members. Party ideology exists in language: in the rhetoric, discourses, mental frameworks, and narratives used among those who identify with the party. Ideology exists in "thinking, speech, and writing" (Elkins and McKitrick 1993, 13). The different parts of an ideology are "elements of political discourse" (Ceaser 2006, 5). The behavior of party members, on the other hand, exists in action. Party ideology constrains the behavior of any given party member depending on a variety of factors including: how embedded they are in the mental frameworks and linguistic patterns of the party ideology, how committed the individual is, personally, to the party ideology, and what other circumstances are involved in their decision-making process. The behavior of political officeholders is the product of innumerable

---

[6] Rodrik and Mukand distinguish between two kinds of ideas that operate in "ideational politics": Ideas about "how the world works" play a role in "worldview politics," while "ideas about voters' self-identity" play a role in "identity politics" (2016, 2).

psychological, sociological, economic, and institutional factors – only one of which is party ideology. According to the political institutional theory of party ideology development tested here, members of a party exercising the powers of government institutions will often act in ways contrary to their party's ideology: Notably, when a new party takes control of government, the members of the party in government will often exercise the powers at their disposal by enacting interventionist policies – even if their party's ideology during the campaign and in the early years of their control of government calls for limited government power and limited intervention.

This is what happened to the Jeffersonian Republicans in the early nineteenth century. Although Republicans had spent the 1790s criticizing executive power, nationalism, and militarism, once he became president, Jefferson found it necessary to send a naval fleet to attack Tripoli and Algiers without a declaration of war from Congress. When the opportunity to purchase the Louisiana Territory presented itself, despite Jefferson's own small-government scruples, and despite his party's limited-government ideology, he took advantage of the opportunity because it served other aspects of the party's ideology and served the interests of party members in the South and West. When the British Royal Navy impressed American sailors into service and seized their cargo, the Jeffersonian Republican Party, despite their free trade ideological commitments, passed the Embargo Act of 1807 because of the opportunity it gave Republicans, who were generally more hostile to England, to strike back. After enacting these policies, and many others that contrasted with the party's ideology, the Jeffersonian Republican Party faced incentives to change their party's ideology to justify these actions. Over time, they gradually did change their ideology.

Similarly, this is what happened to the Democrats in the 1930s. With the national crisis of the Great Depression in full force – despite their previous critiques of Republican big government – the Democratic Party spent, regulated, and intervened beyond what their predecessors had attempted. President Roosevelt quickly used his party's control of unified government to pass New Deal legislation despite the party's previous theory of governance and theory of economic intervention.[7] The Democratic Party used the powers at its disposal to pursue other aspects of party ideology like equality, support for agriculture, and support

---

[7] If Democrats had nominated John Nance Garner or Al Smith in 1932, it might have taken longer for President Garner or President Smith to come around to active intervention in the national economy than it took for the relatively progressive President Roosevelt.

for the urban poor, and to benefit the various groups that made up the burgeoning New Deal coalition. The Southern wing of the party, represented by Democrats like John Nance Garner, benefitted from New Deal programs like the AAA, REA, and TVA. The urban, working-class wing of the party, represented by city machines like Tammany Hall, benefited from New Deal programs like the CCC, FERA, NIRA, and WPA. The progressive wing of the party, represented by upper-class and/or intellectual Democrats like FDR, were happy to see the Democratic Party return to the policies of Woodrow Wilson. To justify these interventions, the party rapidly changed its ideology during the 1930s to emphasize and promote Progressive ideas while discarding their previous limited government ideas.

We should keep in mind that just because political actors can participate in the creation and transformation of political ideologies does not mean that they can do so exogenously or at will. These political actors are embedded in a language community that limits the way they even think about the activity of party ideology change. As Elkins and McKitrick explain, new "ascriptions of meaning, then, must in the most basic sense be fashioned out of what is already there. The clusters of ideas, the values attached to them, and the modes whereby they are put into words must be drawn from some common reservoir; otherwise, there can be no echoes, no recognition, no meaning" (1993, 13). This linguistic character of ideology means that transformations of ideology are limited. Any radical changes in some part of an ideology must be paired with consistency in other parts of the ideology for it to make sense and remain relevant. For example, when Democratic Party ideology changed in the early twentieth century from advocating limited national power and limited economic intervention to advocating expansive national power and expansive economic intervention, other aspects of the party's ideology remained consistent, and familiar terms were put to new uses. Notably, Democrats refashioned the term "liberal" to no longer refer to *laissez-faire*, free-market policies, but to refer to expansive government power and intervention on behalf of the "common man" (Milkis 1993, 49).

Even though ideologies are politically constructed, subject to change over time, and tools used by political parties, we must not fall into the trap of thinking that ideologies are merely artificial rationalizations masking real, subterranean interests.[8] Ideologies are systems of ideas that

---

[8] The interests and objectives of political actors are not only mediated by ideas and beliefs about the world around them, but they are also shaped by those ideas (Goldstein and Keohane 1993).

are sincerely held by individuals and groups of people, and they reflect facts about the world in which we live with varying levels of accuracy. As sincerely held belief systems, political ideologies have real constraining power on the ideas, attitudes, and actions of political actors. They are powerful systems of ideas.

Finally, it is important to note that a party ideology may or may not be different from other general ideologies shared by groups of people such as liberalism, conservatism, and socialism. For most of American history, the ideologies of the two major parties have been distinct from other general ideologies, but in recent years the changing meaning and content of Republican Party ideology (what we might call Republicanism) has tracked very closely to the changing meaning and content of conservatism. Likewise, the evolution of Democratic Party ideology has tracked very closely to the evolution of liberalism and progressivism (Noel 2013). Regardless of the labels we use to describe them, at all points in American history the two major parties have articulated some ideology (Hinich and Munger 1994, Gerring 1998, 61).

3 THE STRUCTURE OF AMERICAN PARTY IDEOLOGIES

This book's treatment of party ideologies is based on the conceptualization of ideologies as structures composed of "idea-elements" in a hierarchy with "different levels of generality" and stability (Ceaser 2006, 5). At the base of this pyramid, the most general and stable idea-elements that anchor a party's ideology are "foundational concepts" (Ceaser 2006) that explain the party's "fundamental principles" (DiSalvo 2012), "fundamental beliefs" (Peffley and Hurwitz 1985, 872) or "ends." These fundamental aspects of a party's ideology – like the Democratic Party's current language about social equality or the Republican Party's recent rhetoric about economic liberty – are not immutable, but they rarely change. Another type of idea that helps constitute a party's ideology, less stable than the party's foundational ideas, are "theories of intervention" that "designate the areas and extent to which government should intervene" in society and the world (DiSalvo 2012, 32). A third type of idea within a party ideology, also more subject to change than the party's foundational ideas, are "theories of governance" that outline how governing powers should be distributed among various institutions. Many observers of politics have noticed how Democrats and Republicans have changed their attitudes toward, for example, executive power or judicial power over the years. Finally, at the top of this pyramid are specific issue positions, which are perhaps the most visible and mutable part of a party's ideology. Thus, ideologies not only bundle issue positions together (Noel 2013), but they also bind issue positions to "more abstract or fundamental" idea-elements within the ideology (Peffley and Hurwitz 1985).[9]

Previous scholarship has focused on how fixed and stable "foundational ideas" interact with changing historical circumstances to lead to new theories of intervention, theories of governance, issue positions, and political behavior. While I agree that this process is an important part of party ideology change, one of the contributions of this book is to show how the causal arrow can also run in the other direction. That is, changes in political behavior can lead to changes in party issue positions, theories of governance, and theories of intervention, which can then lead to change in foundational ideas. While this book necessarily engages with all of these different parts, or levels, of a party's ideology, it focuses specifically on the development of the two major parties' theories of governance and theories of intervention.

4 A POLITICAL INSTITUTIONAL THEORY OF AMERICAN PARTY IDEOLOGY DEVELOPMENT

Building on previous scholarship, which explains that politicians almost universally seek to maximize their power,[10] this book argues that the tendency for politicians to expand their power has implications for party ideology evolution through a series of steps. First, party control of government institutions provides incentives for members of the party in power to exercise and expand the powers at their disposal. Occasionally, this incentive is strong enough to cause officeholders to act against the constraints of their party's preexisting ideology. Second, actively exercising the powers of government institutions provides incentives for members of the party in power to develop their theory of governance in a way that justifies the exercise of government power by those institutions. Likewise, by the logic of party competition (Lee 2009), members of the party out of power face incentives to develop their party's theory of governance in a way that calls

---

[9] This point is worth repeating. Although ideologies bundle issue positions together, that is not all they do. They are *not* merely a group of issue positions. They are systems of ideas that include ideas about: how the world works, identities, the ends of government, how power should be distributed among governing institutions, what the good society looks like, and a host of other ideas.

[10] See, for example, Neustadt (1960), Skowronek (1997), Moe and Howell (1999), and Howell (2013).

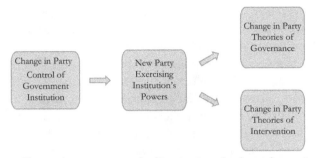

FIGURE 2.1 Change in party control of institutions leads to change in party ideologies

for restraint by those institutions. Third, and in a similar way, actively exercising the powers of government institutions provides incentives for members of the party in power to develop their theories of intervention in ways that justify those institutions intervening in society and the world. Likewise, by the logic of party competition, members of the party out of power face incentives to develop their party's theories of intervention in ways that call for less intervention by those institutions (see Figure 2.1).

This book examines the implications of this model for three different aspects of party ideology: economic policy, foreign policy, and judicial policy. Chapter 3 shows how members of the party in control of the White House often change their party's theory of governance to advocate for a strong presidency, centralized bureaucratic administration, and unilateral executive action. Since intervening in foreign affairs is one of the primary powers that the party in control of the presidency can exercise, they also advocate for more foreign intervention. Conversely, members of the party in opposition to the White House change their party's theory of governance to advocate for limited presidential power, decentralized bureaucratic administration, and working jointly with Congress. They also change their party's theory of intervention in a way that advocates for less foreign intervention.

Chapter 4 shows how members of a party in simultaneous control of the presidency and Congress have incentives to change their party's theory of governance to advocate for a strong national government, centralization of power in Washington, and judicial deference to Congress and the president. Since intervening in the economy is one of the primary powers that the party in control of government can exercise, they are also likely to advocate for more economic intervention. Conversely, members of the party in opposition to unified government have incentives to change their party's theory of governance to advocate for limited national government power, decentralized federalism, and judicial checks on the elected branches of government. Furthermore, the opposition party is likely to advocate for less economic intervention.

Chapter 5 shows how members of a party in control of the Supreme Court have incentives to change their party's theory of governance to advocate for a strong judiciary, judicial independence, and judicial supremacy. Since intervening judicially to change politics and society is one of the primary powers that the party in control of the Supreme Court can exercise, they are also likely to advocate for more judicial intervention. Conversely, members of the party in opposition to the Supreme Court have incentives to change their party's theory of governance in a way that advocates for limited judicial power and judicial deference to the elected branches of government. A party that changes its theory of governance to advocate for less judicial power is also likely to change its ideology to advocate for less judicial intervention.

These three aspects of party ideology are, of course, not exhaustive. Many other aspects, like monetary policy or immigration policy, do not seem to be explained by party control of government institutions. The political institutional theory of party ideology development has implications for some, but certainly not all, aspects of party ideologies. The three dimensions of party ideology examined in this book were selected, in part, because they have an identifiable relationship to party control of government institutions, and thus provide useful tests of my novel theory that changes in party control of government lead to changes in party ideologies. Besides that, I also chose them because these three aspects of party ideology tend to be of particular interest to observers of American politics. Other scholars may identify observable implications of the political institutional theory for other aspects of party ideology not treated here, and they are invited to test those hypotheses accordingly. Before proceeding to the empirical chapters of the book, in this section I will more fully articulate the political institutional theory of American party ideology development. I will identify the premises underlying the theory and define more clearly the causal mechanisms of the theory.

4.1 Theoretical Premises

There are two theoretical premises underlying this book's theory. The first premise is that politicians usually want to expand and exercise the powers at their disposal. This is especially true when politicians face what they deem "crisis management" situations: extraordinary events that require an extraordinary response by government officials. This assumption fits with previous scholarship on the presidency.[11] Neustadt (1960) explained that all presidents want to accumulate power in order to accomplish their ends – it is just that some presidents are more effective than others in accumulating this power. According to Skowronek (1997, 12), all presidents have certain constitutional powers that come with the presidential office, and the desire to exercise these powers is "an impulse that all presidents share" in order to "realize their ambitions." Moe and Howell explain: "whatever else presidents might want, they must at bottom be seekers of power" (1999, 854). The desire to respond to events, exercise the powers at their disposal, and expand the powers at their disposal is a general disposition that characterizes most politicians – including presidents, members of Congress, and Supreme Court justices.

This first premise also fits with the American Founders' "Whig" theory of politics. At the Constitutional Convention, George Mason argued that: "From the nature of man we may be sure, that those who have power in their hands ... will always ... increase it" (Farrand 1911, 578). In the ratification debates, James Madison argued that Americans should adopt the newly formed Constitution because it effectively responds to this central problem of human nature and politics: "In framing a government which is to be administered by men over men, the great difficulty lies in this: you must first enable the government to control the governed; and in the next place oblige it to control itself" (Publius 1787). The Anti-Federalists who opposed Madison and his Constitution relied on the same underlying theory of politics in their arguments against ratification: "It is a truth confirmed by the unerring experience of ages, that every man, and every body of men, invested with power, are ever disposed to increase it, and to acquire a superiority over every thing that stands in their way" (Brutus 1787). This fundamental belief also infused early American political thinkers in the years after ratification. According to the Federalist Samuel Williams: "Any body of men who enjoy the powers and profits of public employments, will unavoidably wish to have those profits and powers increased ... The effect seems to be universal. It has ever been the case that government has had an universal tendency, to increase its own powers, revenues, and influence. No people ought to expect that things will have a different tendency among them" (1794).

This premise alone, however, is not sufficient to make us think that changing party control of government will lead to parties changing their

---

[11] For a review of this literature, see Sollenberger (2014).

ideologies. After all, politicians could simply act on their incentives to expand and exercise power without parties changing their ideologies. The second premise underlying this theory, however, is that partisans want to change their party ideology in ways that justify the actions of their co-partisans and vilify the actions of their opponents.

This second theoretical premise is based on the logic of party competition. In the zero-sum, two-party system, partisans have reasons to change their rhetoric in ways that justify the actions of their own party while criticizing the actions of the opposing party. While Frances Lee points out that the logic of party competition gives partisans incentives to act in ways that cannot simply be explained by ideology or preferences (2009), this book goes another step further to argue that the logic of party competition gives partisans incentives to act in ways that actually change their party's ideology. When parties with relatively noninterventionist ideologies take control of government, their preexisting ideology will act as a constraint in making decisions to intervene in society and the world. However, controlling the levers of power will prove tempting because of all the ways that they could intervene on behalf of other, more foundational, aspects of their ideology, and on behalf of themselves and the interests of their party members. Thus, as circumstances arise and as party entrepreneurs act over time, government officeholders will tend to intervene despite their previous rhetoric. To justify the use of these powers, parties often change their theories of governance and theories of intervention.

The desire of politicians to exercise power almost always manifests as a desire to use government power to intervene in society and the world, and this has implications for change in a party's theory of intervention.[12] In the case of the presidency, when a presidential candidate comes to power, they have incentives to exercise the powers of their office even if they previously criticized the exercise of such powers by their predecessor. One of the greatest powers that a president has is that of commander-in-chief in foreign affairs, and so presidents typically become more interventionist on foreign policy than what we would expect from their rhetoric and ideology prior to assuming office. Thus, even though we have had many

---

[12] It is feasible that politicians could exercise the power at their disposal by not intervening, or by even shrinking the size and/or role of government, but this is rare in American politics. Much more often, politicians simply use the power at their disposal to intervene in pursuit of different ends than their predecessors. Chapter 4 shows how the Jeffersonian Republicans briefly used the power at their disposal to shrink the size of government, but quickly changed course and changed their party's theory of national government power and theory of economic intervention accordingly.

presidential candidates criticize incumbent presidents for hawkish or interventionist foreign policy since the turn of the twentieth century, it is something to reflect upon that few presidents – if any – have governed as noninterventionists during that time.

4.2 Ripple Effects of Changes in Party Theories of Governance and Intervention

Although parties frequently change their theories of intervention, differences in more fundamental aspects of party ideology may cause party leaders in control of government to intervene in ways different from how the previous party intervened. Arguably, the Republican Party's foreign interventionism during the Bush 43 administration was directed at different ends, and undergirded by different ideological foundations, than the Democratic Party's foreign interventionism during the Clinton administration. Similarly, in the case of unified government, the economic interventionism of the Democratic Party's New Deal was arguably directed at different ends, and undergirded by different ideological foundations, than the economic interventionism of the Republican Party's Square Deal. Finally, in the case of the Supreme Court, the Democratic Party's judicial interventionism in the postwar era was directed at different ends, and undergirded by different ideological foundations, than the Republican Party's judicial interventionism during the Lochner Era.

Nonetheless, these changes in party theories of intervention often have ripple effects on other aspects of party ideology. For example, when the Democrats became more interventionist on foreign policy – relative to the Republicans – during World War I and World War II, this helped transform other aspects of the Democratic Party's ideology. As Gerring (1998) points out, the party shifted from a "populist" era to a "universalist" era in the mid-twentieth century, and the party's emphasis on spreading democracy – articulated by Wilson and FDR – helped bring about this change in a more fundamental aspect of party ideology. Democrats evolved from being relatively more nationalist to relatively more internationalist in the twentieth century.

4.3 The Ingredients for Party Ideology Change

This book hypothesize that long-term changes – but not short-term changes – in party control of government institutions lead to party ideology transformation. The reason I focus on long-term changes is because the incentives that party actors face (to exercise power when in office and to justify co-partisans and criticize opponents) are not sufficient, on their own, to cause party ideology development. Ideologies, like institutions, are structures that are not easily changed. First of all, party leaders face incentives to maintain existing ideological positions: If ideologies are changed too often and too cavalierly, then they lose their usefulness as reputational signaling mechanisms to voters (Hinich and Munger 1994, 75). Second of all, because group ideologies are language discourses shared by millions of people, they typically cannot change their meaning for so many people all at once. It usually takes a long time for parties to stop using their previous rhetoric and for the new rhetoric to gain currency among politicians, interest groups, writers, activists, and party identifiers in the electorate. Finally, due to path dependence, the longer the two parties have held divergent ideological positions, the more calcified these ideologies become and the more difficult they are to change (Pierson 2004).

Thus, several ingredients need to come together before we would expect this inertia to be overcome, and this typically takes several years. First, there must be a salient political issue (like the government's response to the Great Depression) for the parties to divide over (Stephenson 1999). Ideological change requires the articulation and exchange of political ideas. In the case of party theories of foreign intervention, a political issue must arise within foreign policy that "entangles" the president and the parties in political debate. In the 2000s, the Iraq War was a catalyst for changing party theories of governance (e.g., the role of the president in the American political system), party theories of intervention (e.g., how much America should intervene militarily in the world), and party theories of ends (e.g., the objective of spreading democracy).

Second, there must be party leaders in government willing to act in ways contrary to the party's previous ideological commitments. For the Democrats of the 1930s, this was Franklin Roosevelt and his Democratic New Deal Congress. For the Republicans of the 2000s, this was George W. Bush and his Iraq War.

Third, once government officeholders have acted contrary to party ideology, and there is a new incentive to change party ideology to justify co-partisans and criticize opponents, there must be party entrepreneurs – often the leaders of a party faction – who can recognize opportunities, and assemble the necessary resources, to act on these new incentives (Sheingate 2003). This approach appropriates Terry Moe's "logic of institutional development": On occasion, certain actors, operating in particular institutional settings, have the necessary incentives and resources to successfully change a party's ideology (1985).[13] For example, recognizing an opportunity for change, Van Buren and Jackson provided the political entrepreneurship needed to change their party's ideology in the 1820s from "national" republicanism, which advocated for a stronger national union and more government intervention, to "democratic" republicanism, which advocated for a more limited national government and less intervention in the economy.[14] Similarly, Franklin Roosevelt provided the political entrepreneurship, and his bully pulpit as president provided the resources, needed to change his party's ideology in the 1930s from "classical" liberalism, which advocated *laissez-faire* economic policies, to "new" liberalism, which advocated for active government involvement in regulating the capitalist economy and its outcomes.

Fourth, when these party entrepreneurs are successful, different groups within the parties rise and fall in importance in accordance with the party's changing ideology. To say that party ideologies evolve over time does not necessarily mean that the people who make up the two parties are constantly switching parties or changing their minds (although both phenomena do happen, and they are an important part of party ideology development).[15] It can also mean that certain strands of thought within the two parties become more vocal or muted depending on circumstances. For example, the Antiwar Left has long been a part of the Democratic Party: It was suppressed during the Kennedy and Johnson administrations (a suppression resulting in riots at the 1968 party convention) but received the party's presidential nomination in 1972 once Republicans controlled the White House and oversaw the Vietnam War. It was vocal during the Reagan administration, muted during the Clinton administration, and vocal again during the Bush administration's Iraq War. Similarly, isolationists in the Republican Party lost their dominance in the 1950s during the Eisenhower administration, were revived in the 1990s during the Clinton administration, muted again in the 2000s

---

[13] In the twentieth century, this has usually meant collaboration between elite political actors and political thinkers referred to by Noel (2013) as "academic scribblers."

[14] Despite not controlling the presidency, Van Buren's political connections to various party machines and factions, and Jackson's national popularity, provided the resources necessary for such a change.

[15] Karol (2009) has shown that members of Congress do frequently change positions on a variety of issues.

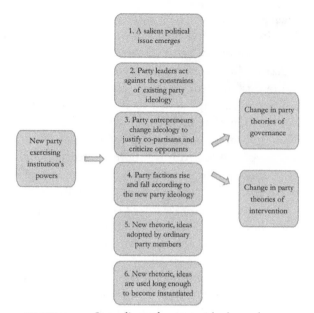

FIGURE 2.2 Ingredients for party ideology change

during the Bush administration, and revived again in the 2010s during the Obama administration. This shift in emphasis – some groups within the party becoming more influential in shaping party platforms, candidate selection, and party stances at some times more than others – is a key ingredient in party ideology evolution (DiSalvo 2012).

Fifth, it is not enough for party elites in government to change a party's issue positions, talking points, and narratives. These new ideas, discourses, and rhetoric must be adopted by ordinary party identifiers in the electorate. Sixth, and finally, the new narratives, ideas, and rhetoric must be employed long enough that they become instantiated in discourse (see Figure 2.2).

Given that so many ingredients need to come together before party ideologies durably change, under normal circumstances, only a long-term (but not short-term) change in party control of government provides enough time for all of the necessary ingredients to emerge. All parties face incentives on day one of unified control of government to expand the powers of the national government and intervene in the economy. How long it takes for them to act on these incentives in opposition to their ideology, how long it takes for the ideology to change in a way to justify these actions, and whether or not any ideological changes end up being durable depend on many different factors. In general, however, we should expect it to take at least two presidential terms for all six of the necessary ingredients to come together. As a result, the independent variable of this study is not simply a change in party control of government, but a *long-term* change in party control lasting eight years or longer.

4.4 No Long-Term Change in Party Control

Just as this book hypothesizes that change in long-term party control of government institutions leads to change in party theories of governance and intervention, it also hypothesizes that the absence of change in long-term party control of government institutions leads to relative stasis in party theories of governance and intervention. This is due to the path-dependent nature of party ideologies. Absent external forces (like socioeconomic changes), we expect that the meaning and content of ideologies will remain relatively static. The ideologies held and espoused by parties at time 1 are likely to be held and espoused at time 2, and the ideologies held and espoused by parties at time 2 are likely to be held and espoused at time 3, etc.

Because this book focuses on long-term changes in party control of government institutions, I will not discuss all the numerous short-term changes in American history. For example, even though there have been thirteen instances of the relatively less interventionist party taking control of unified government, because these are almost always short-term changes in control, they almost never lead to durable shifts in party theories of economic intervention. In 1801, 1829, 1835, 1845, 1853, 1857, 1893, 1913, 1933, 1953, 2001, 2003, and 2017 the relatively less interventionist party took control of unified government, but only the changes in 1801 and 1933 led to durable changes in the relative ideological positions of the two parties with respect to national government power and economic intervention. In these two instances, the new party in power held on long enough to durably change the parties' ideologies. In every other instance, the new party's control of government was quickly reversed one or two congressional elections later. In these cases, there was not a long enough period for all of the ingredients necessary for ideological change to come together before the new party's unified control of government was disrupted, and the two parties lost their institutional incentives for ideological change. Only in 1801–1825, when the Republican Party had a stranglehold on unified government, and 1933–1947, when the Democratic Party dominated the national government, did the two parties' ideologies durably change on economic policy. In those instances, the changes in party ideologies became instantiated long enough to outlast the time when they lost unified control.

4.5 Relative Ideological Movement vs. Absolute Ideological Positions

Because political structures are not entirely plastic, early ideological choices made by party members create path dependence for future choices. This path dependence limits how much and how often party ideologies can change. New changes do not completely overturn or replace the content of previous ideologies but are layered on top of them. Thus, the theory does not imply that a party's ideology at any given time will correspond to its institutional position – only that parties will, in general, tend to move in the direction of their institutional positions.

In the case of the presidency and party foreign policy, we would not expect the *absolute* ideological *positions* of the parties to switch on foreign intervention with every change in party control of the White House; instead, we expect the *relative* ideological *movement* of the parties to change on foreign intervention in accordance with change in control of the presidency. For example, during the eight years of the Clinton administration, we would expect Democratic Party ideology to move in a more interventionist direction *relative* to Republican Party ideology, and for GOP ideology to move in a less interventionist direction *relative* to Democratic Party ideology, but it remains to be seen whether the two parties would move enough, relative to each other, to actually switch positions on an absolute scale of foreign intervention ideology. The eight years of the Clinton administration may not result in enough *relative* ideological movement between the two parties to overcome the *absolute* ideological distance created by twenty years of Republican control between 1969 and 1992. Thus, the theory predicts that in the 1990s, the gap between the two parties will at least narrow (if they do not actually change positions in ideological space) rather than widen.

Historical contingencies or secular developments that have a similar impact on both parties will cause the two parties' ideologies to change in the same way, but without a change in long-term control of government institutions, the hypothesis predicts that the *relative* positions of the parties will remain the same. For example, the bombing of Pearl Harbor caused almost all Americans – in both parties – to become more interventionist on foreign policy. However, if Democrats were already more hawkish than Republicans before December 1941, then this theory predicts that Democrats will continue to be *relatively* more hawkish than Republicans in 1942 – even though both parties moved in a more interventionist direction.

It is possible that particular historical contingencies or secular developments could affect the two parties differently, and that the relative ideological positions of the parties change without a change in long-term party control of government institutions. For example, the agrarian revolt of the 1890s affected the Democratic Party, which dominated the South and West where the agrarian revolt occurred, more than the Republican Party. Thus, even though there was no long-term change in party control of unified government, the relative ideological positions of the two parties changed as Democrats in the 1890s moved more toward economic intervention than Republicans. Such historical contingencies are beyond the scope of the political institutional theory examined in this book, but they are the kinds of "society-centered" factors that have been focused on by previous scholars.

5 RESEARCH DESIGN

To see if this theory can improve our understanding of American party ideology development, the following three chapters evaluate three different hypotheses derived from the political institutional theory outlined above. Chapter 3 tests the hypothesis that parties in long-term control of the presidency tend to become more interventionist on foreign policy, while parties in opposition tend to become less interventionist (see Table 2.1). Chapter 4 tests the hypothesis that parties in long-term control of unified government tend to become more interventionist on economic policy, while parties in opposition tend to become less interventionist on economic policy (see Table 2.2). Finally, Chapter 5 tests the hypothesis that parties in long-term control of the Supreme Court tend to become more interventionist on judicial policy, while parties in opposition tend to become less interventionist (see Table 2.3). This section outlines how the independent variable (change in long-term party control of government institutions) and dependent variable (change in party ideologies) will be measured.

5.1 Measuring Change in Long-Term Party Control of Government Institutions

A change in long-term party control is defined here as a change lasting for at least eight years. This time span is chosen based on Skowronek's work on reconstructive politics (1997). In American politics, a one-term president is considered a blip or an aberration. A party that only captures the presidency for one term, and is then forced to relinquish power, is a party

TABLE 2.1 *Party control of the presidency and party theories of foreign intervention (expectations)*

Time period	Independent variable: Change in long-term party control of the presidency	Dependent variable: Expected change in relative party ideologies
1 Progressive Era and Republican Empire 1900–1913	Republican presidents	Republicans should move more toward intervention than Democrats
2 World War I and Wilsonian internationalism 1913–1921	Democratic president	Democrats should move more toward intervention than Republicans
3 Interwar Era 1921–1933	Republican presidents	Republicans should move more toward intervention than Democrats
4 Democratic New Deal and World War II 1933–1953	Democratic presidents	Democrats should move more toward intervention than Republicans
5 Republican anti-communism 1953–1961	Republican president	Republicans should move more toward intervention than Democrats
6 Democratic Cold War 1961–1969	Democratic presidents	Democrats should move more toward intervention than Republicans
7 Republican Cold War 1969–1993	Republican presidents	Republicans should move more toward intervention than Democrats
8 Clinton internationalism 1993–2001	Democratic president	Democrats should move more toward intervention than Republicans
9 Bush War on Terror 2001–2009	Republican president	Republicans should move more toward intervention than Democrats
10 Obama internationalism 2009–2017	Democratic president	Democrats should move more toward intervention than Republicans

with only tenuous control of government that leaves a smaller mark on the course of American political development. "Reconstructive presidents" (and parties) are always at least two-term presidents, who then have successors from their same party continue their reconstructive work. Thus, in identifying periods of long-term party control of a

TABLE 2.2 *Party control of unified government and party theories of economic intervention (expectations)*

Time period	Independent variable: Change in long-term party control of unified government	Dependent variable: Expected change in relative party ideologies
1 Federalist Era 1789–1801	Government divided between Federalists and Republicans	Federalists and Republicans should maintain their relative positions on intervention
2 Jeffersonian Era and Era of Good Feelings 1801–1825	Republican government	Republicans should move more toward intervention than Federalists
3 Emergence of mass, two-party system and competitive politics 1825–1861	Government divided between Democrats and Whigs	Democrats and Whigs should maintain their relative positions on intervention
4 Civil War, Republican Reconstruction, Gilded Age, and Progressive Era 1861–1933	Republican government	Republicans should move more toward intervention than Democrats
5 Democratic New Deal, liberal consensus, Great Society, and party sorting 1933–present	Democratic government	Democrats should move more toward intervention than Republicans

government institution, this book looks for party control that lasts for at least eight years.

In identifying periods of change in long-term party control, I look at moments when the new institutional configuration is in tension with the existing party ideologies. Thus, I examine only instances in which one party transfers long-term control to the opposing party. A party's institutional position may shift from a long period of control to a short period of opposition and back to another long period of control, but this would not represent a new party taking long-term control. This is what happened to the presidency between 1969 and 1993. Republicans had long-term control from 1969 to 1977, Democrats had short-term control from 1977 to 1981, and Republicans regained long-term party control from 1981 to 1993. Only the change in 1969, but not the changes in 1977 or 1981 represented a change in long-term party control of the presidency.

TABLE 2.3 *Party control of the Supreme Court and party theories of judicial intervention (expectations)*

Time period	Independent variable: Change in long-term party control of the Supreme Court	Dependent variable: Expected change in relative party ideologies
1 Federalist Era and Marshall Court 1790–1836	Federalist Supreme Court	Federalists should move more toward intervention than Republicans
2 Taney Court and Chase Court 1836–1874	Democratic Supreme Court	Democrats should move more toward intervention than Whigs and Republicans
3 Gilded Age and the Lochner Era 1874–1937	Republican Supreme Court	Republicans should move more toward intervention than Democrats
4 Postwar liberal consensus and conservative response 1937–1991	Democratic Supreme Court	Democrats should move more toward intervention than Republicans
5 Rehnquist Court and Roberts Court 1991–present	Republican Supreme Court	Republicans should move more toward intervention than Democrats

5.2 Measuring Change in Party Ideologies

Ideology is a notoriously difficult political phenomenon to measure (Converse 1964), but in order to test theories that purport to explain party ideology change over time, a better measure than roll call scaling applications is required. The empirical sections that follow rely on different measures of party ideology corresponding to the three different parts of political parties recognized by political scientists: the party organization, the party-in-government, and the party-in-the-electorate.

To measure party ideology, as it exists in the party organization, I have read every major party platform in American history and made note of every sentence that talks about party theories of governance and party theories of intervention. Party platforms are useful samples of the kinds of narratives that party members tell themselves at any given time, and they are useful records of the issue positions that party members take at any given time.[16] Unfortunately, mass party organizations only emerged in the 1840s, so party platforms are largely unavailable before that time.

To measure party ideology as it exists among the party-in-government, I rely on, in addition to party platforms, the writings and speeches of party leaders in government. Whether a particular presidential candidate or member of Congress *truly* believed what they were writing or speaking is largely irrelevant for the purposes of measuring party ideology because we are interested in measuring not so much what any particular person believed about the role of government in society, but the kinds of things that party leaders, office seekers, and office holders told each other, and their constituents, about the proper role of government. This is where party ideology exists – in the narratives, mental frameworks, and discourses used by party members in discussing public policy. To measure ideology at the level of the party-in-government, I also rely on votes cast by members of Congress and the bills signed or vetoed by presidents. I do not subscribe to the assumption that roll call votes perfectly reveal ideology, but to the extent that mental frameworks, ideological narratives, and belief systems constrain the behavior of a party's members of Congress, then the voting decisions of a party's MCs can be a useful second-best proxy measurement of ideology.[17]

Finally, to measure party ideology as it exists among the party-in-the-electorate, I rely on survey data where individuals who identify with one of the two major parties express their ideas and attitudes about governance and intervention. Unfortunately, survey data only emerged in the twentieth century, so we know less about party ideology in the electorate prior to the twentieth century. Nonetheless, using survey data, voting data, party platforms, and the speeches and writings of party leaders together can give us useful measurements of party ideology developments over the course of American history.

---

[16] Several scholars have noted the consistency between campaign rhetoric (platforms and speeches) and subsequent issue positions (Pomper 1968). Others have argued that party platforms and campaign speeches are *just* rhetoric, but even if this claim is true, it does not discount them as accurate expressions of party ideology. It is true that voters no longer read party platforms, but that does not make them any less representative of party ideology. Platforms include the narratives that partisans tell themselves and the ideas that ideological partisans want to communicate – whether or not the nonpartisan electorate is listening.

[17] I also do not follow DW-NOMINATE in simply attaching ambiguous ideological labels to vote choices (e.g., labeling whatever Democrats vote for as "liberal" and whatever Republicans vote for as "conservative"). Instead, I look at specific bills to see if a party is voting for more or less national government power, presidential power, judicial power, economic intervention, foreign intervention, and judicial intervention.

6 CONCLUSION

In this chapter, I have laid the groundwork for what will follow in the rest of the book. As a preliminary matter, I have defined the important terms and concepts that are employed in the book, including "parties," "ideologies," and "party ideologies." Furthermore, I have articulated the theory that will be tested in the following three chapters that tell the story of American party ideology development. Finally, I have outlined the research design that will be used in each of these three chapters.

3

The Presidency and Party Theories of Foreign Intervention

We can't be all things to all people in the world, Jim. And I think that's where maybe the Vice President and I begin to have some differences. I'm worried about over-committing our military around the world. I want to be judicious in its use. You mentioned Haiti. I wouldn't have sent troops to Haiti. I didn't think it was a mission worthwhile. It was a nation-building mission. And it was not very successful. It cost us a couple billions of dollars and I'm not sure democracy is any better off in Haiti than it was before.

–George W. Bush (2000)

I INTRODUCTION

In the 2000 US presidential debates, George W. Bush criticized Vice President Al Gore for his role in the Clinton administration's foreign interventionism. Governor Bush pledged, instead, to have a "humble" foreign policy that would be "judicious in its use" of the American military. If elected, Bush would differ from the Democratic administration by not "over-committing our military around the world," and by not engaging in a costly, "nation-building mission" that left the invaded country no better off than it was before (Bush 2000). The foreign policy positions of the two candidates were not surprising. They represented the two different ideologies of the parties during the Clinton administration: Democrats defending US intervention in world affairs and Republicans arguing for less intervention (Schlesinger 1995).

From our contemporary standpoint, we know that the parties changed positions in the ensuing years. Just a few years later, the Democratic Party was criticizing Republicans for reckless war making, "over-committing our military around the world," a foolish "nation-building mission," and wasting American money and lives. This change was not only reflected in the discourse of party elites, but also in the attitudes of ordinary party identifiers. The American National Election Studies regularly asks Americans whether they agree or disagree with the statement "this country would be better off if we just stayed home and did not concern ourselves with problems in other parts of the world." In 1998, more Democrats than Republicans gave the interventionist response, but by 2002, significantly more Republicans than Democrats gave the interventionist response. This evolution in Republican Party ideology, becoming relatively more interventionist under Bush, and the corresponding change in the Democratic Party, becoming relatively less interventionist, is just one of numerous instances in American political history of the two major parties changing their positions, rhetoric, and ideologies with regard to foreign policy.

2 HYPOTHESIS

This chapter examines the hypothesis that parties in control of the presidency tend to change their ideologies in ways that justify more presidential power and more interventionist foreign policy, and that parties in opposition to the White House tend to change their ideologies in ways that call for less executive power and less foreign intervention. A party's advocacy of more foreign intervention includes calls for declaring war on foreign nations, sending troops into international conflicts, funding and otherwise aiding foreign nations, increasing spending on the military to prepare for foreign conflict, and greater involvement in international organizations that intervene in foreign affairs. This interventionist position has taken on many different names including internationalism, realism, nation-building, entanglements, humanitarianism, spreading democracy, hawkishness, spreading peace, or imperialism – depending on if it is being praised or criticized. Similarly, a party's advocacy of less foreign intervention includes opposition to declaring war on foreign nations, to sending troops into international conflicts, and to funding and aiding foreign nations, while expressing support for remaining neutral in international conflicts, decreasing spending on the military, and less involvement in international organizations that intervene in foreign affairs. This position has also assumed many different names, including isolationism, realism, pacifism, or dovishness – depending on if it is being praised or criticized.

The dependent variable in this chapter measures change in the *relative movement* of party positions with regard to more or less presidential power and foreign intervention. For example, at the start of the Eisenhower administration in 1953, Democratic Party ideology called for more foreign intervention than Republican Party ideology. Since the Republican Party took long-term control of the presidency between 1953 and 1960, this chapter predicts that the Republican Party would have changed its ideological position to move farther in the direction of foreign intervention than their Democratic opponents. The prediction is not necessarily that the two parties will actually switch positions in ideological space (although that is possible), but that the gap between the two parties will at least narrow. Furthermore, it is possible – due to secular shifts in American history – that both parties moved in the direction of more foreign intervention during this period. Within this general movement by society at large, however, this theory predicts that the Republican Party will move farther in that direction than the Democratic Party. Thus, it is the *relative movement* of the two parties' ideologies that is being measured rather than their *absolute positions*.

As explained earlier, given the stickiness and path dependence of ideologies, and the need for several factors to emerge simultaneously, under normal conditions it usually takes long periods of time for party ideologies to change as expected. The ingredients necessary for party ideology change include a political issue for the two parties to debate and divide over, a party entrepreneur with sufficient resources willing to act in ways to try to change the party's ideology, the rise and fall of different party factions, and the adoption of new narratives and language discourses among ordinary party identifiers. Furthermore, the new rhetoric and ideas must be in use long enough – before party control of government institutions changes back – for these changes to instantiate a durable shift in party ideology. Thus, this chapter on foreign policy looks at moments when a new party takes control of the presidency for at least eight years.[1]

Since this book focuses on long-term party control of government institutions, in order to record enough observations to be able to draw conclusions about a trend, it must look at a long stretch of US history. This chapter examines party control of the presidency and party ideologies since 1900 because the turn of the twentieth century represented a new era of American foreign affairs. These twelve decades of US history yield ten observations of long-term change in party control of the presidency (see Table 3.1). In every instance but one (1961–1969) the parties' ideologies with regard to foreign policy evolved as expected

---

[1] A party's institutional position may shift from a long period of control to a short period of opposition and back to another long period of control, but this would not represent a new party taking long-term control.

TABLE 3.1 *Party control of the presidency and party theories of foreign intervention (expectations)*

Time period	Independent variable: Change in long-term party control of the presidency	Dependent variable: Expected change in relative party ideologies
1 Progressive Era and Republican empire 1900–1913	Republican presidents	Republicans should move more toward intervention than Democrats
2 World War I and Wilsonian internationalism 1913–1921	Democratic president	Democrats should move more toward intervention than Republicans
3 Interwar Era 1921–1933	Republican presidents	Republicans should move more toward intervention than Democrats
4 Democratic New Deal and World War II 1933–1953	Democratic presidents	Democrats should move more toward intervention than Republicans
5 Republican anti-communism 1953–1961	Republican president	Republicans should move more toward intervention than Democrats
6 Democratic Cold War 1961–1969	Democratic presidents	Democrats should move more toward intervention than Republicans
7 Republican Cold War 1969–1993	Republican presidents	Republicans should move more toward intervention than Democrats
8 Clinton internationalism 1993–2001	Democratic president	Democrats should move more toward intervention than Republicans
9 Bush War on Terror 2001–2009	Republican president	Republicans should move more toward intervention than Democrats
10 Obama internationalism 2009–present	Democratic president	Democrats should move more toward intervention than Republicans

3 THE PROGRESSIVE ERA AND REPUBLICAN EMPIRE, 1900–1913

Between 1900 and 1913, Republicans controlled the presidency, and the two parties' ideologies developed as expected. Republicans developed a theory of governance that involved a strong presidency – typified in the administration of Theodore Roosevelt – and an increasingly intervention-ist foreign policy. In contrast, Democratic criticisms of presidential power became a central aspect of party platforms and rhetoric. At the same time, the Democratic Party's foreign policy, articulated by three-time presiden-tial nominee William Jennings Bryan, became critical of US military interventions and imperialism.

3.1 Historical Context

The turn of the twentieth century was a time of imperial American foreign policy. This represented an important secular shift in public ideology, with respect to foreign intervention, from the early American republic when Americans largely wished to be left alone by foreign powers (Schle-singer 1995). Over the course of the nineteenth century, American ideol-ogy – including the ideology of both major parties – became more interventionist on foreign policy for a variety of reasons, including the American appetite for territorial expansion and the rise of American economic and military power. During that time, the United States stopped fearing the military prowess of the nations of Europe and took its place as a leading world power itself.

In 1898, the American public supported, Congress declared, and the president executed war with Spain over its colonial possessions. American victory in the war resulted in the acquisition of Spain's colonies, and further embroiled the United States in foreign interventions in the following years. The Spanish-American War, and the issue of American territorial expansion, provided a foreign policy issue over which the parties could debate and distinguish themselves and their principles. Political scientist Woodrow Wilson, who had previously complained about Congressional government and the lack of executive statesmanship in the United States (Wilson 1885), recognized in a later edition of his book that the emergence of American imperial foreign policy during the McKinley administration had transformed the presidency from a weak institution that had been subject to Congressional control to a strong executive that "may put this whole volume hopelessly out of date"

(Wilson 1901). During this time of increasing presidential power and increasingly interventionist foreign policy, McKinley, Roosevelt, and Bryan were three of the party entrepreneurs most involved in developing their parties' ideologies.

3.2 Party Control of the Presidency and Party Theories of Governance

In the half-century between 1860 and 1912, just one Democrat was elected president. In long-term control of the presidency, the Republican Party's theory of governance called for a strong executive. While Lincoln articulated the doctrine of executive discretion most intelligently, by the first decade of the twentieth century, the party's ideology had expanded and been influenced by the ideas of executive power propounded by Theodore Roosevelt (Yarbrough 2012). By the end of his presidency, TR had moved his party's theory of governance a long way from the Whig Party of the 1830s–1850s and the Republican Party that impeached Andrew Johnson.[2] While the Whigs adopted their party name to indicate their opposition to executive power, Republicans at the turn of the twentieth century laid the foundations for the modern, strong executive with Presidents McKinley and Roosevelt.

The Democratic Party's theory of governance, in contrast, developed in a way that called for a constrained executive. This was a change from the antebellum period in which Jackson's Democratic Party advocated more presidential power than the Whigs. Living in the presidential wilderness for more than forty years since the Civil War had an impact on the Democratic Party. The 1904 party platform dedicated an entire section to a criticism of "Executive Usurpation":

We favor the nomination and election of a President imbued with the principles of the Constitution, who will set his face sternly against executive usurpation of legislative and judicial functions, whether that usurpation be veiled under the guise of executive construction of existing laws, or whether it take refuge in the tyrant's plea of necessity or superior wisdom.

(DNC 1904)

---

[2] The party's theory of governance during the 1910s can probably be best described as somewhere between the more radical view of executive power held by Roosevelt and the more limited view of executive power held by his successor William Howard Taft. While TR's theories were not the reigning ideology in the party, the GOP had a much different view of executive power by 1912 than it had at the start of its long-term control of the White House in 1861.

The 1908 platform criticized the exponential growth in the number of executive-appointed officeholders. In contrast to this Republican spoils system, the Democrats promised "economy in administration." Finally, the 1912 platform, at the height of Democratic anti-presidential ideology, went so far as to call for a constitutional amendment that would limit presidents to just one term.

3.3 Party Control of the Presidency and Party Theories of Foreign Intervention

Party control of the presidency also coincided with changes in party theories of foreign intervention. The 1900 GOP platform celebrated America's intervention in the Caribbean on the grounds that the United States was spreading freedom to Cuba: The Republican administration "conducted and in victory concluded a war for liberty and human rights ... To ten millions of the human race there was given a 'new birth of freedom' and to the American people a new and noble responsibility" (RNC 1900). After his heroics with the "Rough Riders," Roosevelt became McKinley's Vice President, and soon assumed the presidency. TR helped nurture the GOP's interventionist foreign policy, which included a willingness to have the United States exercise "an international police power" (T. Roosevelt 1904a).

At the same time that the GOP peaked in its interventionist foreign policy with Roosevelt, the Democratic Party moved in the other direction by nominating the outspoken critic of imperialism William Jennings Bryan in 1896, 1900, and 1908. During the second half of the nineteenth century, the Democratic Party had turned its back on the expansionism and imperialism it advocated in the 1840s and 1850s. As a party dominated by rural farmers in the South and West, it absorbed the Populist Party and became increasingly hostile to the internationalism of the urban Eastern elites who controlled the Republican Party. The 1900 platform specifically denounced America's interventions in the Philippines: "We condemn and denounce the Philippine policy of the present administration. It has involved the Republic in an unnecessary war, sacrificed the lives of many of our noblest sons, and placed the United States, previously known and applauded throughout the world as the champion of freedom, in the false and un-American position of crushing with military force the efforts of our former allies to achieve liberty and self-government." It also condemned "militarism" in general, arguing, in an echo of the Jeffersonian Republicans, that a large standing army is a threat to freedom and requires burdensome taxes (DNC 1900). The 1904 platform dedicated an entire section to what it called "imperialism":

We favor the preservation, so far as we can, of an open door for the world's commerce in the Orient without unnecessary entanglement in Oriental and European affairs, and without arbitrary, unlimited, irresponsible and absolute government anywhere within our jurisdiction. We oppose, as fervently as did George Washington, an indefinite, irresponsible, discretionary and vague absolutism and a policy of colonial exploitation, no matter where or by whom invoked or exercised. We believe with Thomas Jefferson and John Adams, that no Government has a right to make one set of laws for those "at home" and another and a different set of laws, absolute in their character, for those "in the colonies."

(DNC 1900)

The platform further criticized the Roosevelt administration for making war without Congressional approval. Like the Whigs of the nineteenth century, the Democrats were now invoking George Washington's non-interventionist rhetoric.

In the first decade of the twentieth century, the Republican and Democratic Parties developed distinct ideologies in accordance with GOP control of the presidency. The Republican Party's theory of governance advocated for a strong president, while the Democratic Party's theory of governance criticized "executive usurpation." The GOP's theory of foreign intervention advocated for a strong international presence and a "big stick," while the Democratic theory of foreign intervention criticized "imperialism" and "militarism."

4 WORLD WAR I AND WILSONIAN INTERNATIONALISM, 1913–1921

Between 1917 and 1918, American casualties in the Great War cooled the American appetite for military conflict. This critical juncture revived a strain of noninterventionism and isolationism that persisted in American culture for a quarter-century until the attack on Pearl Harbor. Both parties became less interventionist than they had been in the preceding decades. Nonetheless, party control of the presidency helped shape how the ideologies of the two parties developed in relation to each other within this broader sphere. During the two presidential terms of Woodrow Wilson, the Democratic Party came to embrace presidential power, and relatively more foreign intervention, while the GOP adopted the anti-internationalist rhetoric of isolationist Americans like Bryan. Given the character of the two parties' ideologies in

1912, with Republicans being much more interventionist than Democrats, it took a World War and several years of party control of the presidency for Democrats to finally become as interventionist as Republicans. The old ideas and narratives were powerful and difficult to discard.

4.1 Party Control of the Presidency and Party Theories of Governance

After finally taking control of the White House in 1913, the Democratic Party stopped advocating for a constitutional amendment to bar presidents from running for reelection. They also stopped talking about executive usurpation. Woodrow Wilson was one of the nation's leading theorists of a strong presidency in the American constitutional system. He called for a leader democracy in which the president would lead responsible party government. Symbolic of his efforts to strengthen the presidency, Wilson became the first president since the eighteenth century to deliver the State of the Union Address in person. Upon reaching the conclusion of the 1916 platform, the Democratic Party exclaimed that "Woodrow Wilson stands to-day the greatest American of his generation" (DNC 1916). The party entrepreneurship of Woodrow Wilson, who just happened to have a background as a political scientist advocating for executive power, allowed the Democratic Party to change its theory of governance relatively quickly. If another politician had received the Democratic nomination and become president, it probably would have taken longer.

The Republicans were relatively slower to change their theory of governance and did not immediately switch to criticizing presidential power. However, by 1920, the GOP's theory of governance called for a constrained executive. Specifically, the Republican Party platform criticized President Wilson for executive "usurpation" and for continuing to exercise the emergency powers of the president after the end of the Great War: "The President clings tenaciously to his autocratic war time powers. His veto of the resolution declaring peace and his refusal to sign the bill repealing war time legislation, no longer necessary, evidenced his determination not to restore to the Nation and to the State the form of government provided for by the Constitution. This usurpation is intolerable and deserves the severest condemnation" (RNC 1920).

4.2 Party Control of the Presidency and Party Theories of Foreign Intervention

As the two parties' theories of governance changed, so did their theories of foreign intervention, but this was more gradual. In 1913, Democrats were still employing the rhetoric and ideology of anti-imperialism that they had been using since Reconstruction. Shortly after taking office, Democratic President Woodrow Wilson promised a noninterventionist crowd in Alabama that "the United States will never again seek one additional foot of territory by conquest" (Wilson 1913). However, Wilson's ideology, and the ideology of the Democratic Party he led, changed on foreign policy as all of the necessary ingredients came together over the course of his administration.

President Wilson faced several opportunities in which the incentive to exercise the foreign policy powers at his disposal conflicted with his incentive to act according to the party's preexisting non-interventionist ideology. In April 1914, despite the party's previous denunciation of "militarism" and "imperialism," Wilson sent troops to occupy Veracruz in response to the Tampico Affair, and in July 1915 Wilson sent 330 US Marines to occupy Haiti to protect American business interests. When it became apparent, in 1915, that Wilson's diplomacy was leading America into intervening in the Great War in Europe, antiwar Secretary of State William Jennings Bryan resigned from Wilson's cabinet. The split between Wilson and Bryan shows that the hold of political ideology, or political principles, is greater on some political actors than others. Bryan the principled ideologue was unwilling to change his foreign policy views just because his party now controlled the presidency. However, many other Democrats and Republicans were willing to change their views in order to justify co-partisans and criticize opponents.

The President's interventionist actions, in opposition to Bryanism, led to factional infighting. As Wilson ran for reelection in 1916, a newly emergent interventionist wing of the party began to show its influence on the party's platform:

The circumstances of the last two years have revealed necessities of international action which no former generation can have foreseen. We hold that it is the duty of the United States to use its power, not only to make itself safe at home, but also to make secure its just interests throughout the world, and, both for this end and in the interest of humanity, to assist the world in securing settled peace and justice. We believe that ... the time has come when it is the duty of the United States to join the other nations of the world in any feasible association that will effectively serve those principles.

(DNC 1916)

The 1916 platform was the first Democratic Party platform to call for a military buildup since the Civil War. Wilson requested and received a declaration of war from Congress in April 1917.[3] After the end of the war in 1918, Wilson was the key player in attempting to form an international league of nations. As a president popular among his co-partisans, Wilson had sufficient resources and opportunities to significantly influence the party's ideological development.

The Republican Party's theory of foreign intervention moved in the opposite direction. In 1916, the Republicans nominated an internationalist, Charles Hughes, as they had always done, but by the end of the war, American political ideology had undergone a secular shift toward less foreign intervention, and the GOP led the country's move in this direction. After Wilson's second term in office, Republicans nominated their first non-internationalist candidate in Warren Harding, who called for a "return to normalcy." In a remarkable change from the days of Theodore Roosevelt and William Jennings Bryan, the Republican candidate won by criticizing the Democratic Party's foreign interventionism.

Although Democrats held the White House for just eight years, the issue of World War I and the party entrepreneurship of Wilson provided enough incentives and opportunities for the Democratic and Republican parties to change their ideologies in ways that had long-lasting effects. These changes in relatively transient party theories of governance and party theories of intervention also had an impact on changes in relatively durable party theories of ends. During Wilson's administration, an internationalist faction emerged within the Democratic Party for the first time, and that faction has been present ever since with varying levels of importance. Likewise, an isolationist faction emerged within the Republican Party for the first time, and that faction has also been present ever since with varying levels of importance. This era helped to shape Democratic Party ideology such that the party's current theory of ends includes international humanitarianism – an aspect of party ideology that was not present prior to the Wilson administration. If anything, prior to this time, international

---

[3] Wilson also requested and received the Selective Service Act in 1917, which drafted 2.8 million soldiers. Like the Federalists during the Quasi War and the Republicans during the Civil War, the Democrats prosecuted seditious speech during the war.

humanitarianism was a tenet of GOP ideology. This development fore-shadowed the emergence of "universalism" as a defining characteristic of Democratic Party ideology (Gerring 1998).

5 REPUBLICAN INTERWAR ERA, 1921–1933

Because the horrors of World War I resulted in a secular shift in American foreign policy toward isolationism, and because Republicans led the country's move in this direction, the presidential election of 1920 wit-nessed the largest popular vote landslide in American history. With Republicans in the White House from 1921 to 1933, the two parties' ideologies evolved as expected. However, as there were no wars during this period, the changes were not as dramatic or rapid as those witnessed in the 1910s. The two parties' preexisting ideologies were political struc-tures resistant to change and difficult to overcome.

5.1 Party Control of the Presidency and Party Theories of Governance

After losing two consecutive presidential elections, in 1920 and 1924, the Democratic Party returned to its rhetoric of opposition to executive power and bureaucratic centralization. In the aftermath of the Harding and Coolidge administrations, the 1928 platform declared its opposition to "bureaucracy and the multiplication of offices." Instead of nationaliza-tion, the Democrats defended "the rights of the states" as "a bulwark against centralization." The platform devoted an entire section, "Econ-omy and Reorganization," to explaining how it would shrink and reorganize the executive branch. Similarly, after the Hoover administra-tion, the first thing the 1932 Democratic Party platform promised, as a solution to the Great Depression, was "an immediate and drastic reduc-tion of governmental expenditures by abolishing useless commissions and offices, consolidating departments and bureaus, and eliminating extrava-gance." Such a call for shrinking the executive branch, and decreasing spending, is ironic given the policies pursued by the Democratic Party during the New Deal. Republicans also promised economy in government in 1932, but they insisted this was a "nonpartisan" issue, and since, according to them, "the President is particularly fitted to direct meas-ures," their proposed solution was to give him "the required authority" to reorganize the bureaucracy.

5.2 Party Control of the Presidency and Party Theories of Foreign Intervention

Like their theories of governance, the two parties' theories of foreign intervention also slowly and gradually developed in the expected way. In the 1924 presidential campaign, Democrats still advocated for the League of Nations, while the GOP still opposed it. By 1928, however, the Democratic Party was returning to the rhetoric of nonintervention that it had used during the era of Grover Cleveland and William Jennings Bryan. Echoing the 1900 platform, the 1928 platform expressed an "abhorrence of militarism, conquest and imperialism," and advocated "freedom from entangling political alliances with foreign nations" (DNC 1928). Democrats also returned to the practice of criticizing Republican administrations for conducting foreign policy without the consent of the Senate. The 1932 Democratic platform demanded "no interference in the internal affairs of other nations." Their presidential candidates in 1920, 1924, and 1928 resembled the candidates of the pre-Wilson years more than they did Wilson. In 1924, William Jennings Bryan's brother, Charles, was put on the presidential ticket with John Davis.

The Republicans also moved slowly back to their pre-Wilson positions. Although Harding and Coolidge had campaigned in 1920 on retreating from foreign interventions and a return to normalcy, almost all presidents end up engaging in more foreign intervention than they anticipate. The party's theory of foreign intervention gradually changed to justify these actions.

First, political instability and international conflict in Central America in the 1920s provided an opportunity for Republican presidents to act. Second, President Coolidge was willing to act somewhat against the party's noninterventionist rhetoric espoused in the 1920 campaign: In 1924, he sent troops to Honduras, and in 1926 he sent troops to Nicaragua. Third, party entrepreneurs began to change the party's ideology and different factions within the GOP rose and fell. Although the Republican Congress was more resistant than the Republican presidency in this return to internationalism, and rejected Coolidge's request that America join the World Court, the president's actions were still influential on party ideology development. For example, the 1928 GOP platform called for the "full ratio" of "Navy armaments" allowed under the limitations of the Navy Armaments Treaty and the presidential "power to draft people and resources in times of war" (RNC 1928).

Democrats, on the other hand, began to back away from the strong internationalist position of the Wilson years, and criticized Republican interventionism in the 1928 presidential campaign. Franklin Roosevelt, sensing a winning issue to use against Republicans, penned an article in *Foreign Affairs* criticizing the Coolidge administration for its military policy. "We can for all time," Roosevelt proclaimed, "renounce the practice of arbitrary intervention in the home affairs of our neighbors" (1928, 586). This ideological position only became remarkable once FDR became president and Republicans began accusing him of "war-mongering" in the late 1930s.

Since non-interventionism was popular in America in the 1920s, Roosevelt's editorial stance showed how politicians of both parties sought to align themselves with the popular side of the issue. By 1928, the two parties were not as clearly divided on the issue as they had been in 1920. While not as anti-interventionist as FDR in 1928, presidential candidate Herbert Hoover backed away from the Coolidge administration's foreign policies toward Latin America (McPherson 2014). While there was substantial diversity of thought within both parties on foreign policy, we can still detect some trends in party ideology development. In his study of roll call votes on American foreign policy, George Grassmuck (1951) found that "during the twenties Republican congressmen tended to support the foreign policy of the Republican presidents, and this policy favored a strong international position. Throughout this same period Democratic congressmen tended to oppose this position." Without a war or foreign crisis to sharply demarcate foreign policy positions, the ideological developments of the 1920s were not as sharp as the changes in the 1910s. The inertia of ideological structures resisted change. Nonetheless, the two parties' ideologies changed in relation to each other as predicted. After being staunchly less interventionist than the Democrats in 1920, the GOP became at least as interventionist as the Democratic Party – if not more so – during the 1920s. This is what we would expect from the political institutional theory of party ideology development.

6 DEMOCRATIC NEW DEAL AND WORLD WAR II, 1933–1953

Former critic of foreign intervention, senator Arthur Vandenberg (R-MI), recorded in his diary that his "convictions regarding international cooperation and collective security took form on the afternoon of the Pearl Harbor attack. That day ended isolationism for any realist" (Vandenberg

1952, 1). World War II ended isolationism for most Americans, in general, and this represented a secular shift in American ideas about foreign intervention. Within this broader change in public opinion, however, the relative change in ideologies between the parties was influenced by party control of the White House.

Franklin Roosevelt established long-term Democratic Party control of the presidency by winning four consecutive elections from 1932 to 1944. During this period, the Democratic Party clearly became more supportive of presidential power and foreign intervention than the Republican Party. The anti-executive and isolationist wing of the GOP, led by Senator Robert Taft, emerged as the dominant voice of the party during this time. While ultimately supporting FDR's intervention in World War II, after the Japanese attack on Pearl Harbor, Democratic control of the presidency meant that Republicans moved more slowly into support for the war. Just as Wilson provided political entrepreneurship to change Democratic Party ideology during the opportunity provided by World War I, Roosevelt provided political entrepreneurship to change Democratic Party ideology during the opportunity provided by World War II.

6.1 Party Control of the Presidency and Party Theories of Governance

Before changing their theories of foreign intervention, the parties first changed their theories of governance. Between 1933 and 1952, advocacy for a strong executive and presidential leadership became an important part of Democratic Party ideology. FDR's administration is widely seen as defining the modern presidency, and the Democratic Party largely justified this expansion of presidential power while the Republican Party mostly criticized it. The 1936 GOP platform opened by attacking not only the economic interventions of New Dealism but also, interestingly, its expansion of executive and bureaucratic power:

America is in peril ... The powers of Congress have been usurped by the President. The integrity and authority of the Supreme Court have been flouted ... The New Deal Administration ... has promoted investigations to harass and intimidate American citizens, at the same time denying investigations into its own improper expenditures. It has created a vast multitude of new offices, filled them with its favorites, set up a centralized bureaucracy, and sent out swarms of inspectors to harass our people ... It has coerced and intimidated voters by withholding relief to those opposing its tyrannical policies ... To a free people, these actions are insufferable. This campaign cannot be waged on the traditional differences between the Republican and Democratic parties. The responsibility of this election transcends all previous political divisions. We invite all Americans, irrespective of party, to join us in defense of American institutions.

(RNC 1936)

According to Republicans, the 1936 election could not be "waged on the traditional differences between the Republican and Democratic parties" because the election was not only about the ends of government in society, but also about the constitutional balance of institutional powers (theories of governance). The GOP made a call for a "defense of American institutions" by which they meant a return to limited executive power.

The fight over Roosevelt's Third New Deal, in which he attempted to expand the power of the presidency at the expense of Congress and the Courts, also illustrates the changing theories of governance within the two parties. In March 1938, the Senate passed FDR's executive reorganization bill 49–42 (Milkis 1993, 122). However, not a single Republican joined the forty-seven Democrats, one Progressive, and one Independent who voted in favor of the bill (Congressional Quarterly 1950). When the Executive Reorganization Act of 1939 finally passed the House, 98 percent of Democrats, but just 5 percent of Republicans, supported the bill. Similarly, when the Senate passed the House version, 63–23, 95 percent of Democrats, but just 9 percent of Republicans, voted in favor of the bill (Poole and Rosenthal 2015).

Although these roll call votes are not a direct measure of ideology, they are a useful indirect measure of ideology. When Republicans voted overwhelmingly against, and Democrats voted overwhelmingly for, the Executive Reorganization Bill, their actions matched their rhetoric. The narratives, discourses, and ideologies articulated by the two parties during this time included clearly different theories of governance. The Democratic theory of governance called for more presidential power, while the Republican theory of governance called for less.

6.2 Party Control of the Presidency and Party Theories of Foreign Intervention

In the 1930s and 1940s, all of the necessary ingredients for party ideology change came together. In particular, the emergence of a Second World War and the actions of President Roosevelt, as commander-in-chief and party leader, helped change the two parties' theories of foreign intervention. Changes in the Democratic Party's ideology included the rise and fall of party factions. Many ideological pro-New Dealers like John L. Lewis turned against Roosevelt over his hawkish foreign policy. Isolationist Democratic senators including Burton Wheeler (MT) and David Walsh (MA) became less influential in the party and ultimately lost their seats in Congress. Some of these disaffected Democrats tried to pursue a third-party option by drafting a presidential candidate in 1940 who would be interventionist on economic policy but noninterventionist on foreign policy – what these principled ideologues believed to be the true, progressive faith.

At the same time that Democratic Party ideology was becoming more interventionist on foreign policy, the old GOP isolationism of 1920 was revived. As early as 1936, Republican Party platforms began criticizing FDR for Wilsonian internationalism, and – like the Whigs and Bryan Democrats before them – reviving the words of Washington: "Obedient to the traditional foreign policy of America and to the repeatedly expressed will of the American people, we pledge that America shall not become a member of the League of Nations nor of the World Court nor shall America take on any entangling alliances in foreign affairs" (RNC 1936). By 1940, as FDR looked to involve America in the Second World War that had broken out in Europe, GOP isolationism reached its peak:

The Republican Party is firmly opposed to involving this Nation in foreign war. We are still suffering from the ill effects of the last World War: a war which cost us a twenty-four billion dollar increase in our national debt, billions of uncollectible foreign debts, and the complete upset of our economic system, in addition to the loss of human life and irreparable damage to the health of thousands of our boys.

(RNC 1940)

Even after the GOP admitted that United States involvement in World War II was the correct course of action, the party again resisted the Democratic Party's internationalism. "We shall seek to achieve such aims through organized international cooperation and not by joining a World State" (RNC 1944). It is true that from 1941 to 1944, even though they were out of power, the GOP became more interventionist than they had been in the past. However, the hypothesis tested in this chapter is not whether a party becomes more or less interventionist on some absolute scale, but how much more or less interventionist it becomes in relation to the other party. In this instance, the GOP, in opposition to the president, moved more slowly than Democrats toward the new position of international intervention that the United States adopted in the 1940s.

The Democratic Party, in contrast, was proud of its internationalism and interventionism. The party defended FDR against charges by the GOP that he was engaging in "war-mongering" (DNC 1940). In 1947, President Truman outlined his Truman Doctrine, committing America to intervene internationally to protect free peoples against Soviet aggression. In 1950, Truman sent troops to protect South Korea against invasion from the Communist North with the blessing of the United Nations but not the United States Congress. The two parties once again split over their support for internationalism. Making the case for foreign interventionism, 1952 Democratic presidential candidate Adlai Stevenson proclaimed that "the Democratic Party stands foursquare behind [the United Nations] and behind the war in Korea" (Stevenson 1952).

By the end of two decades of Democratic Party dominance of the presidency, the party had become fully more interventionist than they were during the GOP administrations of the 1920s. Twisting the historical record, and telling themselves that they had always been the party of internationalism, the 1952 platform boasted: "The return of the Democratic Party to power in 1933 marked the end of a tragic era of isolationism fostered by Republican Administrations which had deliberately and callously rejected the golden opportunity created by Woodrow Wilson for collective action to secure the peace." An important part of the process of party ideology change over time is party narrative change. Parties constantly rework their narratives to assure themselves that they have continuity with their past, and the 1952 DNC platform is an excellent example of that.

In keeping with the party ideology developed during the 1930s and 1940s, Republicans opposed President Truman sending troops to Korea in 1950 without Congressional authorization of war – the first time a president had committed troops in a major conflict without following the Constitution's prescription that Congress should declare war. In this way, the Republican Party's theory of governance and theory of foreign intervention supported each other. Robert Taft ("Mr. Republican") articulated GOP foreign policy ideology from the Senate floor in this way: "We have a situation in which in a far distant part of the world one nation has attacked another, and if the President can intervene in Korea without congressional approval, he can go to war in Malaya or Indonesia or Iran or South America."

The differences in party ideology can be seen in the way that GOP nominee Dwight Eisenhower – who had only recently declared himself to be a Republican – began changing his views to fit within the GOP's noninterventionist ideology. In a September 1952 editorial entitled "The New Eisenhower," the noninterventionist *Chicago Tribune* approvingly chronicled "how far Gen. Eisenhower has moved in Mr. Taft's direction," including his abandonment of universal military training and his new support for cutting military spending (Chicago Tribune 1952). In October of 1952, Eisenhower promised that, as president, he would "bring the Korean war to an early and honorable end" (Eisenhower 1952).

These changes in party ideologies between 1933 and 1952 are not only manifest in party platforms and candidate speeches, but also in the attitudes expressed by ordinary party identifiers. In 1952, after twenty straight years of Democratic presidents, the newly created American National Election Studies asked its survey respondents whether they agreed or disagreed with this statement: "Since the end of the last world war this country has gone too far in concerning itself with problems in other parts of the world." Thirty-eight percent of Democrats, but just 25 percent of Republicans, disagreed with that statement (Campbell, Gurin, and Miller 1999). Thus, significantly more Democrats than Republicans expressed the more interventionist attitude on foreign policy in 1952.

7 REPUBLICAN COLD WAR, 1953–1961

In the 1950s, a foreign policy issue (the Cold War) and an entrepreneurial party reformer (Dwight Eisenhower) helped bring about party ideology change once again. Despite his noninterventionist rhetoric on the campaign trail in the fall of 1952, after taking office Eisenhower and the Republicans began to depart from the isolationism of the Taft era.

One way to chronicle changes in the two parties' theories of governance and theories of foreign intervention during the 1950s is to chronicle the history of the Bricker Amendment. In July 1951, during Truman's second term in office and after almost two decades of Democratic control of the White House, Senator John Bicker (R-OH) introduced a constitutional amendment that would limit the president's ability to take the United States into war. The proposed amendment "was the embodiment of the [Republican] Old Guard's rage at what it viewed as twenty years of presidential usurpation of Congress's constitutional powers" (Caro 2003, 528). Republicans continued to push for this amendment in 1952 – during Truman's last year in office – and Senator Bricker reintroduced his amendment in 1953 with GOP support even though Republicans had won control of the White House. In the first months after the election, they continued to vote according to the ideological dispositions they had built up over the previous two decades. While it is difficult to reverse twenty years of ideological developments, through Eisenhower's entrepreneurship and the resources at his disposal, the party eventually backed away from its previous anti-presidential and noninterventionist ideology over the course of his administration. By the time the Bricker Amendment came up for a passage vote in the Senate on February 26, 1954, after Eisenhower worked against the legislation for a year, the parties took roughly the same positions: Thirty-three Republicans and thirty Democrats supported the Bricker Amendment, while fourteen Republicans and eighteen Democrats opposed it. Although the two parties had not entirely switched positions in ideological space, the enormous gap between the two parties that existed in 1952 had narrowed considerably by the fall of 1954.

Political scientists who studied political parties in the 1950s noticed this change in the two parties' ideologies. "Before 1952, the Republican Party, represented largely by its Congressional leaders, had tended to oppose the active internationalism of the Democratic Party. In 1953 and thereafter, when the focus for the Republican Party shifted to the White House, the general adherence of the Eisenhower Administration to the internationalist policies of its predecessors served to minimize party differences in foreign affairs" (Campbell et al. 1960, 199–200).

The relative movement of the two parties' ideologies, with respect to both party theories of governance and foreign intervention, can be seen in changes in their platforms. For example, despite its earlier opposition to the UN, in 1956 the GOP stated its intention to "vigorously support the United Nations" (RNC 1956). After two terms of a Republican administration, the party articulated its newfound interventionist ideology in this way:

The pre-eminence of this Republic requires of us a vigorous, resolute foreign policy—inflexible against every tyrannical encroachment, and mighty in its advance toward our own affirmative goals ... The countries of the free world have been benefited, reinforced and drawn closer together by the vigor of American support of the United Nations ... We believe military assistance to our allies under the mutual security program should be continued with all the vigor and funds needed to maintain the strength of our alliances at levels essential to our common safety. The firm diplomacy of the Eisenhower-Nixon Administration has been supported by a military power superior to any in the history of our nation or in the world. As long as world tensions menace us with war, we are resolved to maintain an armed power exceeded by no other.

(RNC 1960)

It is true that, in the aftermath of the Korean War, the Eisenhower administration was less willing to use American ground troops in fighting Communism than the Truman administration had been. Eisenhower resisted French requests for American troops to help fight the Communists in Vietnam in 1954. However, Republicans demonstrated interventionist attitudes in other ways: Eisenhower relied more on threats of nuclear force, supplying weapons and money to nations fighting against Communist aggression, and use of the CIA.

Party theories of presidential power and foreign intervention are not usually overturned on election night or as soon as a new party takes control of the presidency. As ideological structures, they continue to shape the behavior of party members until the ideology can be transformed, which typically takes years. Due to previous ideological predilections, Eisenhower was less in tune with the reigning ideology of his party than others, like Senator Robert Taft, who might have been nominated by the Republicans in 1952 (Milkis 1993, 168). Given the incentives that presidents almost universally face to exercise the powers at their disposal, Eisenhower faced incentives to intervene more in foreign affairs, and with more reliance on executive discretion, than the ideological position of the party as a whole. To justify their president, the party gradually began to change its ideology with regard to presidential power and foreign intervention.

For example, the dramatic change in party theories of foreign intervention can be seen in the responses that Democrats and Republicans in the electorate gave to survey questions on foreign policy during this time. As noted, in 1952 Democrats had given the more interventionist response to the ANES question about foreign policy by a difference of thirteen points. In 1956, the ANES asked survey respondents if they agreed or disagreed with the statement that "this country would be better off if we just stayed home and did not concern ourselves with problems in other parts of the world." This time, 61 percent of Republicans, and 57 percent of Democrats, disagreed with that statement. Thus, by 1956, more Republicans than Democrats were giving the interventionist response. By 1960, after eight years of the Eisenhower presidency, Republican-identifying respondents had become a full eight points more interventionist than Democratic-identifying respondents. While both parties became more interventionist on foreign policy during the 1950s, Republicans moved farther in that direction than Democrats.

8 DEMOCRATIC COLD WAR, 1961–1969

Long-term party control of the White House shifted to the Democrats in the 1960s with Presidents John F. Kennedy and Lyndon B. Johnson, and the two parties' theories of governance developed as predicted by the political institutional theory of party ideology development. For example, the 1964 GOP platform pledged an "elimination of excessive bureaucracy" and the 1968 platform complained that "an entrenched, burgeoning bureaucracy has increasingly usurped powers, unauthorized by Congress." Sounding like Democrats during the Hoover administration, Republicans went on to claim that the "decentralization of power, as well as strict Congressional oversight of administrative and regulatory agency compliance with the letter and spirit of the law, are urgently needed to preserve personal liberty, improve efficiency, and provide a swifter response to human problems" (RNC 1968).

However, contrary to the hypothesis tested here, in this one decade there was no obvious and clear relative movement in party theories of foreign intervention. At the start of this period, both parties were roughly equally hawkish and anti-communist, and both parties boasted of their toughness toward, and willingness to intervene against, the Soviet Union. By the end of Johnson's administration in 1968, both parties were again roughly equally interventionist. Although the Democratic Party nominated cold war liberal Hubert Humphrey in 1968, and defeated an antiwar platform plank by a vote of 1,568 to 1,041, the party's interventionist stance led to rioting by antiwar Democrats in Chicago. The Democrats were not an entirely hawkish party. An analysis of the two parties' platforms in 1964 and 1968 do not reveal clear differences on the issue of foreign intervention. The Democrats had not clearly moved in a more interventionist direction than Republicans over the course of eight years of White House control.

Although surveys of ordinary party identifiers indicate that the two parties' theories of foreign intervention evolved somewhat as expected, these do not carry as much weight as a textual analysis of party rhetoric. In the 1968 ANES survey, roughly equal numbers of Democrats (74 percent) and Republicans (76 percent) disagreed with the noninterventionist sentiment that "this country would be better off if we just stayed home and did not concern ourselves with problems in other parts of the world." Thus, the eight-point gap between the parties seen in 1960 had narrowed to a two-point gap by 1968. However, that change alone is not substantive enough to indicate an incontrovertible shift in the relative ideological positions of the parties. Although it is a useful proxy measure, survey data is a less direct measure of ideology than the rhetoric espoused by the two parties. Furthermore, in testing my theory of party ideology change, I insist on a high burden of proof. An observation can only be coded as following the hypothesis if the two parties clearly and unambiguously changed as predicted. Thus, in this one instance, the two parties' theories of foreign intervention did not change entirely as expected.

The party history of the 1960s makes it clear that other factors, besides party control of the presidency, influence the development of party ideas about foreign policy. A historical contingency, the emergence of the antiwar New Left and the hawkish New Right in the postwar era, worked in opposition to the logic of party ideology development. This may have to do with the fact that the parties had polarized over a different aspect of party ideology – attitudes toward social democratic reforms – during the previous three decades. Since the GOP had developed an anti-communist identity in the aftermath of the Democratic New Deal, and scored considerable political points for this position in the 1950s, the nature of foreign policy during the Cold War encouraged GOP hawkishness in the 1960s despite opposition to the presidency. The ideological changes of the 1950s, in which an anti-communist Republican Party became hawkish on foreign policy, established structures of Republican Party ideology that had lasting influence for several decades afterward.

Based on party attitudes expressed in response to the ANES survey question about foreign intervention, Republicans have almost always been more interventionist than Democrats since they first surpassed the Democrats in 1956 (see Figure 3.1). The exceptions to this rule can be partly explained by party control of the presidency. Since Republicans established an eight-point difference between the two parties in 1960, that gap has only narrowed to less than four points in years that occurred after Democratic control of the presidency. In 1968, after the Kennedy and Johnson administrations, the gap narrowed to two points. In 1980, after the Carter administration, the gap narrowed to three points. During the Clinton administration the gap narrowed to two points in 1996, and by 1998 the Democrats actually became one point more interventionist. Most recently, in 2016, during the Obama administration, Democrats again became more interventionist than Republicans.

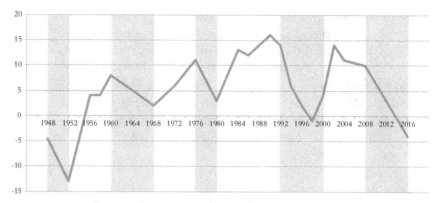

FIGURE 3.1 Differences between Republican and Democratic levels of foreign interventionism, 1948–2016
Note: Shaded time periods represent Democratic Party control of the presidency. The y-axis is based on NES survey questions asking respondents if Americans should "not concern ourselves with problems in other parts of the world" (dataset variables VAR 480040, VAR 520051, and VCF0823). It is calculated by subtracting the percentage of Democrats giving the interventionist response from the percentage of Republicans giving the interventionist response (see Appendix 1 for complete data). Thus, positive numbers indicate that a greater percentage of Republicans gave the interventionist response, while negative numbers indicate that a greater percentage of Democrats gave the interventionist response.

9 NEW RIGHT REPUBLICANS AND NEW LEFT DEMOCRATS, 1969–1993

Winning four of five presidential elections between 1968 and 1988, the Republican Party gained long-term control of the presidency. During that time period, GOP ideology embraced a strong presidency and remained more interventionist on foreign policy. The Democratic Party, on the other hand, moved quickly away from the strong executive theory of governance that had dominated the party since the New Deal. In its place, the party embraced the New Left's anti-executive and antiwar sentiments. This relative shift in the two parties' ideologies is in accordance with the hypothesis.

9.1 The Antiwar Left and Democratic Doves

After relinquishing control of the presidency in 1969, the Democratic Party quickly moved to oppose both an imperial presidency and an imperial foreign policy. The party was able to move quickly because all of the necessary ingredients for party ideology change were present from the moment Nixon took office, including a political issue to debate (the Vietnam War), an insurgent party faction (the Antiwar Left), and party entrepreneurs with resources. In 1972, the party nominated antiwar candidate George McGovern. The 1972 platform retained some of the internationalist planks of previous Democratic Party platforms, but the McGovern wing of the party dominated, and the platform also made explicit criticisms of the Vietnam War now being carried on by Republicans:

We believe that war is a waste of human life. We are determined to end forthwith a war which has cost 50,000 American lives, $150 billion of our resources, that has divided us from each other, drained our national will and inflicted incalculable damage to countless people. We will end that war by a simple plan that need not be kept secret: The immediate total withdrawal of all Americans from Southeast Asia … The U.S. will no longer seek to determine the political future of the nations of Indo-China.

(DNC 1972)

In 1976, the party once again nominated a candidate, Jimmy Carter, who drew a contrast with the executive imperialism and foreign intervention-ism of the Nixon administration. The 1976 platform criticized GOP unilateralism and secret conduct of foreign policy, and called for a reduc-tion of spending by 5–7 billion dollars.[4]

After the Watergate scandal, the Democrats' criticism of Republican imperialism was effective and the party regained control of the White House in 1977. After taking office, Carter was soon met with inter-national emergencies that caused him to question the noninterventionist ideology of his party. Even though Carter made interventionist moves during his term in office, he lost his reelection bid in 1980, and so the period from 1977 to 1980 did not represent a long-term change in party control of the presidency. As such, it was less likely that all of the necessary components would emerge within that short time period, and that party ideology changes would last long enough to instantiate a durable change. As expected, there was no durable shift in the relative ideological positions of the party. In nominating Reagan in 1980, the GOP had become no less interventionist on foreign policy, vis-à-vis the Democrats, than they had been in 1976. The 1984 Democratic Party

---

[4] After one term of President Carter, however, the Democratic Party boasted in its 1980 plat-form of increasing defense spending every year since 1976.

platform criticized the Republican administration for an arms race, and called for disarmament instead. The party continued to call for decreased defense spending – especially with the Cold War coming to a close.

9.2 Neoconservatives and Republican Hawks

In 1968, after eight years of Democratic presidents, the GOP was still using the antiwar rhetoric that would shortly become a key part of Democratic Party ideology.

The entire nation has been profoundly concerned by hastily extemporized, undeclared land wars which embroil massive U.S. armed forces thousands of miles from our shores. It is time to realize that not every international conflict is susceptible of solution by American ground forces ... We will return to one of the cardinal principles of the last Republican Administration: that American interests are best served by cooperative multilateral action with our allies rather than by unilateral U.S. action.

(RNC 1968)

However, in the 1970s, with a GOP president prosecuting the war in Vietnam, Republican ideology evolved to become more interventionist. As the antiwar New Democratic Left grew in importance, neoconservatives began leaving the Democratic Party for the Republican Party. The 1972 GOP platform criticized the Democratic Party's new-found dovishness and isolationism:

The nation's frustrations had fostered a dangerous spirit of isolationism among our people. America's influence in the world had waned ... We believe in keeping America strong. In times past, both major parties shared that belief. Today this view is under attack by militants newly in control of the Democratic Party. To the alarm of free nations everywhere, the New Democratic Left now would undercut our defenses and have America retreat into virtual isolation, leaving us weak in a world still not free of aggression and threats of aggression. We categorically reject this slash-now, beg-later, approach to defense policy.

(RNC 1972)

Nixon's successor after his resignation, Gerald Ford, retained Secretary of State Kissinger and largely continued Nixon's foreign policies. The 1976 ANES survey found that Republican respondents were now eleven points more interventionist than Democrats.

Despite the Democratic Party's short-term control of the presidency from 1977 to 1980, Republicans remained more interventionist on foreign policy than Democrats, and neoconservatives continued to change party affiliation. In the 1980 campaign, Ronald Reagan brought on

Democratic Party hawk Jeane Kirkpatrick as a foreign policy advisor. After the 1980 election, Kirkpatrick became ambassador to the United Nations. During the Reagan administration, the GOP continued its hawkish foreign policy and continued to criticize Democrats for being isolationists (RNC 1984). Defense spending rose to record peacetime levels in the 1980s, and America intervened in a variety of international conflicts whether through funding, supplying weapons, CIA operations, or military intervention. The 1990 ANES survey found that Republicans were a record sixteen points more interventionist than Democrats. After the Cold War, Reagan's successor, George H. W. Bush, continued Republican interventionist foreign policy by sending troops to Panama and the Persian Gulf in quick, decisive military victories. As predicted by the hypothesis, between 1969 and 1992, the Republican Party became clearly more interventionist while the Democratic Party became clearly less interventionist on foreign policy.

10 INTERNATIONALIST DEMOCRATS AND PALEOCONSERVATIVE REPUBLICANS, 1993–2001

During the eight years of Bill Clinton's Democratic presidency, the two parties' ideologies concerning foreign intervention shifted as different factions within the parties became more vocal. Within the Democratic Party, the antiwar McGovernites began to hold less sway. In their place, a "New Democrats" faction – led by Bill Clinton, Al Gore, and the Democratic Leadership Council – held the ideologically dominant position. Within the Republican Party, the hawkish neoconservative branch of the party became less prominent, while an isolationist paleoconservative strand emerged.

The Clinton administration continued the foreign interventionist policies of the GOP: Like his Republican predecessors, Clinton was not afraid for America to assume its new role as the world's lone superpower. Democratic Party ideology developed in a way that called on the use of force to spread democracy, and changed to support an increased defense budget: "The Clinton-Gore Administration has actively promoted the consolidation and spread of democracy and human rights ... The Administration has ensured that America is prepared to fight alongside others when we can, and alone when we must. We have defeated attempts to cut our defense budget irresponsibly" (DNC 1996). Following the foreign policy of his Republican predecessor, Clinton ordered military interventions in Somalia, Yugoslavia, Haiti, and Iraq. As the GOP criticized the

Democratic Party for these interventions, Democrats responded in their 1996 and 2000 party platforms by calling the Republicans isolationists. In 1996, they wrote: "The Dole-Gingrich Congress and the Republican Party have a different approach to America's security. Too often they would force America to go it alone – or not at all ... The Republican Party too often has neglected diplomatic opportunities [and] slashed the budgets necessary for diplomatic successes" (DNC 1996). The 1998 ANES survey found that, for the first time since 1952, Democratic respondents had become more interventionist than Republican respondents. In 2000, the platform explained: "Some Republicans believe America should turn away from the world. They oppose using our armed forces as part of international solutions, even when regional conflicts threaten our interests and our values" (DNC 2000).

As the Democratic Party turned away from Antiwar Left, and toward New Democratic, foreign policy ideology, the Republican Party turned toward its older isolationist ideology. Republicans in Congress criticized the Clinton administration's foreign interventions. The 2000 platform wrote: "The current administration has casually sent American armed forces on dozens of missions without clear goals, realizable objectives, favorable rules of engagement, or defined exit strategies" (RNC 2000). One Democratic columnist observed in 1994: "These days, Republicans are intent on gaining partisan profit from President Bill Clinton's foreign-policy travails. Yet, GOP leaders agree on little other than their opposition to administration policies that, ironically, often mirror those of Republican predecessors. GOP rhetoric has grown more partisan even as the President's policy has become less so" (Borosage 1994). In 1996, populist isolationist Republican Pat Buchanan had his best showing in the Republican Party presidential primaries. The 1996 platform was the first since the 1940s to criticize the United Nations – and did so at length. In the 2000 presidential debates between George W. Bush and Al Gore, Governor Bush criticized the Clinton administration's international interventionism, and famously pledged to have a "humble" foreign policy that focused on American interests. This position only became remarkable when President Bush prosecuted the war in Iraq and justified it on the idea of spreading democracy.

Between 1993 and 2001, the ideologies of the two parties developed as predicted by the political institutional theory. While it is debatable whether or not Democratic Party ideology became more interventionist than Republican Party ideology during this time, the massive gap that existed in 1992 was at least considerably narrowed.

11 HAWKISH REPUBLICANS AND DOVISH DEMOCRATS, 2001–2009

From 2001 to 2009, long-term party control of the presidency shifted to the Republican Party. During this time, the two parties' ideologies reverted to the 1969–1993 dynamics: The GOP once again became significantly more interventionist than the Democratic Party. The 1960s–1970s antiwar wing of the Democratic Party, dormant during the 1990s, was revived during the Iraq and Afghanistan Wars instigated by a Republican administration.

The 9/11 attacks ensnared the parties in foreign policy debate in a way that shifted party theories of intervention much more quickly than typically occurs with change in party control of the White House. According to the 2002 ANES survey, Republicans returned to being a full fourteen points more interventionist than Democrats (a spread not seen since 1992), and this double-digit gap persisted throughout the Bush administration. As the Iraq War became more and more unpopular, Democratic Party ideology became more and more dovish, and more and more critical of a now-hawkish Republican Party. The 2004 platform criticized President Bush for unilateralism and militarism: "The Bush Administration ... rush to force before exhausting diplomacy. They bully rather than persuade. They act alone when they could assemble a team" (DNC 2004). In 2008, the Democratic Party nominated antiwar candidate Barack Obama, and the 2008 platform criticized the Bush administration for "rushing us into an ill-considered war in Iraq" (DNC 2008). The Republican Party, on the other hand, nominated foreign policy hawk John McCain. The evolution of the two parties between 2001 and 2009 can be understood in the light of the institutional logic of party ideology development.

12 INTERNATIONALIST DEMOCRATS AND TEA PARTY REPUBLICANS, 2009–2017

In 2009, Democrats regained long-term control of the presidency with Barack Obama. Although it took several years for all of the necessary ingredients to come together, the ideologies of the two parties changed as predicted. During the Bush 43 administration, opposition to executive imperialism was an article of faith among Democrats, while Republicans embraced a strong presidency. During this time, conservative political and legal theorists renewed their development of a "unitary theory" of the executive (Skowronek 2009). However, after a change in party control of the presidency, Democrats and Republicans changed roles with Republican supporters of a strong executive taking a back seat in the party to those critical of executive usurpation. In 2014, President Obama decided to bypass an intransigent Congress by using the "pen" and "phone." Republicans decried Obama's decision to govern unilaterally as unconstitutional. As expected, during the Obama administration, the two parties' theories of presidential power became very different from what they were during the Bush administration.

The two parties' theories of foreign intervention likewise changed dramatically. Between 2009 and 2017, a "Tea Party" faction within the Republican Party, dormant during the Bush administration, emerged in opposition to Democratic control of the national government. Tea Party Republicans who criticized domestic intervention in the economy and foreign intervention overseas began to have a more prominent voice in the party. While the 2012 GOP nominee, Mitt Romney, refused to reverse the GOP's previous interventionist stance on foreign policy, the 2016 nominee, Donald Trump, explicitly criticized the Iraq War and Bush era foreign interventionism, and instead called for an "America First" foreign policy.

13 CONCLUSION

The popularity of Trump's isolationism among Republican Party primary voters in 2016 surprised many political observers, but it was entirely expected by the theory tested here. What has been interesting to see is how President Trump has already begun to act in opposition to Republican Party ideology, articulated during the Obama administration, about limiting presidential power and limiting foreign intervention. For example, in 2013, during the Obama administration, citizen Trump foreshadowed his isolationist, "America First" presidential campaign of 2016 by tweeting at the incumbent president: "President Obama, do not attack Syria. There is no upside and tremendous downside ... To our very foolish leader: Do not attack Syria–if you do many very bad things will happen ... What will we get for bombing Syria besides more debt and a possible long term conflict?" Shortly after taking the oath of office, in April 2017, Trump could not resist the temptation to do the "very foolish" thing that he warned President Obama against. In doing so, Trump has followed a long line of US presidents who seek to exercise

TABLE 3.2 *Party control of the presidency and party theories of foreign intervention (results)*

Time period	Independent variable: Change in long-term party control of the presidency	Dependent variable: Change in relative party Ideologies
1 Progressive Era and Republican Empire 1900–1913	Republican presidents	Yes: Republicans moved more toward intervention than Democrats
2 World War I and Wilsonian internationalism 1913–1921	Democratic president	Yes: Democrats moved more toward intervention than Republicans
3 Interwar Era 1921–1933	Republican presidents	Yes: Republicans moved more toward intervention than Democrats
4 Democratic New Deal and World War II 1933–1953	Democratic presidents	Yes: Democrats moved more toward intervention than Republicans
5 Republican anti-communism 1953–1961	Republican president	Yes: Republicans moved more toward intervention than Democrats
6 Democratic Cold War 1961–1969	Democratic presidents	No: Democrats did not move more toward intervention than Republicans
7 Republican Cold War 1969–1993	Republican presidents	Yes: Republicans moved more toward intervention than Democrats
8 Clinton internationalism 1993–2001	Democratic president	Yes: Democrats moved more toward intervention than Republicans
9 Bush War on Terror 2001–2009	Republican president	Yes: Republicans moved more toward intervention than Democrats
10 Obama internationalism 2009–2017	Democratic president	Yes: Democrats moved more toward intervention than Republicans

and expand the powers at their disposal – even when their party's ideology calls for presidential restraint and noninterventionist foreign policy. What will be interesting to watch is to see if this presidential hawkishness continues, and if the two parties' ideologies change during the Trump administration in an effort to justify their co-partisan and criticize their opponent.

From 1900 to 2017, long-term party control of the presidency changed ten times, and in every instance but one (1961–1969) the parties' ideologies with regard to foreign policy evolved as expected (see Table 3.2). The political institutional theory of party ideology development hypothesizes that changes in long-term party control of the presidency provide incentives for party actors to change their parties' theories of foreign intervention, but that party actors do not always have the resources and opportunities to act upon those incentives because of a multitude of other factors that influence party ideology dynamics. That the ten instances of change in long-term party control of the presidency resulted in nine instances of change in party ideologies is remarkable. It is unlikely that these two factors appeared together so often by coincidence.

4

Unified Government and Party Theories of Economic Intervention

For over two years our Federal Government has experienced unprecedented deficits, in spite of increased taxes ... The first and most important and necessitous step in balancing our Federal budget is to reduce expense ... You cannot go very far with any real Federal economy, without a complete change of concept of what are the proper functions and limits of the Federal Government itself ... [The Hoover administration] is committed to the idea that we ought to center control of everything in Washington as rapidly as possible ... Ever since the days of Thomas Jefferson, that has been the exact reverse of the democratic concept, which is to permit Washington to take from the States nothing more than is necessary ... I regard reduction in Federal spending as one of the most important issues of this campaign. In my opinion it is the most direct and effective contribution that Government can make to business.

–Franklin D. Roosevelt (1932)

I INTRODUCTION

In 1932, after three years of crippling economic depression in America, the Democratic Party was hoping to accomplish a rare feat: capturing the White House. In the seventy-two years since Abraham Lincoln, eleven Republicans – but just two Democrats – had been elected President of the United States. In October of that year, the Democratic challenger to incumbent President Herbert Hoover gave a speech in Pittsburgh in which he did what Democratic presidential candidates had frequently done: criticized the Republican Party's policies of big government, too much economic intervention, excessive taxes, and reckless spending. Governor

Roosevelt articulated standard "Jeffersonian" Democratic Party ideology
about the proper role of government in domestic affairs: limited government, less centralization at the national level, less spending, and lower
taxes. From our contemporary perspective, we know that FDR went on to
repudiate these ideas during his New Deal presidency, durably changing
the Democratic Party in the process.

The Republican Party likewise changed its ideas about economic intervention in response to the Democratic Party's New Deal. For seven
decades after the Civil War, Republicans had almost always advocated
more national government power and more economic intervention than
their Democratic opponents. However, once FDR outlined a "New Deal"
to increase government intervention in the economy to unprecedented
levels, Republicans increasingly adopted the rhetoric of limited government and nonintervention. For those who lived through this transformation, the change in the parties' positions, rhetoric, and ideology was
striking. Looking back on the 1932 campaign, New Deal Federal Reserve
Board Chairman Marriner Eccles remarked: "Given later developments,
the campaign speeches often read like a giant misprint, in which Roosevelt and Hoover speak each other's lines" (Kennedy 1999, 102).

This change in Democratic Party ideology during the 1930s, from an
advocacy of less government intervention to more, and the corresponding
switch in the Republican Party, is just one of numerous instances in
American political history of the two major parties changing their positions, rhetoric, and ideologies. This chapter examines whether change in
party control of government can help explain these changes in party
ideologies.

2 HYPOTHESIS

This chapter hypothesizes that a party in long-term control of unified
government tends to develop its ideology in a way that advocates for, and
justifies, relatively more national government power and economic intervention. A more interventionist economic policy includes advocacy for
more government spending, more economic regulation, more infrastructure projects, more redistribution of wealth and income, and more government social programs. This position has taken on many different
names and appeared in many different ideological forms over the past
230 years, including mercantilism, Federalism, National Republicanism,
Whiggery, "the American System," social democracy, progressivism,
liberalism, and social justice. Similarly, this chapter examines whether a

party in opposition to unified government tends to develop its ideology in a way that advocates for, and supports, relatively less national government power and economic intervention. This includes advocacy for less government spending, lower taxes, less economic regulation, fewer infrastructure projects, less redistribution of wealth and income, and fewer government social programs. This position has also assumed many different names and forms, including whiggery, liberalism, Jeffersonian Republicanism, the "Principles of '98," constitutionalism, Democratic Republicanism, democracy, *laissez-faire*, standpatism, conservatism, classical liberalism, and libertarianism. This aspect of party ideologies is similar to the "first" dimension of ideology discussed in much of the literature on party ideology development (Poole and Rosenthal 2007).

The dependent variable here is change in the *relative movement* of party positions with regard to more or less national government power and economic intervention. For example, at the start of the Jeffersonian Era in 1801, Federalist Party ideology called for significantly more economic intervention than Republican Party ideology. Since the Republican Party took long-term control of unified government between 1801 and 1825, this chapter predicts that the Republican Party would have changed its ideological position to move farther in the direction of more economic intervention than their Federalist opponents. The hypothesis is not necessarily that the two parties will actually switch positions in ideological space (although that is possible), but that the gap between the two parties will at least narrow. Furthermore, it is possible that, due to secular shifts in American history, both parties moved in the direction of more economic intervention during this period. Within this general movement by society at large, however, this theory predicts that the Republican Party will move farther in that direction than the Federalist Party. Thus, it is the *relative movement* of the two parties' ideologies that is being measured rather than their *absolute positions*.

While it is difficult to measure party theories of economic intervention, it is easy to measure party control of unified government. Determining party control of Congress and the presidency is clear in American history as each of the forty-five presidencies has represented one of the two major parties, and each of the 116 Congresses have been controlled, or split between, the two major parties. Under normal conditions, it usually takes a long time for party ideologies to change as expected. As a result, I focus on changes in party control of government institutions lasting for at least eight years. In identifying periods of change in long-term party control, this chapter looks at moments when the new institutional configuration is in tension with the existing party ideologies for a sustained period of time.[1]

This chapter presents data for the independent and dependent variables going back to the emergence of the two-party system in the 1790s. Narrowing the time frame to a particular era or slice of history has the added benefit of being able to do in-depth case study analysis, and broadening the time frame to all of US history has the danger of treating each case too superficially. But, because there have been so few cases of change in long-term party control of unified government, in order to record enough observations to be able to draw conclusions about a trend, we must look at all of US history going back to the first parties.

These twenty-three decades of US history give us five eras of long-term party control of unified government to examine (see Table 4.1). The first time period is the infant years of the United States under the Constitution from 1789 to 1800.[2] The second time period is the quarter century after the Jeffersonian Republicans took control of unified government in the "Revolution of 1800." The third time period is the antebellum era following the presidential election of 1824, which ended the one-party system as Republicans split between "National" Republicans and "Democratic" Republicans. This period is distinguished as a separate era because two new parties emerged – Democrats and Whigs – and not because either party took long-term control of unified government.[3] The fourth time period is the seven decades following the election of Abraham Lincoln in 1860 when his new Republican Party took control of unified government. The fifth time period is the current period following the election of Franklin Roosevelt in 1932 when his Democratic Party took

---

[1] For example: Democrats had long-term control of unified government during the seven sessions of Congress that began with FDR as President (1933–1946), government was divided during the 80th Congress (1947–1948), Democrats had short-term control of unified government during Truman's second term (1949–1952), Republicans had short-term control during the 83rd Congress (1953–1954), government was divided during the rest of Eisenhower's administration (1955–1960), and Democrats regained long-term party control during the Kennedy and Johnson administrations (1961–1968). Only the change in 1933, but not the changes in 1947, 1949, 1953, 1955, or 1961 represented a change in long-term party control of unified government.

[2] The Federalists controlled the presidency for all three presidential terms, the Senate for all six Congresses, and the House for four of the six Congresses. That is, there were eight years of Federalist government (1789–1793 and 1797–1801) and four years of divided government (1793–1797).

[3] It would not make sense to include 1825–1861 as part of the era of "Jeffersonian Republican" government because there was no longer a "Jeffersonian Republican" Party.

TABLE 4.1 *Party control of unified government and party theories of economic intervention (expectations)*

Time period	Independent variable: Change in long-term party control of unified government	Dependent variable: Expected change in relative party ideologies
1 Federalist Era 1789–1801	Government divided between Federalists and Republicans	Federalists and Republicans should maintain their relative positions on intervention
2 Jeffersonian Era and Era of Good Feelings 1801–1825	Republican government	Republicans should move more toward intervention than Federalists
3 Emergence of mass, two-party system and competitive politics 1825–1861	Government divided between Democrats and Whigs	Democrats and Whigs should maintain their relative positions on intervention
4 Civil War, Republican Reconstruction, Gilded Age, and Progressive Era 1861–1933	Republican government	Republicans should move more toward intervention than Democrats
5 Democratic New Deal, liberal consensus, Great Society, and party sorting 1933–present	Democratic government	Democrats should move more toward intervention than Republicans

long-term control. The rest of this chapter will analyze the development of the two major parties' ideologies during each of these eras.

3 FEDERALIST ERA, 1789–1801

During the 1790s, the first political parties emerged under the new Constitution and the ideologies they developed matched their institutional positions. The two parties first divided over the "great principle": determining "how strong and active the new federal government was to be" (Aldrich 1995, 72). Under the umbrella of the "great principle," the first Congresses debated issues such as the assumption of state debts, increased taxation, the creation of a national government mint, and the creation of a national bank. The party in power, the "Pro-administration" or "Hamiltonian" Federalists, advocated for a stronger national government and more government intervention in the economy. The party out of power, the "Anti-administration" or "Jeffersonian" Republicans, advocated for a less powerful national government and less government intervention in the economy. While many different factors contributed to the ideological positions these two parties first established, over the course of the 1790s, the party ideologies remained relatively stable as predicted by the theory. There was no change in party control of unified government that would lead us to expect a change in the two parties' relative ideological positions with regard to national government power and economic intervention.

3.1 Historical Context of the Federalist Era

The Federalist and Republican parties were generally parties-in-government only, and not mass-based parties in the electorate (Aldrich 2011). The political entrepreneurs who played a critical role in shaping the new parties' ideologies during this decade included Alexander Hamilton and John Adams, for the Federalists, and Jefferson and Madison for the Republicans. Hamilton outlined a bold economic plan for the new Congress to adopt that included more government intervention in the economy than his opponents wanted. Hamilton hoped his policies would help the fledgling republic to become a notable industrial and commercial empire. In addition to advocating the national government assumption of state debts, and the creation of a Bank of the United States, Hamilton called for the national government to intervene in the economy through a system of tariffs, subsidies, and infrastructure spending. While Jefferson opposed Hamilton's policies in the administration, and Madison opposed Hamilton's policies in Congress, the party battle spilled over into the public realm in 1798 when the Alien and Sedition Acts were passed by the Federalist Congress and signed by President Adams. The debates of partisan elites in Congress and in the administration became the subject of popular discussion.

3.2 Party Control of Unified Government and Party Ideology Development

For most of the 1790s, Federalists controlled unified government and Republicans opposed them. Given that their ideological positions already matched their institutional positions, it is not surprising that the two parties' ideologies did not change dramatically. The Federalists, following the British mercantilist school of thought, continued to advocate for more national government power and more economic intervention, while the Republicans, following the French physiocratic school of thought, advocated for less. The Federalist Party passed most of Hamilton's policies into law, while the Republican Party criticized these interventions into the economy as unconstitutional and imperial.

3.3 Other Factors that Explain Party Ideology Development in the Federalist Era

Previous scholarship has rightfully pointed to the political economy of America at the turn of the nineteenth century to help us understand differences in the ideologies of the two parties. The first party divisions were, to some extent, regional divisions within the country. The Federalists in government largely came from the North, and New England in particular, where the economy was relatively industrial, commercial, urban, and based around manufacturing and shipping. This economic arrangement gave Northerners incentives to support tariffs, internal improvements, and national government financing. Northern manufacturers competed with British manufacturers to sell their goods in the United States, and high tariffs would protect their goods from this competition. Northern merchants needed a stable currency, and access to credit, that could be supplied by a national banking system. The Republicans in government largely came from the South, Virginia in particular, and from the Middle States. These Republican farmers did not have the same policy preferences as Northern manufacturers and merchants. These socioeconomic factors worked in concert with the institutional positions of the two parties to help the parties develop their different theories of economic intervention in the expected way.

3.4 The Federalist Era and the Liberal Conservative Myth

The history of party ideologies in the 1790s that I have just described demonstrates the uselessness of the "left-right" spectrum in measuring party ideologies. If you had forced the Federalists and Republicans of the 1790s to use the language of "left" and "right" that had just emerged during the French Revolution, you might label the Republicans (relatively more sympathetic to the French Revolution) as the "left" party and the

Federalists (relatively less sympathetic to the French Revolution) as the "right" party. Notably, this is how Poole and Rosenthal code the roll call votes of Republicans and Federalists during this era for their DW-NOMINATE model. However, in this scenario, the "left" party is calling for limited government, less government intervention in the economy, and free trade. In contrast, the "right" party is calling for more national government power and more government intervention in the economy. Certainly, the meanings of "left" and "right" have changed drastically since then. Thus, it makes no sense to try to make claims about the two major parties moving to the "left" or the "right" from the time of the Founding to the present.

4　JEFFERSONIAN REPUBLICAN ERA, 1801–1825

In 1801, the Republican Party took long-term control of unified government that lasted until 1825, and the two parties' ideologies changed as this theory predicted. The Republicans began the period as much less interventionist on economic policy than the Federalists, but over the course of the Jeffersonian Era, Republicans began to change their party's ideas, and they closed the gap between the two parties. Over the course of their time in power, Republicans eventually adopted almost all the policies that Hamilton had previously recommended, and that Republicans had previously excoriated. As Republican ideology adopted Federalist ideas, the Federalist Party dissolved and left a one-party system. While the Republicans changed their theory of governance and theory of economic intervention, the more foundational aspects of their party ideology remained largely intact.

4.1　Historical Context of the Jeffersonian Era

In the early nineteenth century, the American people, including both major parties, moved to embrace more national government power and more intervention in the economy than was generally acceptable in the late eighteenth century. The second war for independence, the War of 1812, exposed many of the weaknesses of the American state, and in "the first few years following the war ... the spirit of nationalism was in vogue" (Risjord 1965, 8). This resulted in greater support by both parties for a stronger army, a national bank, and more national infrastructure. The expansion of American settlers beyond the Appalachian Mountains also resulted in a call for more national infrastructure projects to unify the expanding republic. Since the Republican Party ran the US government, it was responsible for most of the nationalist legislation of this period, and its ideology changed to catch up with its institutional and policy positions. While the nation, as a whole, generally moved in a direction welcoming more national government power and more economic intervention, the two parties moved differently, in relation to each other, as predicted by the political institutional theory of party ideology development: The party in power moved farther in the direction of government intervention than the party out of power.

4.2 Party Control of Unified Government and Party Ideology Development

In his First Inaugural Address, Jefferson articulated his party's ideas about limited government, which were formulated during the campaigns and elections of the 1790s:

What more is necessary to make us a happy and a prosperous people? Still one thing more, fellow citizens, a wise and frugal government, which shall restrain men from injuring one another, shall leave them otherwise free to regulate their own pursuits of industry and improvement, and shall not take from the mouth of labor the bread it has earned. This is the sum of good government; and this is necessary to close the circle of our felicities.

(Jefferson 1801a)

In the early years of the Republican regime, Jefferson's party acted in accordance with this ideology. The first Republican Congress repealed the Whiskey Tax of 1791 and the direct tax of 1798, along with the naturalization laws of 1798. In addition to signing these repeals, Jefferson pardoned prisoners who had been prosecuted under the Sedition Act. The new government reduced the size of the military, decreased the national government's debt, and decided not to renew the charter on Hamilton's Bank of the United States. Early in the years of Republican control, party politicians seemed happy to follow the script set out by the party's ideology. However, the longer Republicans remained in control of government, the more they began to adopt the policies and ideas of their Federalist predecessors.

Between 1801 and 1825, the originally anti-nationalist Republican Party gradually moved away from its roots in anti-federalism toward "national republicanism." One of the first temptations to act against the party's theory of governance was the opportunity to purchase the Louisiana Territory. The acquisition would serve the party's theory of ends because it would make possible the ideal of an agrarian republic of egalitarian yeoman farmers spread out over the vast continent, but it would also violate the party's ideology because, to act quickly on the deal, Jefferson would have to exercise more national government power, in general, and more executive power, in particular, than Republicans had previously believed was proper. Given this tension between the party's theory of ends and the party's theories of governance and intervention, the more foundational theory of ends won out, and Jefferson went ahead with the executive action (Risjord 1965, 5–6).

However, it is not as though the theories of governance and intervention were merely instrumental in the service of party ends. These theories were powerful ideas, and Jefferson's "strict-constructionist scruples" caused him much trepidation and anxiety about going forward with the purchase to more than double the size of the United States (Wilentz 2005, 111).

The leader of the party that had blasted executive usurpation under John Adams had no illusions about the fact that he lacked explicit constitutional authority to acquire the new territory, let alone an acquisition as large as the nation itself ... For a moment, as Jefferson contemplated proposing a constitutional amendment that would provide a clear ground for this sweeping exercise of power, it appeared that he might actually force a debate over the legitimacy of the action when everyone else seemed anxiously eager to accept it on its face. With hints of second thoughts in France, the prospect of a delay that might jeopardize the purchase agreements became unbearable, and Jefferson decided not to let the question of propriety get in the way of the achievement.

(Skowronek 1997, 70)

In this instance, the more foundational aspect of Republican Party ideology (the theory of ends) held more weight in shaping the behavior of a political actor than the less foundational aspects of party ideology (the theories of governance and intervention).

In the years following the Louisiana Purchase, Republicans faced additional incentives to act against their theories of governance and intervention to serve the economic interests, and other ideological interests, of their constituents in the South and West. In 1806, with a majority of Federalists and a minority of Republicans, Jefferson signed into law the bill creating the Cumberland Road: the first internal improvement of its kind. In 1807, Jefferson's concerns about foreign affairs led him to push through the Republican Congress an embargo act that restricted trade. This embargo represented an unprecedented use of government power to intervene in the economy. In 1808, Jefferson's Republican Secretary of the

Treasury, Albert Gallatin, offered a report that called for $20 million in internal improvements. Commenting on these Republican actions, in opposition to the party's previously articulated ideology, Herbert Croly explained:

Jefferson, who had been a lion in opposition, was transformed by the assumption of power into a lamb. Inasmuch as he had been denouncing every act of the Federalists since the consummation of the Union as dangerous to American liberties or as inimical to the public welfare, it was to be anticipated, when he and his party assumed office, that they would seek both to tear down the Federalist structure and rear in its place a temple of the true Republican faith. Not only did nothing of the kind follow, but nothing of the kind was even attempted.

(Croly 1909, 46)

Because of the dissonance between the party's ideology and the party's actions in government, Republicans faced incentives to modify their theories of governance and intervention to justify their behavior.

As we observe the language and rhetoric used by Republicans in the years following their takeover in government, we see that the party's ideology began to change accordingly. As the historian Henry Adams noted, when Republicans took control of unified government, they changed their minds on a variety of issue positions, including the national debt, the size of the navy, and the national bank.

Four years had not passed since Jefferson and his party had clamored against attempts to give energy to government; and no one could ever forget that they claimed and received power from the people in order to defend State-rights, restrict Executive influence, and correct strained constructions of the Constitution. Who upheld State-rights in 1804, and complained of Executive influence and strained constructions? Certainly not Jefferson or his friends ... Whenever Jefferson had occasion to discuss the aims and opinions of the two parties, he did not allude to the principles set forth in 1798.

(H. Adams 1891, 203–204)

Although Adams was correct to point out the hypocrisy, Jefferson was not entirely a man of political expediency. As a principled ideologue, the transformation of the Republican Party caused Jefferson pangs of conscience, and he blamed the Hamiltonian policies of the 1790s as the original sin responsible for the mercantilist policies of his own administration: "It mortifies me to be strengthening principles which I deem radically vicious, but the vice is entailed by the first error" (Jefferson 1801c, 344, fn. 1).

Despite the remorse he expressed, it is clear that Jefferson behaved "differently as President than his earlier utterances would have suggested" (Reichley 2000, 52). Jefferson's betrayal of the "Revolution of 1800" caused a split within the Republican Party between "moderate and ardent republicanism" (Jefferson 1807, 424). During his second term in office, a faction of Republican ideologues, led by John Randolph, broke with the president over what they perceived as Federalist policies being promoted by the Republican administration. These Republicans became known as "Quids" to distinguish themselves from the main body of the party, and they opposed Jefferson's administration on the Yazoo land fraud compromise, the attempt to purchase West Florida from Spain, and the trade restrictions with England (Risjord 1965, 40–71). The rise and fall of party factions that accompanies party ideology change saw the nationalist faction become increasingly important and the "Quid" faction become increasingly irrelevant.

Madison's two terms as president moved the party in an increasingly nationalist direction. In 1810, Republican "war hawks" like Henry Clay and John Calhoun from the backcountry were elected to Congress, and they called for an even stronger national government that would bind the separate states together and provide a powerful military force in international affairs. The rise of these young Republican nationalists was opposed by the previous generation of anti-nationalist Republicans, including the Quids, who became known as "Old Republicans" (Risjord 1965, 7). The difference between these two factions was not only a difference in issue positions, but also a difference in the bundle of ideas they articulated (a difference in ideology).[4]

The Federalist and Republican ideological positions became closer during this period because of changes in Republican, rather than Federalist, Party ideology: The Republican theory of governance became significantly more nationalist and the Republican theory of economic intervention became significantly more interventionist. While there were some Federalists who moved in a less nationalist direction in the early

---

[4] By changing their party's ideology after taking power, the Republicans represented the first such change in American party history, but they were following a pattern that had been established even earlier. Notably, the Republicans resembled the Whigs of eighteenth-century British politics. When Whig Party ideology began to change after taking control of Parliament, the party split between the main body of the party and a dissenting faction known as "Old Whigs," who wished to maintain the original principles of the party. Similarly, when Republican Party ideology began to change in the 1800s after taking control of unified government, the party split between the main body of the party and a dissenting faction known as "Old Republicans," who wished to maintain the party's original principles (Banning 1978, 283).

1810s (some even flirting with New England secession from the Union), the party largely maintained its earlier principles as the country as a whole moved toward Federalist ideas about national power and economic intervention. Still, Federalist opposition to the War of 1812, and their connection to the Hartford Convention, soon doomed the party to irrelevance. By the early 1820s, many former Federalists had joined the majority Republican Party, but they were not required to change their principles concerning the role of the national government. Although the Old Republicans blamed Jefferson for starting the party down the path of nationalism and interventionism, after his presidency he, too, worried that the party was going too far. In 1822, Jefferson wrote to Henry Dearborn that the Federalists, discredited as a national party, now promoted "consolidated government" from within Republican ranks like foxes hiding "in the midst of the sheep." As a result, Jefferson explained, "you see so many of these new [R]epublicans maintaining in Congress the rankest doctrines of the old [F]ederalists" (Jefferson 1822a, 265). Jefferson was not simply concerned with changes in Republican Party issue positions, but he was concerned with changes in Republican Party "doctrines" (or ideology). The accession of John Quincy Adams, the son of the old Republican nemesis, to the presidency in 1825 symbolized the party's newly developed nationalist theory of governance.

Although Republican ideology continued to embrace economic intervention as more and more Republican nationalists joined Congress, the old party ideology still worked as a partial constraint on the behavior of party members, and, of course, political actors still exercised agency in opposition to the general forces at work. For example, in two different instances, Madison the constitutionalist vetoed legislation passed by his more interventionist co-partisans in Congress. First, in 1814, the Republican Congress chartered the Second Bank of the United States, but President Madison, given his background in the original Republican Party, worried about its constitutionality and vetoed it. However, in the aftermath of the war, Madison changed his mind. In his annual message to Congress in December 1815, "the great architect of the old Republicanism called upon Congress to consider federal support for certain internal improvements, tariff protection for new industries which had been encouraged by the argument with England, and creation of a new national bank" (Banning 1978, 299). Second, in 1817, Madison the constitutionalist vetoed the Bonus Bill explaining that, although he supported Congressional funds being spent on internal improvements, such an authorization required a Constitutional amendment before he could sign it (Madison 1817).

Despite occasional vetoes by presidents from the Virginia Dynasty, Republican nationalists like Henry Clay, John Calhoun, and John Quincy Adams "dominated the party after the War of 1812" (Milkis and Nelson 2008, 113). They moved the party's ideology toward more national government power as they pursued an "American System" of economic interventions – including tariffs, subsidies, and internal improvements – that echoed the mercantilist policies of the Hamiltonian Federalists, but were aimed at benefitting different constituencies and used toward different ends (John 2003). These party entrepreneurs, acting with resources in Congress and the administration, took advantage of opportunities to change their party's ideology in accordance with the incentives they faced.

While the Republicans changed their party's theory of economic intervention, the Federalists, such as they were, simply maintained their old theory of government intervention in the economy. They continued to advocate for mercantilist policies like a national bank, high tariffs, and internal improvements. As the Republican Party expanded its dominance of American politics, and as it adopted the Federalist theory of economic intervention, the Federalist Party dissolved. In retirement, Jefferson followed the political events unfolding in the "Jeffersonian Era," and he criticized the new Republican Party's adoption of Federalists and Federalism:

An opinion prevails that there is no longer any distinction, that the Republicans & Federalists are compleatly [sic] amalgamated but it is not so. The amalgamation is of name only, not of principle. All indeed call themselves by the name of Republicans, because that of Federalists was extinguished in the battle of New Orleans. But the truth is that finding that monarchy is a desperate wish in this country, they rally to the point which they think next best, a consolidated government. Their aim is now therefore to break down the rights reserved by the constitution to the states as a bulwark against that consolidation, the fear of which produced the whole of the opposition to the constitution at its birth. Hence new Republicans in Congress, preaching the doctrines of the old Federalists, and the new nick-names of Ultras and Radicals.

(Jefferson 1822b, 251)

It seems that Jefferson was the originator of the "RINO" epithet – criticizing the "new republicans in Congress" as Republicans in "name only." This factional division within the Republican Party would set the stage for the revival of two-party politics in the antebellum era.

4.3   Other Factors That Explain Party Ideology Development in the Jeffersonian Era

Economic factors, of course, also help explain the relative shifts of the two parties during this time. Most of the American pioneers who moved west into and beyond Appalachia in the first quarter of the nineteenth century were Republicans (Wood 2009, 359). These Westerners "needed good roads and canals to communicate and conduct their business with other parts of the country and abroad," and so they supported a change in party ideology that justified a program of internal improvements paid for by the national government (Kolodny 1996, 145). Southerners, on the other hand, were skeptical of a national system of tariffs, internal improvements, and national finance that seemed to disproportionately benefit the North and West. Thus, "Old Republicans" in the South resisted the ideological changes pushed by new Republicans in the West.

Historical contingencies, most visibly the War of 1812, also explain much of the party ideology development observed during this time. The Anglophilic Federalist Party in the North generally opposed the War of 1812, while the Republican Party in the West pressed for it. Once the war was underway, the Federalist opposition to war was seen as unpatriotic and un-American, and this opposition to war caused their demise. Furthermore, the War of 1812 made Republicans believe America needed a stronger national state (Holt 1999). For example, the transportation problems the American military faced during the war caused Republicans to reconsider their opposition to national infrastructure projects (Kolodny 1996, 145). These society-centered factors and historical contingencies, along with party control of institutions, help us understand the party ideology developments we observe during this period. While it is debatable whether or not the Republican Party became as nationalist and as interventionist as the Federalist Party during this time period, it is clear that the gap between the parties that existed in the 1790s had narrowed considerably during the first quarter of the nineteenth century.

4.4   The Jeffersonian Era and the Ingredients Necessary for Party Ideology Change

During this period, all of the necessary ingredients came together for Republican Party ideology to dramatically change. First, a variety of salient political issues emerged, including the opportunity to purchase the Louisiana Territory, the call for more internal improvements and trade protection, a growing national debt, the call for a national bank, and war with England. Second, at certain times – and to varying degrees – Jefferson, Madison, James Monroe, and Republicans in Congress were willing to act in ways contrary to previous party orthodoxy on those issues. Third, seeking to justify these actions, important party entrepreneurs like Clay and John Quincy Adams changed the party's ideology by putting familiar terms to new uses. "Republicanism" became associated with nationalism, and defenders of the original faith adopted the label "Old Republican" to distinguish themselves from the new ideology that had emerged. Fourth, these new nationalists in the party – many of them "war hawks" elected from the frontier – rose in importance within the party as the "Old Republicans" became less influential. Fifth, ordinary Republicans in the electorate began using the new narratives, rhetoric, and ideas despite the dissenting opinions of Republicans like John Taylor and an aging Jefferson, who complained that Federalists now hid like foxes in the midst of the Republican fold. Finally, the new language and ideas were used long enough that they became instantiated among the public. This represented a durable shift in Republican Party ideology between 1801 and 1825 that would remain largely unchanged throughout the succeeding National Republican, Whig, and Republican parties for over a century until the New Deal.

4.5 The Jeffersonian Era and the Liberal Conservative Myth

The development of Republican Party ideology in the first quarter of the nineteenth century once again shows the uselessness of the "left-right" spectrum in measuring party ideology change. The currently dominant way of thinking about party ideology asks the incoherent question: "Did the Republican Party's move toward nationalism during that period represent a move to the 'left' or the 'right?'" However, this is an unhelpful way of thinking about party ideology change during this time. It is not that the Republican Party became more or less "liberal" or "conservative" by adopting previously Federalist positions on nationalism, a national bank, infrastructure spending, and trade. Rather, the party simply redefined "republicanism" during that period. If we use stable analytical concepts like "national government power" or "economic intervention," then we can coherently talk about a party changing to advocate for more or less national government power, or more or less economic intervention, but we cannot coherently talk about a party becoming more or less "liberal" or "conservative." According to DW-NOMINATE, the

Republican Party changed from being a party of the "left" to being a party of the "right" during this period, but that is not very helpful. Confusingly, in this scenario, a party becomes more "conservative" by calling for more national government power and more government intervention in the economy.

5 EMERGENCE OF A MASS TWO-PARTY SYSTEM AND COMPETITIVE POLITICS, 1825–1861

The ideological divide within the Republican Party, as described in the previous section, led to the creation of a new party system in the antebellum era: Democratic Republicans (later shortened to just "Democrats") generally criticized government intervention in the economy, while National Republicans (most of whom later became Whigs) defended it.[5] During this time period, neither party took long-term control of unified government, and the original ideological divisions of 1825 remained largely intact throughout. The relative stasis in party ideologies observed in this era is predicted by the political institutional theory of party ideology development.

While Democrats and Whigs argued over spending, taxes, internal improvements, tariffs, and a national bank, neither party could satisfy the demands of an emerging abolitionist movement in the North. This period of mass, two-party competition was punctuated by the arrival of a new Republican Party, Abraham Lincoln, and Civil War.

5.1 Historical Context of the Antebellum Party System

As Monroe neared the end of his second term in 1824, it was clear that, in a one-party regime, whichever politician the Republican Party supported in the general election would run unopposed and become the next president. Thus, the party was unable to unify behind a single candidate, and four major candidates emerged instead. John Quincy Adams and Henry Clay, ardent nationalists, were the most clearly in favor of the "American system" of tariffs, internal improvements, and a national bank. William Crawford, the least nationalist of the candidates, received the support of the "Old Republicans" and an endorsement from Jefferson (Kolodny

---

[5] Michael Holt points out that, contrary to popular myth (Binkley 1943, Schlesinger 1945), the American Whig Party was not a continuation of the Federalist Party, but, like the Democratic Party, emerged out of the Jeffersonian Republican Party (Holt 1999, 2).

1996). Crawford also received the support of a first-term Radical Republican senator from New York, Martin Van Buren, who saw the presidential election of 1824 as "the proper moment to commence the work of a general resuscitation of the old democratic party" (Van Buren 1822, 382). Finally, Andrew Jackson was a moderate nationalist, but more popular for his military heroics, and anti-establishment symbolism, than for any ideological issue positions (Holt 1999, 6).[6]

After Adams won the election in the House of Representatives, the Republican Party quickly divided between Adams and Clay supporters, on the one hand, and supporters of Jackson, Crawford, and John C. Calhoun on the other (Holt 1999, 8). The residue of Federalists in New England, led by Daniel Webster, joined in support of the Adams administration. Denied the presidency despite receiving the most votes in the Electoral College, Jackson immediately began planning to oust Adams in 1828, and Van Buren once again hoped to use the election to establish a national two-party system (Remini 1959, Hofstadter 1969, Aldrich 2011). Van Buren successfully orchestrated the support of the Radical Republicans and Old Republicans, and this coalition became known as "Democratic Republicans," or "Jackson men," in opposition to the "National Republicans," or "Adams men." Combining his own supporters, who gave him a plurality of the vote in 1824, with Crawford's supporters, Calhoun's supporters, and Van Buren's political machine, Jackson easily won the election of 1828. Jackson's reelection in 1832 caused National Republicans to join in coalition with a variety of smaller groups opposed to the Jackson administration, and this new party – after considering a return to the "Republican" label – adopted the name "Whig" (Reichley 2000, 79). By 1836, the Democrats and Whigs had emerged as the two major parties.

Between the 1830s and the 1850s, the American public, in general, and both parties, in particular, changed their ideas slightly concerning national government intervention in the economy. Like many public policy issues, the debate over national government intervention in the economy acted like a pendulum, and by the early 1830s, the pendulum had swung back somewhat against national government power

---

[6] Contrary to the myth promulgated by Schlesinger (1945), Jackson did not campaign in 1824 on a noninterventionist platform. Up until this time, Jackson had been a moderate nationalist. "Jacksonian ideology," understood as opposition to the "American System," did not develop until after the election of 1824 (Minicucci 2004, 165).

(John 2003).[7] Jackson successfully campaigned against renewing the charter of the Second Bank of the United States and used his anti-bank campaign to secure reelection in 1832. The "Tariff of Abominations" of 1828 led to the Nullification Crisis of 1832–1833 and helped precipitate a backlash against nationalist economic policies during the Antebellum Era that was tied up with the sectional crisis regarding slavery.

5.2 Party Control of Unified Government and Party Ideology Development

Once the two-party system of Whigs and Democrats was in place, neither party took long-term control of unified government. As expected, the original ideological divisions remained largely intact through the 1850s. The Jackson coalition decided to campaign against John Quincy Adams, in 1828, on the same principles that Jefferson had articulated when he opposed the incumbent's father in 1796 and 1800. Jackson's "neo-Jeffersonian" program leaned toward "the economics of laissez-faire" (Remini 1972, 73). Of course, this coalition of Republicans opposed to Adams included a diverse group of ideological commitments, and the campaign of 1828 would not be all about the "Principles of '98." Indeed, Jackson's vague ideological commitments, but personal popularity, made him the ideal candidate to lead this new heterogeneous party (Minicucci 2004, 183, Aldrich 2011, 113–114). Still, Van Buren assured his political allies back in New York that "we will support no man who does not come forward on the principles & in the form in which Jefferson & Madison were brought forward & this they will in the end all assent" (Remini 1963, 53–54).

The Jacksonian Democratic Party, formed in opposition to Adams and the National Republicans, generally called for less national government intervention in the economy: no federal government role in banking, lower tariffs, fewer internal improvements, and less spending. The 1840 Democratic Party Platform articulated Democratic ideology by emphasizing the party's commitment to Old Jeffersonian Republican

---

[7] In the 1770s, Americans reacted against British mercantilism and the public mood was anti-interventionist. During the critical period of the 1780s, in response to crises at the state level, the public mood became more accepting of national government power and intervention. In the late 1790s, in reaction to Federalist policies, including the Alien and Sedition Acts, the public mood rose up in a "second revolution." In the 1810s, in preparation for – and in the aftermath of – war with Britain, Americans saw a greater need for national government power.

theories of limited national government power and limited government intervention in the economy:

The federal government is one of limited powers, derived solely from the constitution, and the grants of power shown therein, ought to be strictly construed ... The constitution does not confer upon the general government the power to commence and carry on, a general system of internal improvements ... It is the duty of every branch of the government, to enforce and practice the most rigid economy, in conducting our public affairs, and that no more revenue ought to be raised, than is required to defray the necessary expenses of the government ... Congress has no power to charter a national bank ... The liberal principles embodied by Jefferson in the Declaration of Independence, and sanctioned in the constitution, which makes ours the land of liberty, and the asylum of the oppressed of every nation, have ever been cardinal principles in the democratic faith.

(DNC 1840)

The four succeeding party platforms of 1844–1856 essentially reprinted the planks of the 1840 platform verbatim. In this way, the ideology articulated in party platforms tied together the different parts of the party's ideology: foundational ideas, theories of governance, theories of intervention, and issue positions. Throughout this period, the Democratic Party typically campaigned on limited national government power, strict construction of the Constitution, opposition to internal improvements, opposition to tariffs, limited government spending, lower taxes, opposition to a national bank, and the foundational "classical liberal" ideas of Jefferson. The period from 1825 to 1861 is part of the Democratic Party's "Jeffersonian Epoch," which was characterized by "limited government, ... antistatism, and civic republicanism" (Gerring 1998, 162).

The Whig Party, likewise, generally remained true to the economic ideology of the National Republicans that preceded them. Throughout the Antebellum period, the Whigs called for more national government intervention in the economy: for a federal government role in banking, higher tariffs, more internal improvements, and more spending. The 1844 platform indicated that the party's "principles may be summed as comprising, a well-regulated currency; a tariff for revenue to defray the necessary expenses of the government, and discriminating with special reference to the protection of the domestic labor of the country; [and] the distribution of the proceeds of the sales of the public lands" (Whig National Convention 1844). The 1852 platform specifically endorsed the idea that "the Constitution vests in Congress the power to open and repair harbors, and remove obstructions from navigable rivers" (Whig National Convention 1852). The period from 1825 to 1861 is part of the National Republican and Whig Parties' "National Epoch," in which party members were "mercantilists" and "statists" (Gerring 1998, 57).

5.3 The Jacksonian Era and the Ingredients Necessary for Party Ideology Change

These party ideologies were not simply rhetoric, and they were not simply instrumental; they often actually worked to constrain the behavior of political actors. For example, in response to the Panic of 1837, even pragmatic President Van Buren "was sufficiently wedded to Jacksonian principles to resist government-sponsored solutions to the economic crisis" (Milkis and Nelson 2008, 134). This inaction led to Van Buren's defeat in 1840. Political actors are not free to change their party's ideology every time it might suit them. Party ideology change requires many different ingredients, and it typically takes several years for all of those ingredients to emerge.

The stasis in party theories of economic intervention between 1825 and 1861 is partly explained by the absence of change in long-term party control of unified government. For example, during his first term in office, from 1829 to 1833, Jackson enjoyed unified Democratic control of government, but not all of the necessary ingredients showed up during that short time period, and Democrats did not become durably more interventionist relative to National Republicans. During that time, the rechartering of the Second National Bank emerged as an important political issue, but Jackson followed his and Van Buren's neo-Jeffersonian Democratic Party ideology by calling for an end to the national bank. In so doing, he resisted the temptation to simply use the power of the bank to serve his own party's purposes. However, Jackson was not entirely a principled defender of Democratic Party ideology: During his administration, infrastructure spending increased dramatically (Wilentz 2005, 867–868). Furthermore, Jackson enforced the "Tariff of Abominations" in the name of nationalism and in opposition to the states' rights faction of his party. Despite these deviations from party ideology, no party entrepreneur emerged among Democrats to change the party's ideology in a way that would justify the party's nationalism or interventionist economic policies.

Although former National Republicans seized on the issue of executive power – naming their new party "Whigs" during "King Andrew's" second term in office – they did not significantly change their ideas about national government power or economic intervention. After just four years of unified Democratic control of government, the National Republicans won control of the Senate in the election of 1832, and the incentives for party ideology change were lost. Similarly, in 1845, 1853, and 1857, Democrats once again took control of unified government, but in each case government control was short-lived, and it was not enough time for all of the necessary ingredients to come together to expect party ideology change.

5.4 Other Factors That Explain Party Ideology Development in the Jacksonian Era

That the two parties maintained their theories of economic intervention is not, of course, entirely attributable to the path dependent character of party ideologies (the tendency of party ideologies to maintain their pre-existing structure unless acted on by other forces). It is also a product of the political economy of the period. Although founded as a national party, uniting Southern anti-nationalists and northern Federalists opposed to Jackson, the Whig Party became increasingly sectional, and based in the Northeast, over the course of the 1840s and 1850s.[8] As such, they had incentives to push for a national bank, high tariffs, and internal improvements that would disproportionately benefit the manufacturing and mercantile class. In this sense, the explanation offered by previous historians – focusing on the class interests of capital as opposed to agriculture – also helps make sense of this era.

The factor that underlies the entire antebellum period, however, is the issue of slavery, which holds enormous explanatory power. The Democratic Party, based in the South, was generally more supportive of slavery, and its extension into the West, than the Whig Party. The Democrats feared what the national government could do if abolitionists, or opponents of slavery, came to power. As such, Democratic ideology throughout the period emphasized limited national government power and state sovereignty. In each party platform, they resolved:

That Congress has no power, under the Constitution, to interfere with or control the domestic institutions of the several States; and that such States are the sole and proper judges of everything pertaining to their own affairs, not prohibited by the Constitution; that all efforts, by abolitionists or others, made to induce Congress to interfere with questions of slavery, or to take incipient steps in relation thereto, are calculated to lead to the most alarming and dangerous consequences, and that all such efforts have an inevitable tendency to diminish the happiness of the people and endanger the stability and permanency of the Union, and ought not to be countenanced by any friend to our Political Institutions.

(DNC 1844–1856)

---

[8] The Whigs did, however, maintain an important base in Kentucky and Tennessee.

The Democratic Party's strict construction of the Constitution was not only about preventing Congress from passing tariff or internal improvements legislation that disproportionately benefitted the North (as noted earlier, Democrats themselves sometimes supported such legislation); it was also about preventing Congress from interfering with slavery. The election of a president from a third party that was opposed to the expansion of slavery, in 1860, was the impetus for Southern slaveholders' secession from the Union.

5.5 The Jacksonian Era and the Liberal Conservative Myth

The "left-right" spectrum is once again unhelpful in describing party ideology during this period. According to DW-NOMINATE, Jackson's Democratic Party was the party of the "left," while the Whig Party, and its Republican successor, were the parties of the "right." In this way of thinking, pro-slavery Southerners who called for states' rights and less government intervention in the economy were "left-wing liberals," while anti-slavery Northerners who called for more national government power and more government intervention in the economy were "right-wing conservatives." This approach to mid-nineteenth-century party ideology history confuses more than it clarifies.

6 CIVIL WAR, REPUBLICAN RECONSTRUCTION, AND THE PROGRESSIVE ERA, 1861–1933

In 1854, opponents of the Kansas-Nebraska Act, unhappy with the Democratic and Whig Parties' willingness to allow the expansion of slavery into the Western territories, formed a new party that replaced the Whigs as the major opposition to the Democrats. These Northerners chose the name "Republican" to recall the party founded by the author of the Declaration of Independence (RNC 1856), and to recall the nationally dominant party from which both Democrats and Whigs had first emerged. In the 1860s, Republicans took control of unified government, and over the next seven decades they generally remained more supportive of national government power, and economic intervention, than the Democratic Party out of power. While the two parties developed their ideologies mostly in accordance with what we would expect, there are two exceptions during this period.

The first exception, the 1890s, was largely the product of a demographic development and a historical contingency. The emergence of agrarian revolt, along with the political entrepreneurship of William Jennings Bryan, led the Democratic Party to adopt the Populist Party, and to move in a more interventionist direction than the Republican Party. However, this was not a durable change in the party's theory of economic intervention, and by 1904 the Democratic Party had returned to the practice of criticizing Republicans for high taxes, high tariffs, profligate spending, protectionism, economic regulation, and subsidies.

The second exception, the 1910s, was the product of Democrats taking short-term control of unified government (for six years during the administration of Woodrow Wilson). During their control of the national government, Democrats acted in accordance with the political institutional theory by exercising the power at their disposal, and the two parties' theories of economic intervention changed accordingly. Once again, though, this was not a durable change in the party's ideology, and by the mid-1920s Democrats had returned to their neo-Jeffersonian ideology by criticizing Republican interventions in the economy. It was not until the New Deal that the Democratic Party shifted durably in favor of more economic intervention than the Republican Party (Milkis 1992, 109).

6.1 Historical Context

Party ideology in the 1850s and 1860s was dominated by the issue of slavery. The Republican Party's theory of governance argued that the national government should have the power to outlaw slavery in its territories – as it did in the Missouri Compromise of 1820. The Democratic Party's theory of governance, in contrast, argued that the decision about slavery in the territories should be made through local referenda. In addition to its relatively nationalist theory of governance, the Republican Party's relatively interventionist economic policy closely followed the ideas articulated by the Whigs – many of whom became Republicans (Reichley 2000, 100).

Following the Civil War, America experienced dramatic industrialization, immigration, and urbanization. In response to the socioeconomic inequality caused by these forces, several social democratic and Progressive reform movements emerged in American politics. These insurgent reform movements represented a move by the American public, in general, and the two major parties, in particular, toward an increasing acceptance of greater national government power and intervention in the economy. The two parties' ideologies moved in this direction at different times, and in different ways, and these differences can partly be understood through the political institutional theory of American party ideology development.

6.2 Party Control of Unified Government and Party Ideology Development

With the Democratic South out of the Union, the Republican Party dominated the US government starting in 1861. Republicans won six straight presidential contests between 1860 and 1880, controlled the House from 1859 to 1874, and controlled the Senate from 1861 to 1878. After Reconstruction, Democrats began winning the House in the 1870s and 1880s, but they would not gain control of unified government until 1893, and even then, it only lasted two years. During this period of Republican Party control, the GOP had incentives to exercise the powers at their disposal and continue the development of an ideology that justified relatively more economic intervention. Likewise, the post-bellum Democratic Party had incentives to maintain its ideology in a way that criticized Republican intervention in the economy.

6.2.1 Party Ideology Development, 1861–1893

During the Civil War and Reconstruction, Republicans, opposed by Democrats, increased the powers of the national government to prosecute the war and reconstruct the South. Notably, Republicans used their power in service of pursuing their preexisting anti-slavery objectives. They used the expanded power of the national government to abolish slavery; force the Confederate secessionists to surrender; pass the civil rights amendments mandating manumission, citizenship, and voting rights for former slaves; establish the Freedmen's Bureau; and pass a series of Force Acts (Civil Rights or Ku Klux Klan Acts) aimed at ensuring civil and political rights for African-Americans. Republicans also used the expansion of national government powers to intervene in the economy in ways that exceeded even the previous interventionist regimes of the Federalists and National Republicans (Salisbury 1986). The GOP pursued its policies "in a startlingly programmatic fashion, implementing fundamental coercive and redistributive measures" (Skocpol 1992, 86). The Republican program was supported by a party ideology that emphasized the importance of national union and power.

Republican interventions into the economy during this period can be categorized in three ways. First, Republicans intervened by imposing and increasing taxes. They imposed the nation's first graduated income tax, established the Internal Revenue Bureau, imposed real estate taxes, and raised tariff levels to record highs (Stathis 2014, 105–106). Second, Republicans pursued national government infrastructure projects on an unprecedented scale. For example, the Pacific Railroad and Northern Pacific Railroad Acts provided land and financing to build railroads and telegraph lines connecting the West Coast with the Midwest. The National Currency Act of 1863 and the National Bank Act of 1864 reestablished a national bank system, which had dissolved under Jackson in 1836. Third, Republicans began to enact social democratic reforms in the wake of industrialization. For example, in 1868, the Republican Congress passed a law mandating an eight-hour workday for federal laborers, over a veto by Andrew Johnson, which was affirmed by Grant's presidential proclamation after taking office in 1869.

The ideological push for social democratic reforms came from social movements that responded to the socioeconomic inequalities produced by industrial capitalism. Typically, the policy proposals of these reform movements would be adopted, first, by a minor third party, second, by the more interventionist Republican Party in power, and, finally, by the less interventionist Democratic Party in opposition. For example, the labor movement's call for an eight-hour work day (more encompassing than the law passed by Republicans in government) was first adopted as a plank in the platforms of the Labor Reform Party in 1872, the Greenback Party in 1880, the Anti-Monopoly and Republican parties in 1884, and the Democratic Party in 1904. The call for railroad rate regulation was first adopted as a plank in the platforms of the Labor Reform and Prohibition parties in 1872, the Greenback Party in 1880, the Anti-Monopoly and Republican parties in 1884, and the Democratic Party in 1896. The call for regulation ensuring workplace safety was first adopted as a plank in the platforms of the Greenback Party in 1880, the United Labor Party in 1888, and the Socialist Labor, Republican, and Democratic parties in 1892.

Party ideology development between 1861 and 1892 makes sense in light of the political institutional theory. As Republicans dominated the national government in the 1860s and early 1870s, Republican Party ideology advocated more national government power, and more economic intervention, than the Democratic Party. The period from 1861 to 1892 was part of the Republican Party's "National Epoch," in which party members were "mercantilists" and "statists," and part of the Democratic Party's "Jeffersonian Epoch," which was characterized by "limited government" and "antistatism" (Gerring 1998, 57, 162). "The major parties ... projected contrasting stances toward the proper role of government in society and the economy ... Republicans projected activist stances for government, including the federal government ... Democrats championed state and local freedoms from federal intrusions [and] attacked economic interventions" (Skocpol 1992, 80).

Likewise, as the two parties became competitive again, these stark differences moderated. With the readmission of Southern states after Reconstruction, the Democratic Party began to win elections again: The party took the House of Representatives in 1874, and even controlled the Senate in 1879–1881. As Democrats increasingly exercised power in Congress, they moderated their anti-nationalist rhetoric and began following the Republicans in advocating for progressive legislation and social democratic reforms. The Republican penchant for economic intervention also moderated during this period. "Once the southern states rejoined the Union and shook off most Reconstruction controls, the Democratic Party again became closely competitive for national offices. The Republican Party outlived its heroic phase and settled into the normal distributive routines of patronage democracy" (Skocpol 1992, 87). While the political institutional theory helps us understand party ideology developments between 1861 and 1893, it is less useful in explaining the 1890s and 1910s.

6.2.2 *Party Ideology Development, 1893–1909*
The developments of the 1890s are due, in large part, to a society-centered factor: the emergence of agrarian revolt. In the first decades following the Civil War, the GOP created the foundations of the American welfare state through pensions for Civil War veterans (Skocpol 1992, Cogan 2017), but the one-party system of the 1860s and early 1870s also led to corruptions of power and abuses of patronage. Republicans feared no competition from Democrats during this period, and so they often used the suddenly large national government to provide spoils for party machines and corporate interests. By the early 1880s, Republicans had joined Democrats in "politics as usual," and reformers did not see either party advocating their cause (James 2000, 45). At the same time that the Republican Party's "heroic phase" was ending, reformers within the party grew restless, and many third parties emerged to take over the GOP's reform legacy.

The Populist Party's remarkable showing in the presidential election of 1892, and its capture of 10 percent of the vote in the midterm elections of

1894, made the two major parties take notice. As an agrarian movement based in the South and West, it especially caught the attention of the Democratic Party, which took control of unified government in 1893 for the first time since before the Civil War. Up until the 1890s, the Democratic Party in opposition had mostly ignored the Populist movement, and party ideology had continuously affirmed its commitment to Jeffersonian ideas of limited government. Democratic President Grover Cleveland was a *laissez-faire* Bourbon Democrat who had vetoed veterans' pensions and drought relief bills while advocating for lower taxes and less spending. Thus, despite having unified control of government in 1893–1894, Democrats did not have a president willing to take advantage of the power at their disposal.

Although Cleveland, personally, was constrained by party ideology, the Democratic Party did have members of Congress willing to respond to the demands of its party base of populist farmers in the South and West. In 1894, the Wilson-Gorman Tariff Bill lowered the rates of the 1890 McKinley Tariff – a perfectly predictable move by a Democratic Congress – but in order to make up for lost revenue, the bill also included an income tax of 2 percent on income over $4,000. The bill became law without Cleveland's signature. After passing that bill, Democrats lost control of Congress to Republicans for the next sixteen years, and they had no other interventionist economic legislation that they needed to defend. Thus, there was no clear settlement between the Democratic Party's two factions.

The events of the party convention of 1896 illustrate the party's newly ambiguous ideology. Heading into the convention, the party was torn between "Gold Democrats," who opposed monetizing silver and who were less interventionist on economic policy, and "Silver Democrats," who favored monetizing silver and who were more populist and interventionist. However, "a speech by William Jennings Bryan, delivered in defense of the silver plank in the majority platform, played a critical role in shaping the preferences of delegates" at the 1896 convention (Bensel 2005, 27). Bryan's nomination brought the Populist Party into the Democratic fold and alienated the Cleveland Democrats. This historical contingency of political entrepreneurship helps us understand how Democratic ideology moved more toward interventionism than Republican ideology in the late 1890s without a long-term change in party control of unified government.

This development, however, was not a durable shift in the Democratic Party's theory of intervention, and Republicans quickly reestablished themselves as more interventionist. An analysis of party platforms from that period shows how the Democratic Party did not become completely committed to national government power and economic intervention. The 1896 platform, nominating Bryan the populist, still opened with neo-Jeffersonian and neo-Jacksonian ideas about limited national government power:

We, the Democrats of the United States in National Convention assembled, do reaffirm our allegiance to those great essential principles of justice and liberty, upon which our institutions are founded, and which the Democratic Party has advocated from Jefferson's time to our own—freedom of speech, freedom of the press, freedom of conscience, the preservation of personal rights, the equality of all citizens before the law, and the faithful observance of constitutional limitations. During all these years the Democratic Party has resisted the tendency of selfish interests to the centralization of governmental power, and steadfastly maintained the integrity of the dual scheme of government established by the founders of this Republic of republics. Under its guidance and teachings the great principle of local self-government has found its best expression in the maintenance of the rights of the States and in its assertion of the necessity of confining the general government to the exercise of the powers granted by the Constitution of the United States.

(DNC 1896)

In the next three sections, the platform called for bimetallism, opposition to "interest-bearing bonds," and opposition to national banks. The platform then included some interventionist language advocating for enlarging the powers of the Interstate Commerce Commission to regulate trusts and railroads. However, the platform then moved back to traditional Democratic language criticizing tax-and-spend Republicans: "We denounce the profligate waste of the money wrung from the people by oppressive taxation and the lavish appropriations of recent Republican Congresses, which have kept taxes high ... We demand a return to that simplicity and economy which befits a Democratic Government, and a reduction in the number of useless offices, the salaries of which drain the substance of the people" (DNC 1896).

After the unusual campaign of 1896, in which Democrats for the first time seemed to be as interventionist as Republicans, the two parties soon returned to their standard positions. In 1900, the GOP platform called for, among other things, anti-monopoly legislation, national labor insurance, stricter child labor laws, the creation of a national highway system, and rural free postal delivery service. The presidential campaign of 1904, between progressive Republican incumbent Theodore

Roosevelt and Bourbon Democratic challenger Alton B. Parker, marked the GOP as once again significantly more interventionist than the Democratic Party. As TR explained in his autobiography, the ideological developments of the 1890s were an interruption in the general trend of Republicans being more progressive, nationalistic, and interventionist than Democrats:

> The Republican party, which in the days of Abraham Lincoln was founded as the radical progressive party of the Nation, had been obliged during the last decade of the nineteenth century to uphold the interests of popular government against a foolish and ill judged mock-radicalism ... The men who ... claimed to be the radicals, and their allies among the sentimentalists, were utterly and hopelessly wrong. This had, regrettably but perhaps inevitably, tended to throw the party into the hands not merely of the conservatives but of the reactionaries; of men who ... distrusted anything that was progressive and dreaded radicalism. These men still from force of habit applauded what Lincoln had done in the way of radical dealing with the abuses of his day; but they did not apply the spirit in which Lincoln worked to the abuses of their own day. Both houses of Congress were controlled by these men ... I achieved results only by appealing over the heads of the Senate and House leaders to the people, who were the masters of both of us. I continued in this way to get results until almost the close of my term; and the Republican party became once more the progressive and indeed the fairly radical progressive party of the Nation.
>
> (T. Roosevelt 1913, 350–352)

The adoption of Bryanism within the Democratic Party, and the corresponding adoption of "conservatism" in the Republican Party, during the 1890s, was the product of a society-centered factor: the emergence of agrarian revolt in the regions dominated by the Democratic Party. This socioeconomic factor, combined with Bryan's political entrepreneurship, proved more decisive in shaping party theories of economic intervention at the turn of the twentieth century than the political institutional theory, which predicted stasis.

While Democrats continued to call for populist measures in the early twentieth century, they still retained their Jeffersonian rhetoric about limited government. Despite support for progressive legislation by many Democrats in Congress, the party's ideological heterogeneity prevented it from becoming the programmatic reform party that it later became under FDR and LBJ. Although both parties had more and less interventionist factions within their heterogeneous coalitions, Republican Party ideology included a theory of governance that called for more national government power than Democratic Party ideology. Thus, Republican economic ideology was more interventionist than Democratic ideology. Herbert Croly noticed this difference in the parties when he described the differences between William Jennings Bryan and Theodore Roosevelt:

The whole tendency of [TR's] programme is to give a democratic meaning and purpose to the Hamiltonian tradition and method. He proposes to use the power and the resources of the Federal government for the purpose of making his countrymen a more complete democracy in organization and practice; but he does not make these proposals, as Mr. Bryan does, gingerly and with a bad conscience. He makes them with a frank and full confidence in an efficient national organization as the necessary agent of the national interest and purpose. He has completely abandoned that part of the traditional democratic creed which tends to regard the assumption by the government of responsibility, and its endowment with power adequate to the responsibility as inherently dangerous and undemocratic.

(Croly 1909, 169)

Because the country as a whole moved in favor of social democratic reforms and government regulation of the economy in the 1890s–1910s, both major parties moved in this direction. However, the Republicans' theory of governance facilitated TR's bold advocacy in this direction.

6.2.3 Party Ideology Development, 1909–1933

While the GOP had returned to being more interventionist than the Democrats during the Roosevelt administration, the presidential election of 1912 – like the election of 1896 – would interrupt this normal development of party ideologies. When TR chose not to run for reelection in 1908, he turned the presidency over to his protégé William Howard Taft, who agreed with TR's approach "in all essentials of policy," and who TR hoped would have better success in putting their "principles into practice" (T. Roosevelt 1904b, 1043–1044). In some respects, Taft was even more receptive to the progressive factions of the party than Roosevelt (Skowronek 1997, 240–243). However, when Taft pressed the antitrust case against US Steel, after TR had declined to do so for particular reasons that he took great pains to articulate, the former president took this as a personal insult to his progressive credentials. Furthermore, when the Republican coalition of Old Guard conservatives and Progressive reformers began coming apart during the Taft administration, TR decided to seek the party's 1912 nomination to reunify the party. At the contested Republican Party convention in Chicago, chairman Elihu Root – "the dominant force" and a Taft supporter – articulated interventionist and progressive principles that characterized the party's ideology during the previous decade of GOP governance. He argued that when "the conditions of modern industrial life require that government shall intervene in the name of social justice for the protection of the wage earner, the Republican national administrations ... have done their full, enlightened and progressive duty" (Milkis 2009, 116–117).[9]

When the party renominated Taft in 1912, TR bolted from the GOP and a new Progressive Party formed around his "Bull Moose" campaign. By taking the insurgent wing of the GOP with him into the Progressive Party, TR made the Republican Party much less interventionist than it was, and no more interventionist than the Democratic Party. Thus, the 1912 election featured a radically progressive candidate in the Progressive Party, a moderately progressive candidate in the Republican Party, and a moderately progressive candidate in the Democratic Party.[10]

Although the Democratic Party had adopted many populist and progressive issue positions into its party ideology since the 1890s, they still celebrated the "principles of Thomas Jefferson," and they still criticized Republican extravagance in taxing and spending (DNC 1912). The Republican Party, on the other hand, not only continued to fill its platform with planks about labor laws and infrastructure projects, but it also articulated "progressive" ideology that supported those positions: "[The GOP] has been genuinely and always a party of progress; it has never been either stationary or reactionary. It has gone from the fulfillment of one great pledge to the fulfillment of another in response to the public need and to the popular will ... It is prepared to go forward with the solution of those new questions, which social, economic, and political development have brought into the forefront of the nation's interest" (RNC 1912). Nonetheless, to show its opposition to the emerging socialist and radically progressive movements, the 1912 platform was the first in party history to voice limitations on

---

[9] Root specifically praised Republican regulation of the railroads, anti-trust laws, the Pure Food law, natural resource conservation, and the income tax amendment.

[10] As TR explained at the time of the election, "Wilson and Taft both fervidly announce themselves as Progressives, and as regards most of our principles they make believe to be for them, and simply to disagree with us as to the methods of putting them into effect" (T. Roosevelt 1912).

government power. Specifically, the platform defended the freedom of the individual to control "his own justly acquired property."

Although we remember the Wilson administration for its leadership in passing progressive legislation to intervene in the economy, Wilson – like many presidents before him – governed as an interventionist much more than he campaigned as one. The 1912 Democratic Party platform was not very interventionist in comparison with the Progressive and Republican Party platforms. However, Wilson, "whose New Freedom Campaign was far more sympathetic to the decentralized state of courts and parties than TR's, felt compelled—or saw the opportunity—as president, to govern as a New Nationalist Progressive" (Milkis 2009, 25). Between 1913 and 1921, the Democratic Party changed its ideology to justify the interventionist legislation passed by the unified Democratic government. Similarly, the Republican Party changed its ideology to become less interventionist on economic policy and to criticize the legislation passed by a unified Democratic government. While Wilson could have chosen to govern as a progressive outside of the party, he chose instead to make the Democratic Party progressive (Milkis 1993, 30). During the Wilson administration, Democrats came around to the positions of the GOP on defense spending, merchant marine subsidies, women's suffrage, federal funding for education, government subsidies, and internal improvements, despite having criticized Republicans on these very issues in earlier platforms.

In contrast, the 1916 GOP platform was the first in party history to include "free-market" language (the Democrats, in contrast, had used this language throughout their history):

The Republican party believes that all who violate the laws in regulation of business, should be individually punished. But prosecution is very different from persecution, and business success, no matter how honestly attained, is apparently regarded by the Democratic party as in itself a crime. Such doctrines and beliefs choke enterprise and stifle prosperity. The Republican party believes in encouraging American business as it believes in and will seek to advance all American interests.

(RNC 1916)

The 1916 platform criticized Democrats for wasteful spending in national budgeting and for proposing government ownership of the merchant marine instead of just subsidies. In 1919–1920, the Republican Congress repealed Democratic war-time legislation by privatizing the railroads and telegraph and telephone lines. The 1920 platform was the first in

Republican Party history to criticize the expansion of the national government. Reminiscent of Democratic rhetoric during Reconstruction, the GOP platform specifically criticized Democrats for continuing war-time measures after the end of World War I.

Just as in the 1890s, however, these changes in party theories of economic intervention in the 1910s were not permanent. Although Democratic ideology changed during the party's six years of unified government beginning in 1913, they did not maintain control of government long enough for those ideological changes to be made durable in the party at-large. Republicans took back control of Congress in 1919 and the presidency in 1921. For the next dozen years, Democrats returned to being a party in opposition to unified GOP govenrment. During the 1920s, Republicans returned to the economic interventions they had pursued before the Wilson administration, and their party ideology followed suit – but this return took longer than we might otherwise have expected. The succession to the presidency of Calvin Coolidge, upon the death of Warren Harding, helped stall the party's ideological development. Like Madison, Cleveland, and Taft before him, Coolidge's singular commitment to constitutional government caused him to act with more trepidation toward national government power than we would otherwise expect given his party's institutional position.[11] By the time the party nominated progressive politician Herbert Hoover to the presidency, however, the GOP had returned to being more interventionist than the Democratic Party.[12]

A content analysis of party platforms going back to 1920 demonstrates this point. To measure how interventionist the Republican and Democratic Party platforms have been on economic policy, I created a novel index of "economic intervention scores" for each platform using the Manifesto Project Dataset's coding of platform sentences (Volkens et al. 2018). Each platform's score represents the net percentage of the platform's quasi-

---

[11] Skowronek (1997) lists Coolidge as one of "three hard cases," along with Cleveland and Eisenhower. Just as he did not act in accordance with his place in political time in Skowronek's model, he did not act in accordance with his place in control of unified government in this book's model.

[12] For example, in the early 1920s, immediately after the nationalist and interventionist Democratic administration of Wilson, Republicans in Congress generally supported tax cuts more than Democrats in Congress. However, after a decade of Republican control of unified government, more Republicans than Democrats supported tax increases proposed by President Hoover.

sentences advocating economic intervention. To calculate this score, the total percentage of sentences calling for less intervention (based on six MPD categories) were subtracted from the total percentage of sentences calling for more intervention (based on fourteen MPD categories). In 1920 and 1924, the Democratic Party platforms advocated more economic intervention than the Republican Party platforms, but in 1928 and 1932, Republicans called for more intervention. In every presidential campaign since 1936, the Democratic Party platform has advocated for more intervention than the GOP platform (see Appendix 2).

The 1924 GOP platform modestly listed a few of its many economic interventions, but the 1928 platform boasted of the party's interventions. Specifically, the GOP emphasized the Republican government's tariff protections of American labor, reclamation of arid lands, the expenditure of $325 million "for the construction of flood control works," the expansion of the Department of Agriculture, the expansion of Rural Free Delivery routes by the post office, and emergency relief administered by Secretary of Commerce Herbert Hoover in the wake of the Mississippi Valley flood. In the 1932 platform, the GOP peaked in its justification and celebration of economic intervention. Echoing Croly's celebration of Progressive interventions in the economy to solve the problems of the industrial age, and foreshadowing LBJ's rhetoric concerning a war on poverty, the Republican Party announced: "Republicans, collectively and individually, in nation and State, hereby enlist in a war which will not end until the promise of American life is once more fulfilled." The platform listed as its accomplishments, among other programs, stimulus spending toward private and governmental construction, the creation of the National Credit Association, the creation of the Railroad Credit Corporation, the increased injection of capital to federal land banks, the creation of the Reconstruction Finance Corporation, the enlarged powers of the Federal Reserve System, the coordination of public and private relief agencies, government aid to agriculture, aid to veterans, and labor reforms. The platform then concluded with a long list of calls for more intervention in bank regulation, monetary policy, home loans, labor legislation, transportation, and internal improvements, among others.

The Democrats, like the Republicans, also revived some of their pre-Wilsonian rhetoric in the 1920s. The platforms of the 1920s repeatedly criticized Republicans for not repealing, in peace time, the high taxes which Democrats had "devised under pressure of imperative necessity to produce a revenue for war purposes." The 1928 Democratic platform criticized high Republican tax rates not only because of the costs to individuals, but because of the disincentive it provides to business and because of the extravagence it leads to in government expense:

The taxing function of governments, free or despotic, has for centuries been regarded as the power above all others which requires vigilant scrutiny to the end that it be not exercised for purposes of favor or oppression ... tax burdens which, if not unendurable, do in fact check initiative in enterprise and progress in business. Taxes levied beyond the actual requirements of the legally established sinking fund are but an added burden upon the American people, and the surplus thus accumulated in the federal treasury is an incentive to the increasingly extravagant expenditures which have characterized Republican administrations. We, therefore, favor a further reduction of the internal taxes of the people.

(DNC 1928)

Democrats not only criticized Republicans for taxing, but also for too much regulation and spending. Although they proposed some government interventions to help farmers, they criticized Coolidge for proposing relief to agriculture "through a reduction of American farm production" – a policy that the party itself would advocate during the New Deal (DNC 1928). After the onset of the Depression, Democrats blamed the GOP's big government policies and called for "an immediate and drastic reduction of governmental expenditures" and "the removal of government from all fields of private enterprise" (DNC 1932). Thus, it is no surprise that candidate Franklin Roosevelt, on the campaign trail, "argued that Hoover had given the nation too much government and his program was busting the budget" (Skowronek 1997, 282).

Although FDR – who had served in the Wilson administration – considered himself a part of the "progressive" faction of the Democratic Party, when speaking as the Democratic Party's candidate for president in 1932, he often articulated standard Democratic ideology. While it is true that he called for a drastic change from existing practices, and for a "new deal" for the American people, it was not always clear what this would mean. In some speeches Roosevelt called for bold and energetic government action, but in others he worried about the extravagence of federal spending under Republican control, and argued that "the first and most important and necessitous step ... is to reduce expense." He criticized the GOP for being "committed to the idea that we ought to center control of everything in Washington as rapidly as possible." He recommended, instead, the Democratic Party's idea, consistently articulated "since the days of Thomas Jefferson," to "permit Washington to take from the

States nothing more than is necessary." FDR regarded "reduction in Federal spending as ... the most direct and effective contribution that Government can make to business" in the battle to pull the economy out of the Great Depression. In his acceptance speech at the DNC convention, FDR tried to reassure the non-progressive factions of the party that they could trust him despite his last name: "For three long years I have been going up and down this country preaching that Government—Federal and State and local—costs too much. I shall not stop that preaching" (F. Roosevelt 1932a).

Even when he spoke less as a representative of Democratic Party ideology, and more from his own personal views, FDR did not stray far from the party line. In his "Forgotten Man" speech, which he explicitly prefaced as not representative of Democratic Party ideology, FDR bent a little toward government intervention, but he ultimately justified it as simply directing existing government policies away from corporations and big business and toward small farmers. In terms of articulating a theory of economic intervention, FDR criticized the Republican Party's attempts to solve the Great Depression through government spending (what later became known as Keynesianism):

It is the habit of the unthinking to turn in times like this to the illusions of economic magic. People suggest that a huge expenditure of public funds by the Federal Government and by State and local governments will completely solve the unemployment problem. But it is clear that even if we could raise many billions of dollars and find definitely useful public works to spend these billions on, even all that money would not give employment to the seven million or ten million people who are out of work. Let us admit frankly that it would be only a stopgap.

(F. Roosevelt 1932c)

Although he left his suggestions for positive government policy vague, in this speech his one concrete proposal was to decrease government intervention in the economy by decreasing taxes on imported goods. These kinds of proposals were consistent with Democratic Party rhetoric in the years prior to 1932.

By nominating Herbert Hoover as their candidate in 1928 and 1932, the Republican Party demonstrated its progressive bona fides. Contrary to the myth of Hoover as a *laissez-faire*, stand-pat of the Old Guard, he was an active, progressive politician with confidence that government could solve the problems of economic depression. Hoover not only followed TR into the Progressive Party in 1912 and (like FDR) served as a progressive in the Wilson administration, he pursued activist, interventionist, and progressive policies while president, too:

Far from ignoring the severity of the situation, he employed the metaphors of wartime to combat it and became the first American president to meet a downturn in the business cycle with massive governmental interventions. Far from being shocked into paralysis, he secured virtually all his major proposals, including some critical departures from past practice. Far from standing fast against innovation, his administration anticipated much of what would occur during the early years of the New Deal.

(Skowronek 1997, 261)

During the 1920s, the Republican and Democratic Parties developed their theories of governance and economic intervention in accordance with their institutional positions. The two parties' ideologies were not only reflected in their distinct issue positions, but also in the distinct ideas they articulated.

Although Hoover governed as a progressive Republican, FDR and the Democrats were able to paint him as a "do-nothing" president – a mischaracterization that would become a widely accepted myth and legend in the ensuing decades. Much of this is due to how Hoover responded to these attacks.

First, although Hoover and the Republicans often boasted about the bold actions they had taken to intervene in the economy during the Great Depression, during the 1932 campaign the simplistic narrative was "change" vs. "status quo." Any time a presidential election features an incumbent and a challenger, this is the inevitable storyline. In times of international instability or war, this often helps the incumbent as voters fear changing horses in midstream. In times of economic downturn and recession, this often helps the challenger as voters are desperate for a change. Hoover, stuck with the "change" vs. "status quo" narrative, attempted to make the argument that voters should stick with him because times of instabilty call for continuity and a steady hand. Both candidates called themselves "progressives" and "liberals," but Hoover attempted to portray FDR as a dangerous radical that could not be trusted. Roosevelt was more than happy to comply with this framing of the issue, arguing that he offered a "new deal" in opposition to the miserable status quo. Unsurprisingly, during a severe economic depression the "change" candidate won the election.

Second, Hoover felt he was unfairly blamed by Roosevelt for the Great Depression, and argued that the economic recession was the result of global forces outside of his control. He resented FDR's enormous popularity, and he changed his language, rhetoric, and ideas after leaving office. During the New Deal, Hoover argued that America had to return to its classcial liberal tradition of individualism and limited constitutional government. Thus, the former progressive politician eschewed his previous political views and took up a new cause. In his post-presidency, he became one of the most vocal critics of the New Deal and the creation of the welfare, regulatory, and administrative state. The later Hoover did more than anyone else to create the myth of the early Hoover.

6.3 Coding the Republican Era of Civil War, Reconstruction, and Progressivism

Given the ambiguity, at times, in the two parties' ideologies between 1861 and 1933, I refrain from coding this era as supporting my hypothesis. It is true that, from the time of the Civil War to the Great Depression, the parties largely developed their ideologies as predicted by the political institutional theory. During most of this time, Republicans in control of government argued for greater national government power and economic intervention, while Democrats in opposition argued for less. Still, there are some important exceptions during periods when Democrats took short-term control of unified government.

In 1893, the Democratic Party took control of unified government for the first time since before the Civil War, and in this short time period, the first four necessary ingredients for party ideology change all came together. First, a salient political issue – "The absorption of wealth by the few, the consolidation of our leading railroad systems, and the formation of trusts and pools" (DNC 1896) – provided an opportunity for the two parties to debate and disagree. Second, Democratic leaders in Congress (but not in the presidency) were willing to vote in ways contrary to previous party ideology. Third, the political entrepreneurship of William Jennings Bryan at the 1896 national convention provided a new set of narratives, ideas, and discourses to be used by party members. And, fourth, the influence of the Bourbon Democrats waned as the influence of the Populists waxed. However, these new ways of speaking and thinking did not become entrenched in the party, and by the 1900s, Democrats had returned to being less nationalist and less interventionist than Republicans as the GOP took back control of unified government after only a short period of time.

Similarly, in 1913 Democrats once again took control of unified government, and in the 1910s Democratic ideology became just as interventionist – if not more so – than GOP ideology as the first four necessary ingredients came together. First, the social, economic, and political causes promoted by progressive reformers provided a variety of issues over which the parties could disagree and debate. Second, President Wilson and his Democratic Congress were willing to act in opposition to previous Democratic Party ideology. Third, the political entrepreneurship of President Wilson provided a new set of narratives, ideas, and discourses to be used by party members. And, fourth, the influence of traditional Democrats waned as the influence of progressive Democrats waxed. However, these new ways of speaking and thinking did not become entrenched in the ordinary party membership, and by the late 1920s, Democrats had returned to being less nationalist and less interventionist than Republicans as the GOP took back control of unified government.

Although the developments of the 1890s and 1910s were not durable, they were still significant. Therefore, I do not code this era's ideological changes as developing in accordance with the hypothesis. While one could argue that, overall, the parties developed as expected, I only code an era as following the logic of the political institutional theory if the ideologies clearly and consistently developed as expected. There is enough ambiguity during this era that it does not meet the exacting standards of this test.

6.4 The Turn of the Twentieth Century and the Liberal Conservative Myth

Attempts to measure party ideology at the turn of the twentieth century on a left-right static spectrum are incoherent. In gradually embracing Progressive reforms like the income tax, the eight-hour workday, railroad rate regulation, and workplace safety regulations in the 1860s–1880s, was the Republican Party moving to the left or the right? In embracing Populism in the 1890s and Progressivism in the 1910s, was the Democratic Party moving to the left or the right? As explained earlier, these are the wrong questions to ask because the meanings of "left" and "right" (to the extent they were even used in America during this period) were unstable. If we assume, as Poole and Rosenthal claim, that "left" always means more government intervention in the economy and "right" always means less government intervention, then roll call scaling scores are completely wrong. According to DW-NOMINATE, the GOP moved slowly to the "right" in the 1860s–1880s as it adopted Progressive reforms like the income tax, the eight-hour workday, railroad rate regulation, and workplace safety regulations. Similarly, according to DW-NOMINATE, the

Democratic Party moved to the "right" in the 1890s when it adopted the Populist Party, in the 1910s when it adopted Progressive reforms, and in the 1930s when FDR radically changed Democratic Party ideology with his New Deal.

7 DEMOCRATIC NEW DEAL, GREAT SOCIETY, AND PARTY SORTING, 1933–PRESENT

Between 1933 and 1947, Democrats took long-term control of unified government, and during that time the two parties' ideologies changed in accordance with the political institutional theory of party ideology development. After advocating for less national government power and less economic intervention than the National Republican, Whig, and Republican parties for the better part of a century, the Democrats finally began advocating for more national government power and more economic intervention than their partisan rivals. Without another change in long-term party control of unified government since then, the ideological transformations of the 1930s have continued up until the present day.

7.1 Historical Context of the New Deal Era

In the 1920s, with Republicans in control of the national government, federal spending was fairly constant. Under President Coolidge, from 1924 through 1928, the national government spent roughly $2.9 billion each year. Under President Hoover, with the onset of the Great Depression, these numbers began to climb. The federal government spent $3.1 billion in 1929, $3.3 billion in 1930, $3.6 billion in 1931 (creating the first deficit since the 1910s), and $4.7 billion in the election year of 1932 (resulting in a $2.7 billion deficit). In 1932, President Hoover signed into law a revenue act that increased the top marginal tax rate from 25 percent to 63 percent. During the Great Depression, the political ideology of the American public changed to accept more national government power and more economic intervention. Within this general drift, the two major parties' ideologies changed as expected according to party control of government. From 1929 to 1932, Republican ideology moved farther in this direction than Democratic ideology. However, from 1933 to 1946, Democratic ideology moved farther in this direction than Republican ideology.

7.2 The New Deal Era and the Ingredients Necessary for Party Ideology Change

As already mentioned, between 1929 and 1932 Democrats often criticized the Republican Party's policies of big government, too much economic intervention, excessive taxes, and reckless spending. For example, while calling for some of the progressive reforms pushed by both Republicans and Democrats in the early twentieth century, the 1932 Democratic platform called for a "drastic reduction in governmental expenditure," a balanced budget, a curtailment of "extravagant expenditures of governmental and improvement subsidies," and an end to the "extravagance of the Farm Board" (DNC 1932). Even those Democrats who were part of the "progressive" or "Wilsonian" wing of the party, like FDR, were not calling for the kinds of reforms that would later characterize his New Deal administration. During the 1932 campaign, Walter Lippmann famously drew a sharp contrast between the Democratic Roosevelt and his progressive Republican cousin Theodore: "Franklin D. Roosevelt is no crusader. He is no tribune of the people. He is no enemy of entrenched privilege. He is a pleasant man who, without any important qualifications for the office, would very much like to be president" (1932). Responding to this criticism that he was not a principled politician, FDR assured the 1932 Democratic Party convention that he would promote traditional Democratic principles: "I want to make my position clear at the earliest moment of this campaign. That admirable document, the platform which you have adopted, is clear. I accept it 100 percent" (1932a).

Once Democrats took control of unified government in 1933, the necessary ingredients for party ideology change began to come together. First, the economic depression obviously provided an opportunity for Democrats to expand the powers of the national government and increase government intervenention into the economy despite the party's classical liberal tradition. Second, FDR was willing to act in opposition to the party's ideology, and members of Congress were willing to go along with the popular president (Reichley 2000, 213). If Al Smith or John Nance Garner had won the 1932 Democratic nomination contest, they might have been more hesistant to break with the powerful Jeffersonian ideas that had dominated the party for a good part of a century. However, FDR was not a party ideologue or a "Bourbon Democrat." Before embarking on a career as a pragmatic Democratic politician, he had been a

Republican and an admirer of his progressive cousin Theodore. Thus, it is not surprising that the pragmatic and experimental FDR was more willing to act contrary to Democratic Party ideology than other Democratic presidential candidates might have been. Where it may have taken Smith or Garner a few years to fully break with Democratic ideology with regard to national government power and economic intervention, it merely took Roosevelt a few days.

Third, FDR was a party entrepreneur who had the opportunity and resources to change Democratic Party ideology to justify his actions. Famously, Roosevelt utilized the new power of radio to speak directly to the American electorate and explain the reasoning behind his New Deal. He successfully appropriated the term "liberal" to describe his expansion of national government power and economic interventionism – the opposite of what it had previously meant. By putting famliar terms to new uses, FDR was able to radically change the party's ideology.

Fourth, just as the populist and progressive factions of the Democratic Party became ascendant, the "Bourbon Democratic" faction fell into obscurity. In fact, many traditional Democrats left FDR's party and became vocal opponents of his New Deal. Perhaps the most prominent anti-New Deal organizaion in FDR's first term was the American Liberty League, which was directed by many 1920s Democratic Party leaders like John W. Davis (the party's 1924 presidential canddiate), Al Smith (the party's 1928 presidential candidate), and John Raskob (DNC Chair from 1928 to 1932). Traditional Democrats like Smith, who once saw FDR as his protégé, denounced the Roosevelt administration for betraying trad-itional Democratic principles outlined in the 1932 party platform.

I would have them re-establish and redeclare the principles that they put forth in the 1932 platform ... It is the most compact, the most direct, and the most intelligent political platform that was ever put forth by any political party in the country ... and no administration in the history of the country came into power with a more simple, a more clear or a more inescapable mandate than did the party that was inaugurated on the 4th of March in 1933. And listen, no candidate in the history of the country ever pledged himself more unequivocally to his party platform than did [Roosevelt] ... It is all right with me if they want to disguise themselvs as Norman Thomas or Karl Marx, or Lenin, or any of the rest of that bunch, but what I won't stand for is allowing them to march under the banner of Jefferson, Jackson, or Cleveland. What is worrying me is where does that leave us millions of Democrats? ... What happens to the disciples of Jefferson and Jackson and Cleveland? ... There is only one of two things we can do. We can either take on the mantle of hypocrisy or we can take a walk, and we will probably do the latter.

(A. Smith 1936)

Just like the "Old Republicans" during the Jefferson administration, these old Democrats during the FDR administration found themselves without a partisan home.

At the same time that party factions were rising and falling within the Democratic Party, what was left of the Republican Party also began to undergo changes. As mentioned earlier, in 1928 and 1932 the GOP platform was more interventionist on economic policy than the Democratic platform. However, since 1936, Republican platforms have consistently espoused rhetoric calling for less economic intervention than Democratic platforms. These changes in rhetoric and ideology in the 1930s are what have garnered the GOP its repuation as the party of free markets and *laissez-faire*.

Fifth, the new ideas, narratives, and rhetoric adopted by party elites were gradually adopted by partisans in the mass public. Ordinary Democratic voters embraced the New Deal, and they gradually adopted the label "liberal" to characterize their support for expansive national government power and economic intervention. The few remaining Republicans in the electorate (as well as former Democrats) who opposed the New Deal also eventually adopted the previously pejorative term "conservative" to characterize their opposition to a bloated federal government and interventionist economic policy. Sixth, and finally, these changes remained in place long enough to become instantiated in ideological discourse.

7.3 The Modern Era and the Powerful Constraints of Party Ideology

It is important to remember, however, that new party rhetoric and ideology is always layered on top of previous party rhetoric and ideology. Republicans did not all of a sudden become classical Jeffersonian liberals, "Bourbon" Democrats, or "Reagan conservatives" committed to *laissez-faire* and free marekts. Likewise, not all Democrats suddenly became Progressives Republicans on the model of Theodore Roosevelt.

It took until 1964 for Republicans to nominate a presidential candidate whose language and rhetoric was strenuously and explicitly opposed to progressivism, national government power, and economic interventionism. Barry Goldwater was the first Republican candidate to ever label himself a "conservative." In 1936, Republicans nominated progressive Republican governor Alf Landon. In 1940, Republicans nominated former FDR supporter Wendell Willkie, who, after losing the general election, proposed to Roosevelt the creation of a "liberal party." Willkie used that term in the way that FDR had redefined it, and the idea was to replace the heterogeneous two major parties with ideologically homogeneous parties (Reichley 2000, 240). In 1944 and 1948, Republicans nominated progressive Republican governor Thomas Dewey. "Progressives" remained an important faction within the Republican Party from the presidency of Theodore Roosevelt all the way through to the late twentieth century.

Just as it took decades after the election of 1932 for the Republican Party to bury its ideologically progressive past, it took decades for the Democratic Party to rid itself of its Jeffersonian, limited government, states' rights heritage. For example, in the mid-twentieth century, many Southern Democrats joined with non-interventionist Republicans to form a "conservative coalition" in Congress to oppose the New Deal and Great Society programs. However, in the late twentieth century, as FDR's ideological transformation of the Democratic Party became complete, "conservative Democrats" (or "Blue Dog Democrats") disappeared from the national scene. Similarly, as Goldwater and Reagan's ideological transforamtion of the Republican Party became complete, "liberal Republicans" or "progressive Republalicans" also became an extinct species.

The ideological changes inaugurated in the 1930s lasted long enough to become durable developments in party ideology. Democrats took control of unified government in 1933 and held onto unified control through 1946. Since that time, the parties have alternated between divided government, short-term control for the Republicans and Democrats, and long-term control for the Democrats. Without a change in long-term party control of unified government since the New Deal, the political institutional theory of party ideology development predicts that the two parties will maintain their relative positions on national government power and economic intervention. This is exactly what we have observed. The GOP has taken control of unified government on three occasions, for brief periods of time, since 1933. All three instances showed Republicans governing more as nationalists and interventionists than we would have expected from the party's previous rhetoric, but in accordance with our theoretical premise that political actors often use the powers at their disposal to intervene in the economy despite their limited government ideology. However, the party's control of unified government never lasted long enough to expect durable changes in the party's theory of economic intervention.

In 1954 a Republican Congress passed, and President Eisenhower signed, an expansion of social security that increased benefits and covered

10 million more people. The Republicans also passed the St. Lawrence Seaway and the Housing Acts of 1954. We would not have expected these legislative landmarks (Mayhew 2005) given the party's theory of economic intervention in the late 1940s and early 1950s. Although Republicans and Democrats had political issues to debate, and Republicans had party leaders willing to act in opposition to the reigning party ideology, there was not enough time for party entrepreneurs to develop new ideology, for party factions to rise and fall, and for new ideological discourses to become instantiated among ordinary party identifiers.

Similarly, in 2003, a Republican Congress passed, and President George W. Bush signed, a significant expansion of Medicare. The Republicans also passed legislation appropriating $286 billion for transportation infrastructure and $29 billion for Hurricane Katrina relief. Although we would not have expected these bills given the party's ideology and rhetoric in the years leading up to Republicans taking control of unified government, our understanding that politicians want to exercise the powers at their disposal helps explain this contradictory behavior. Just as in the 1950s, although Republicans and Democrats had political issues to debate, and Republicans had party leaders willing to act in opposition to the reigning party ideology, there was not enough time for party entrepreneurs to develop new ideology, for party factions to rise and fall, and for new ideological discourses to become instantiated among ordinary party identifiers.

In 2017–2018, with unified control of government, Republican politicians passed legislation that set records for federal spending: topping $4 trillion for the first time in American history. Despite the fact that the US economy had pulled out of the Great Recession, Republicans in control of government decided to increase national government spending levels – both in real terms and as a percentage of GDP. Based simply on the ideas and attitudes articulated by the Republican Party before assuming control of unified government in 2017, we would have expected federal spending and deficits to decrease. But, knowing what we do about the tendency of almost all politicians to exercise and expand the powers at their disposal, the behavior of President Trump and his Republican Congress was perfectly predictable.

In all three cases, after Republicans gained short-term control of unified government, they passed interventionist economic policies but they did not durably change their party ideologies to have a more interventionist theory of economic intervention. This is exactly what the political institutional theory of party ideology development predicts: When a party takes control of unified government, they tend to exercise the powers at their disposal to intervene in the economy (even if they campaigned on noninterventionist ideas and with noninterventionist rhetoric). Exercising the powers of government gives parties an incentive to change their theory of governance and theory of intervention, but this incentive alone is not sufficient for party ideologies to change. Several other ingredients are necessary for change, and parties often lose control of unified government before all of those ingredients for change come together, and before the changing ideology becomes instantiated.

7.4 The Modern Era and the Liberal Conservative Myth

The ideological developments of the past eight decades continue to prove that using a static spatial spectrum to measure party ideology change is incoherent. According to DW-NOMINATE, the Democratic Party has generally moved to the "left" since the end of the Roosevelt administration. However, does it really make sense to describe the Democratic Party of the 1970s-90s as advocating for more government intervention in the economy than they did at the height of economic planning in the 1940s? For example, Democrats today call for much lower tax rates than they did in 1944 when the "centrist" Democratic Party had increased the top marginal tax rate to 94 percent. According to DW-NOMINATE, the party moved to the "left" when it reformed welfare, cut government spending, balanced the budget, and declared that "the era of big government is over" in the 1990s.

On the Republican side, DW-NOMINATE's ideology scores tells us that the GOP was the least conservative in 1964 when the party nominated Barry Golwater. Since that time, the party has moved to the right – so much to the right that, by the time Newt Gingrich became Speaker of the House in the 1990s, the party had become as "conservative" as it had been during the administration of the progressive Republican president Theodore Roosevelt. These descriptions of party ideology since the 1940s simply do not help us understand the real and important ideological developments that have taken place.

It is not that Democrats have become more "liberal" or that Republicans have become more "conservative," but that the Democratic Party has continually redefined liberalism since that time and the Republican Party has continually redefined conservatism. In the 1930s, Democrats changed "liberalism" to mean expansive national government power and interventionist economic policy. In the 1950s and 1960s, Democrats changed "liberalism" to mean pushing for racial desegregation. In the 1960s–1970s, Democrats changed "liberalism" to mean dovish "Come Home, America" foreign policy. In the 1960s–1970s, Democrats changed "liberalism" to mean pro-choice abortion policy. In the 1980s–2000s, Democrats changed "liberalism" to mean support for same-sex marriage. If you had told someone in the 1920s that the Democratic Party was going to change in those ways, they would not have described those changes as moves to the "left" because "liberalism" meant none of those things at that time.

The history of American conservatism is similarly dynamic. In the 1950s–1960s, certain political intellectuals began using the term "conservative" to refer to opposition to communism and to the welfare, regulatory, and administrative state created by the New Deal. In the 1970s–1980s, Republicans changed "conservatism" to mean pro-life abortion policy and tax-cutting fiscal policy. In the 1990s, Republicans changed "conservatism" to mean opposition to interventionist foreign policy focused on "nation-building" and "spreding democracy." In the 2000s, Republicans changed "conservatism" to mean support for interventionist foreign policy focused on "nation-building" and "spreading democracy." In the 2010s, Republicans changed "conservatism" to mean opposition to free trade agreements like NAFTA. If you had told someone in the 1920s that the Republican Party was going to change in those ways, they would not have described those changes as moves to the "right" because "conservatism" meant none of those things at that time.

It is only retrospectively that we have invested "liberalism" and "conservatism" with these meanings, and then anachronistically claim that these developments show us that the parties have moved to the "left" and the "right." Such an approach is tautological. Whatever issue positions Democrats adopt, we retrospectively label "liberal," and then use these changes in issue positions as "proof" that the party has moved to the "left." Likewise, whatever issue positions Republicans adopt, we retrospectively label "conservative," and then use these changes in issue positions as "proof" that the party has moved to the "right." This is a useless way to describe party ideology development in America.

8 CONCLUSION

American history can be divided up into five eras based on long-term party control of unified government, and this gives us five predictions about party ideology development. In every period but one, the parties' theories of governance and theories of economic intervention developed

TABLE 4.2 *Party control of unified government and party theories of economic intervention (results)*

Time period	Independent variable: Change in long-term party control of unified government	Dependent variable: Change in relative party ideologies as expected?
1 Federalist Era 1789–1801	Government divided between Federalists and Republicans	Yes: Federalists remained more interventionist than Republicans
2 Jeffersonian Era and Era of Good Feelings 1801–1825	Republican government	Yes: Republicans became as interventionist as Federalists
3 Emergence of mass, two-party system and competitive politics 1825–1861	Government divided between Democrats and Whigs	Yes: Democrats remained less interventionist than National Republicans and Whigs
4 Civil War, Republican Reconstruction, Gilded Age, and Progressive Era 1861–1933	Republican government	No: Republicans were not clearly and consistently more interventionist than Democrats
5 Democratic New Deal, Great Society, and party sorting 1933–present	Democratic government	Yes: Democrats became more interventionist than Republicans

as expected (see Table 4.2). The five cases briefly examined here lend support to the idea that changes in party control of unified government lead to changes in party theories of economic intervention. The way in which these parties changed their ideology lend support to the idea that ideologies are powerful ideas resistant to change. Only when several necessary ingredients come together can these ideational structures be overcome and transformed by party entrepreneurs. Finally, the numerous and dramatic changes in party ideologies from the Founding to the present show us the deep problems that arise from trying to measure party ideology history using the Liberal Conservative Myth.

5

The Supreme Court and Party Theories of Judicial Intervention

> We pledge ourselves ... to resist all attempts to impair the authority of the Supreme Court of the United States, the final protector of the rights of our citizens against the arbitrary encroachments of the legislative and executive branches of government. There can be no individual liberty without an independent judiciary.
>
> –Republican Party Platform (1936)

I INTRODUCTION

In the presidential campaign of 1936, the Republican Party praised the Supreme Court's actions in striking down New Deal legislation to protect individual liberties. For their part, Democrats criticized the Supreme Court's judicial intervention into the political process for thwarting the democratic will of the people. The rhetoric of the two parties in 1936 was not surprising. It represented two different party ideologies concerning the role of the Courts: Democrats typically argued for less judicial intervention and Republicans usually defended a strong and independent judiciary. From our contemporary standpoint, we know that the parties changed positions in the ensuing years. In the postwar era, the Republican Party frequently condemned judicial activism and the Democratic Party defended the importance of a strong and independent judiciary in protecting minority rights.

This change in Republican Party ideology, from advocating more judicial intervention to less, and the corresponding switch in the Democratic Party, is just one of several instances in American political history of the two major parties changing their ideologies with regard to judicial policy. This chapter seeks to explain these changes in a way that adds to previous scholarship on both the American judiciary and party ideologies. First, students of legal doctrines and judicial decisions typically ignore parties, but this chapter shows the value of bringing parties into the analysis (Perry and Powe 2004, 643). Second, in studying how party control of the Supreme Court and party ideologies have developed over time, this chapter makes a contribution to recent scholarship on "the role that the Supreme Court plays in American Political Development" (Kahn and Kersch 2006, 13).

2 HYPOTHESIS

The hypothesis examined in this chapter is that parties in long-term control of the Supreme Court tend to change their ideologies in ways that call for a stronger and more independent judiciary, and more judicial intervention, while parties in opposition tend to change their ideologies in ways that call for a more deferential Supreme Court and less judicial intervention. As explained in Chapter 2, this hypothesis is based on two theoretical premises. The first premise is that government officials almost universally seek to maximize and expand their powers, and this includes Supreme Court judges. Thomas Jefferson articulated this idea in a letter to William Jarvis: "Our judges are as honest as other men, and not more so. They have, with others, the same passions for party, for power, and the privilege of their corps. Their maxim is *'boni judicis est ampliare jurisdictionem'*" (1820, 162). Following Jefferson, this chapter argues that judges are apt to maximize and expand their power just like legislators and executives.[1] One of the primary ways that judges exercise their powers is by overturning legislation and intervening in social and political life. This tendency among judges typically promotes the policy goals of the party in control of the Supreme Court and thwarts the policy goals of the party in opposition.[2]

---

[1] Just as with legislators and executives, there are, of course, a variety of constraints that limit the exercise and expansion of their powers, including other institutions, opposition parties, public attitudes, and preexisting ideas about judicial restraint in the party's ideology.

[2] For exceptions to this rule, with regard to Republican control of the Supreme Court in recent decades, see Keck (2004). The reason that it does not always help the party in control of the Court, or hurt the party in the minority on the Court, is that judges not only

The second theoretical premise is that political parties develop their ideologies in ways that justify the actions of their co-partisans in government and criticize the actions of their opponents in government. Just as with the institutions and aspects of party ideology examined in Chapters 3 and 4, this logic of party competition applies to the Supreme Court and party theories of judicial intervention, as well.

A party ideology that advocates for more judicial power and intervention calls for things like judicial independence, the active use of judicial review, and judicial supremacy. Likewise, a party ideology that advocates for less judicial power and intervention criticizes "judicial activism" and "legislating from the bench," and instead advocates for judicial deference to the elected branches of government. For example, my theory predicts that party attitudes toward judicial review (one of the most important ways that the judiciary can intervene in social and political life) will change according to which party has the power to exercise it.

2.1 Dependent Variable: Relative Change in Party Ideologies

The dependent variable in this hypothesis is the *relative movement* of the two parties with regard to more or less judicial intervention. That is, this chapter will focus on how the ideological positions of the two parties *move in relation to each other*. For example, both major parties envision a greater role for judicial intervention today than they did in the 1790s (Whittington 2007). However, this chapter will focus on how the two parties' ideologies changed *relative* to each other. That is, given that both parties developed more interventionist ideas over the course of American history, has one party moved more in that direction than the other in different historical eras?

It is also important to note that this chapter measures *party* ideology as distinct from *judges'* ideology or *judges'* behavior. While party ideology is certainly an important independent variable that helps explain a justice's ideology and behavior, judicial behavior is not the dependent variable of interest here.[3] In measuring change in *party* theories of governance and judicial intervention, this chapter focuses on the ideas expressed by party

---

act as partisans in their judicial decision-making, but also as ideologues and institutionalists, which may or may not conflict with their partisan incentives (Keck 2007).

[3] Measuring party ideology, rather than justices' preferences, is a different project than that engaged in by many judicial scholars, including attitudinalists (Segal and Spaeth 1993) and scholars of American political development (Graber 2000), who seek to explain the votes cast by judges and the theories of jurisprudence articulated by judges.

leaders and party members who are most representative of a party's ideology: presidents and leaders of Congress (representing the party-in-government), presidential candidates (often representing the party organization), and ordinary party members (the party-in-the-electorate). Because they are not elected, and do not face reelection, federal judges are less representative of the party's ideology than the president and party-in-Congress (Keck 2007). As a result, this chapter differs from the other empirical chapters of this book in which the government actors who represent a change in party control of a government institution were also the political actors analyzed to measure change in party ideology. This chapter does not do that.

2.2 Independent Variable: Change in Long-Term Party Control of the Supreme Court

It is more difficult to determine party control of the Supreme Court than it is to determine control of Congress or the presidency, but it is still possible. Even though they do not campaign for election with party labels, all justices were nominated by a partisan president, and most justices were party politicians before being nominated to the Court.[4] Thus, with a few exceptions, we can determine a justice's operational party affiliation during their tenure on the Supreme Court based on the party affiliation of the president who nominated them.[5] To measure the independent variable, party control of the Supreme Court, I created a novel dataset that codes an operational party affiliation, while on the Court, for each of the 114 Supreme Court justices in American history.[6] The default coding of a judge's party

---

[4] It has become less common in recent decades for presidents to nominate party politicians, but it was the norm for most of American history.

[5] In this way, parties are able to entrench their ideologies on the Court even after they lose control of the presidency and Congress – a phenomenon that Balkin and Levinson (2001) term the "temporal extension of partisan entrenchment."

[6] Data for the independent and dependent variables were gathered from US history going back to the emergence of the two-party system in the 1790s. Narrowing the time frame to a particular era or slice of history has the added benefit of being able to do in-depth case study analysis, and broadening the time frame to all of US history has the danger of treating each case too superficially. However, because there have been so few cases of change in party control of the Supreme Court, in order to record enough observations to be able to draw conclusions about a trend, we must look at all of US history going back to the first parties. These twenty-three decades of US history give us five observations of change in party control of the Supreme Court to examine.

affiliation is the party of the nominating president.[7] However, in a few cases, I coded a judge's operational party affiliation as different from their nominating president if they clearly and consistently sided with a different political party in their judicial decisions on the bench. In determining these exceptions, I looked at the judge's prior party affiliation and I relied heavily on Urofsky's *Biographical Encyclopedia of the Supreme Court* (2006) and Hall's *Biographical Dictionary* (2001). I found that, although most justices followed the judicial preferences of the political party who nominated them, sixteen of them did not (see Appendix 3).

However, this finding requires a couple important caveats. First, the two parties have not held clearly divergent ideological positions on all issues in all periods of American history, and in order for a justice's judicial decisions to be identified as divergent from the party that appointed them, the appointing party must have a clear ideological difference with the opposition. For example, on the dimension of economic intervention, as explained in Chapter 4, the ideological differences between Republicans and Democrats were less clear in the late nineteenth and early twentieth centuries when both parties had social democratic reformers within their ranks (mostly "populists" in the Democratic Party and "progressives" in the Republican Party). Given the two parties' ambiguity on business regulation at the turn of the twentieth century, it is difficult to say that one group of justices defected from their parties' ideological positions and another group held true. This limits the number of justices coded as diverging from their nominating party's positions.

Second, as should be clear by now, the ideological preferences of the two major parties have changed many times over the course of American history. Thus, if a justice served during a time of ideological change (especially if they had a long tenure on the Court), a justice who was consistent throughout their tenure may have been faithful to the ideological preferences of the party that appointed them but unfaithful to the ideological preferences of the party that emerged after their appointment.[8]

---

[7] Viewing justices as partisan actors promoting the interests of the presidential party that nominated them to the Court is a long-held practice among political scientists (Dahl 1957).

[8] This is arguably the case with Harlan Fiske Stone, Charles Evans Hughes, Earl Warren, Charles Whittaker, Potter Stewart, Harry Blackmun, and John Paul Stevens. Each justice was a Republican appointed by a GOP president when the Republican Party was ideologically heterogeneous and had significant "liberal" and "progressive" factions within the party. However, as the party became increasingly homogeneous and conservative in the postwar era, these justices found themselves siding with the Democratic Party (Gillman 2006, 142).

This second consideration, in contrast to the first, increases the number of justices coded as diverging from their party's positions.

The sixteen judicial "traitors" were appointed almost exclusively in two particular historical eras. First, most of the Republican appointments to the Court during the Jeffersonian Era followed the jurisprudence of John Marshall, and the Federalist majority that preceded them, rather than the jurisprudence of Jefferson and his Republican Party. This includes Henry Livingston, Thomas Todd, Gabriel Duvall, Joseph Story, and John McLean. Second, about half of the Republican appointments to the Court between the 1920s and the 1970s were "liberal" or "progressive" Republicans who ended up in opposition to the "conservative" Republican Party that emerged after their appointments. They tended to follow the jurisprudence of the liberal Democratic Party during the New Deal and postwar era. This group includes Harlan Fiske Stone, Benjamin Cardozo, Earl Warren, Harry Blackmun, and John Paul Stevens.[9]

In determining when a change occurs in party control of the Supreme Court, I use the coding of each justice's *operational* party affiliation on the Court. This is because what matters to a party, in developing its attitudes toward judicial intervention, is whether the justices serving on the Court at any given time are supporting or overturning their party's policy preferences – not whether the justices were appointed by their party's presidents or not. Thus, it did not matter to the Jeffersonian Republicans that their presidents had appointed a majority of the Court's membership

---

[9] Stone was a liberal Republican nominated by Calvin Coolidge in 1925. As one of the "Three Musketeers," Stone supported the Democratic Party's New Deal. Cardozo was a progressive Democrat nominated by Herbert Hoover in 1932. Cardozo joined Stone and Brandeis as one of the "Three Musketeers." Warren was a progressive Republican nominated as chief justice by Eisenhower in 1953. As chief justice, Warren led the Court's left-leaning civil rights jurisprudence in the postwar era. William Brennan was a progressive Democrat nominated by Eisenhower in 1956. Serving on the Court until 1990, he was arguably the most liberal member of the Supreme Court during his tenure. Blackmun was a liberal Republican nominated by Nixon in 1970. He sided with the liberal justices on the Burger and Rehnquist Courts like Brennan and Thurgood Marshall. Blackmun wrote the Court's majority opinion in *Roe v. Wade*. Stevens was a moderate Republican appointed by Ford in 1975. In his eleven years as part of the Burger Court, from 1975 to 1986, Stevens tended to side with the conservatives on the Court and opposed affirmative action and upheld capital punishment. However, in his twenty-four years as part of the Rehnquist and Roberts Courts, from 1986 to 2010, Stevens tended to side with the liberals on the Court, and was more liberal than Ronald Reagan's Republican Party from 1980 to 2010. By 2006, Stevens was considered the leading liberal on the Court (Gillman 2006, 142).

TABLE 5.1 *Party control of the Supreme Court and party theories of judicial intervention (expectations)*

Time period	Independent variable: Change in long-term party control of the Supreme Court	Dependent variable: Expected change in relative party ideologies
1 Federalist Era and Marshall Court 1790–1836	Federalist Supreme Court	Federalists should move more toward intervention than Republicans
2 Taney Court and Chase Court 1836–1874	Democratic Supreme Court	Democrats should move more toward intervention than Whigs and Republicans
3 Gilded Age and the Lochner Era 1874–1937	Republican Supreme Court	Republicans should move more toward intervention than Democrats
4 Postwar liberal consensus and conservative response 1937–1991	Democratic Supreme Court	Democrats should move more toward intervention than Republicans
5 Rehnquist Court and Roberts Court 1991–present	Republican Supreme Court	Republicans should move more toward intervention than Democrats

in the 1810s and 1820s because the majority of justices did not decide cases according to Republican Party preferences. Similarly, it did not matter to conservative Republicans that their presidents had appointed a majority of the Court's membership in the 1950s–1980s because the majority of justices did not decide cases according to Republican Party preferences.

Based on this coding of each justice's operational party affiliation while on the Court, we observe that party control of the Supreme Court has changed five times (see Table 5.1). Federalists took control in 1790 when Washington appointed Wilson, Jay, Cushing, Blair, Rutledge, and Iredell. Democrats took control in 1836 after Jackson appointed Baldwin, Wayne, and Taney to join Thompson. Republicans took control in 1874 when Grant appointed Strong, Bradley, and Waite to join Swayne and Miller. Democrats took control in 1937 when FDR appointed Black to join Brandeis, Stone, Hughes, and Cardozo. Republicans took control in 1991 when Bush appointed Thomas to join

Rehnquist, O'Connor, Scalia, and Kennedy.[10] These five periods of party control of the Supreme Court generate five predictions for party ideology development (see Table 5.1). The following sections will examine whether party theories of jurisprudence have evolved in the expected way.

3 FEDERALIST ERA, JEFFERSONIAN ERA, AND THE MARSHALL COURT, 1790–1836

Between 1790 and 1836, the ideologies of the two major parties, with respect to judicial intervention, evolved as predicted. The Federalists, in control of the Supreme Court, developed a theory of governance and a theory of judicial intervention calling for a strong judiciary and more judicial intervention. The Republicans, in opposition to the Court, generally argued for a weak judiciary and for less judicial intervention. The two parties had established their ideological positions by the end of the 1790s, and their theories of judicial intervention persisted in the succeeding decades. Although Republicans took control of the elected branches of government in the "Revolution of 1800," the previously appointed Federalist justices on the Supreme Court, holding life terms, continued to intervene in political life in order to rule in favor of Federalism's (and National Republicanism's) policies long after the Federalists last won a national election in 1798.[11]

3.1 Historical Context of the Federalist Era and Marshall Court

During the debates over ratification of the Constitution, the issue of the Supreme Court's power and authority to intervene in social and political life was a point of contention. Anti-Federalists, opposed to ratification, argued that the Court's implied power to review the constitutionality of legislation passed by Congress, combined with life terms, would make

---

[10] GOP control of the Supreme Court since 1991, however, has been tenuous. This is because the majority has never expanded beyond 5–4, and because that bare majority requires counting swing voters like O'Connor and Kennedy as party of the Republican majority. Over a period of twenty-seven years, depending on the composition at any given time, the Democratic appointees only had to pick off one these unreliable GOP appointees on any given case.

[11] The Federalists extended their "partisan entrenchment" for almost four decades until the death of John Marshall (Balkin and Levinson 2001).

tyrants of the justices on the Supreme Court (Brutus 1788).[12] In Federalist 78, Alexander Hamilton assured Americans that, under the new Constitution, the Supreme Court would be the least susceptible to tyranny, and insisted that justices should not only have life terms and the power of judicial review, as proposed by the Constitution, but that they should have the *sole* power of judicial review (Publius 1787).

In the 1790s, when the partisan divide between Hamiltonian Federalists and Jeffersonian Republicans replaced the divide between Federalists and Anti-Federalists, the two parties once again divided over the issue of the power and place of the judiciary. A series of Supreme Court cases in the mid-1790s, with rulings favorable to the Federalist Party, made Republicans disgruntled, and the federal judiciary's enforcement of the Alien and Sedition Acts brought about a passionate debate between the two parties over which institutions are authorized to determine the constitutionality of Congressional legislation. This issue made the judiciary a focus of the presidential campaign of 1800 (Stephenson 1999). After Republicans took control of Congress and the presidency, the disjunction between a Federalist judiciary and a Republican national government led to continued tensions over the power and place of the Supreme Court until the Democratic Republicans finally took control of the Court in 1836.

3.2 Party Control of the Supreme Court and Party Ideology Development

After the First Congress passed, and Washington signed, the Judiciary Act of 1789, the president set to work appointing judges to staff the federal court system. John Jay and James Wilson, two of the leading Federalist proponents of the Constitution, were the first Supreme Court justices to take the oath of office later that year. They were followed by William Cushing, John Blair, John Rutledge, and James Iredell in 1790. Given the existing theories of government intervention and theories of ends held by the two parties in the early 1790s, it is entirely plausible that the Republicans would have wanted a strong and interventionist judiciary for the

---

[12] While both Federalists and Anti-Federalists believed that the Constitution provided the Supreme Court with the power to interpret the Constitution in order to determine the constitutionality of federal legislation, Hamilton's normative position in favor of judicial supremacy – in which the Supreme Court should have the sole power of judicial review – was less common.

precise reason that they wanted a weak and limited national government: The courts could have been used to strike down legislation passed by the Federalist Congress and president that gave too much power to the national government over the states (R. Ellis 1971, 12–13). However, in the ensuing years, Republicans quickly despaired of finding allies in the federal judiciary.

3.2.1 Party Ideologies during the First Party System

Rather than intervening in ways that Republicans wanted, for the most part the federal judiciary intervened to overturn state laws rather than nationalist legislation passed by the Federalist Congress (Treanor 2005). As the federal judiciary intervened in American political and social life in ways that limited state power and strengthened national government power, Republicans spoke out against the judiciary while the Federalists defended it. In 1795, Jefferson complained that the "judiciary branch of the government" had become too involved in politics by becoming an "auxiliary to the Executive in all its views" (1795, 209). Having taken control of the House of Representatives during Washington's second term, Republicans argued for a weaker executive and a weaker Supreme Court to defer to the democratic will expressed in the House.

In the aftermath of the Alien and Sedition Acts, Republicans argued that the Federalist national government had become tyrannical in its suppression of dissent and its use of the Federalist judiciary to enforce the unpopular laws. Jefferson and Madison's Virginia and Kentucky Resolutions claimed that the states, and not the national judiciary alone, had the authority to determine the constitutionality of Congressional legislation (in this case, the authority to determine that the Alien and Sedition Acts were unconstitutional). In response, several Federalist-controlled state legislatures passed resolutions arguing that it is the prerogative of the Supreme Court, and not the state legislatures, to exercise judicial review.

As the Supreme Court became entangled in the presidential campaign of 1800, the two contending parties took opposing sides: The Republicans argued for less intervention by the judiciary in political affairs, and the Federalists defended the prerogatives of the Court (R. Ellis 1971, Wood 2009, 400–432). As the historian Gordon Wood noted: "With good reason, the Jeffersonian Republicans had become convinced by 1800 that the national judiciary had become little more than an agent for the promotion of the Federalist cause" (2009, 418). In this time of party ideology development, Jefferson and Madison were the party entrepreneurs who acted to shape the Republican Party's ideology in a way that called for a weaker and less interventionist judiciary.

After the "Revolution of 1800," Republicans controlled the presidency and Congress, but not the Supreme Court. Just prior to the change in government control, Congress passed, and President Adams signed, the Judiciary Act of 1801, which strengthened the Courts against the oncoming hostility of the new regime. Gouverneur Morris explained the purpose of the law: "The Leaders of the federal party may use this opportunity to provide for friends and adherents ... They are about to experience a heavy gale of adverse wind. Can they be blamed for casting many anchors to hold their ship through the storm?" (Morris 1801, 405) What the Federalists viewed as an anchor in the storm, the Republicans viewed as a thorn in their side.

The most radical members of the party were ready to dismantle the entire judicial system that the Federalists had put in place. Writing to Jefferson, William B. Giles, the representative of Virginia's 9th District, explained the feeling of Republicans upon taking office in 1801: "What concerns us most is the situation of the Judiciary as now organized. It is constantly asserted that the Revolution is incomplete, as long as that strong fortress is in possession of the enemy ... No remedy is competent to redress the evil system, but an absolute repeal of the whole Judiciary" (R. Ellis 1971, 20–21). While Jefferson did not go that far, he did believe "that the growing pretensions of the Judiciary must be curbed" (Warren 1922, 209). The new Republican Congress repealed the Judiciary Act of 1801 immediately upon taking power. In a speech on the Senate floor recommending repeal, Kentucky Republican John Breckenridge gave his interpretation of departmentalism: "The Legislature have the exclusive right to interpret the Constitution, in what regards the law-making power" (Breckenridge 1802).

In addition to the Repeal Act, Jefferson conceived of a plan to amend the Constitution so that the president could remove a justice from the Supreme Court upon request from Congress. Republicans also proposed an amendment that would have limited federal judges to a fixed term. They pursued the impeachment of Federalist judges, including John Pickering, who was removed from the District of New Hampshire, and Supreme Court Justice Samuel Chase, who was acquitted. The period between 1801 and 1807, in which Republicans first came to power and faced an entrenched Federalist judiciary, is identified by Engel (2011) as the first of a dozen periods of "court-curbing" in American political history.

During the first quarter of the nineteenth century, the Jeffersonian presidents from Virginia appointed six justices to the Supreme Court, but this failed to change the balance of power on the Court. Two Republican-appointed justices, William Johnson and Smith Thompson, voted in ways that supported the Republican Party, but the other four tended to side with Marshall and the Federalists more often than with Johnson and Thompson.[13] This inability to change the Court's behavior meant that the two parties maintained their ideological positions throughout the period.

3.2.2 Party Ideologies during and after the Era of Good Feelings

Between 1819 and 1824, the Marshall Court issued a cluster of important and controversial decisions that once again entangled the judiciary in partisan debate. In *McCulloch v. Maryland* (1819), *Cohens v. Virginia* (1821), and *Green v. Biddle* (1823), the Marshall Court ruled in favor of national power over the states, which resulted in the second era of court-curbing by the Republican Congress and presidency (Engel 2011). Jefferson, once again, was not shy to express his antipathy toward the federal judiciary. In a letter to William Jarvis, Jefferson took issue with Jarvis' assumption that the Supreme Court has the final say in determining the constitutionality of legislation, and instead articulated his doctrine of departmentalism:

You seem ... to consider the judges as the ultimate arbiters of all constitutional questions; a very dangerous doctrine indeed, and one which would place us under the despotism of an oligarchy ... not responsible, as the other functionaries are, to the elective control. The constitution has erected no such single tribunal, knowing that to whatever hands confided, with the corruptions of time and party, its members would become despots. It has more wisely made all the departments co-equal and co-sovereign within themselves.

(Jefferson 1820, 162)

To Charles Hammond, he wrote that "it has long been my opinion ... that the germ of dissolution of our federal government is in the constitution of the federal judiciary; an irresponsible body ... working like gravity by night and by day, gaining a little today and a little to-morrow,

---

[13] According to Stephenson (1998, 58), "only William Johnson, Jefferson's first pick for the high court, had maintained independence and was in a position to challenge Marshall intellectually." Nonetheless, the timing of change in party control of the Supreme Court identified in Appendix 3 (1836) remains the same whether Smith Thompson is viewed as an operational Republican or Federalist. See, also, Abraham (2008, 68).

and advancing in noiseless steps like a thief over the field of jurisdiction"
(Benson 1911, 2). Jefferson's proposed solution to this problem was to
make federal judges subject to reappointment every six years like senators
(Jefferson 1821, 214).

As explained in Chapter 4, the election of 1828 officially divided the
Republican Party between "National Republicans," supporting John
Quincy Adams, and "Democratic Republicans," supporting Andrew
Jackson. The Nationalist Republicans included most of the former Feder-
alists who were now too embarrassed to use that name, while the Demo-
cratic Republicans included most of the "Old Republicans" and "Radical
Republicans." In this party divide, the Nationalists continued to support
the national judiciary, while the Democrats sought to revive the original
Jeffersonian Republican opposition to the judiciary. After Jackson
defeated Adams in 1828, the National Republican Party dissolved. The
Whig Party emerged in opposition to President Jackson and executive
power, but not in opposition to judicial power.[14]

The Democrats, like the Old Republicans before them, attacked the
judiciary in response to Marshall Court decisions that ruled in favor of
national over state sovereignty. The Nullification Crisis of the late 1820s
and early 1830s revived the 1790s issue of who had the authority to
interpret the Constitution: the individual states or the national judiciary.
In response to Whig politician Daniel Webster's claim that the Supreme
Court held the power of judicial review, and not the states, Missouri
Democratic Senator Thomas Hart Benton claimed in 1830 that this
theory led to "a despotic power over the States" and "a judicial tyranny
and oppression" (Stephenson 1999, 71).

The controversy over the recharter of the Second Bank of the United
States also placed the two parties on opposing sides of the question of
judicial authority. In response to the Whig Party's theory of judicial
supremacy, President Jackson, in his bank veto message, argued for the
old Jeffersonian doctrine of departmentalism:

If the opinion of the Supreme Court covered the whole ground of this act, it ought
not to control the coordinate authorities of this government. The Congress, the
executive, and the court must each for itself be guided by its own opinion of
the Constitution ... It is as much the duty of the House of Representatives, of the

---

[14] "Democrats, and before them the Jeffersonians, had been the antijudiciary party in
    national politics. The Whigs, in contrast, were the intellectual heirs of the national
    Republicans and the Federalists, who had been strong supporters of the federal judiciary"
    (Stephenson 1999, 88).

Senate, and of the President to decide upon the constitutionality of any bill or resolution which may be presented to them for passage or approval as it is of the supreme judges when it may be brought before them for judicial decision. The opinion of the judges has no more authority over Congress than the opinion of Congress has over the judges, and on that point the President is independent of both. The authority of the Supreme Court must not, therefore be permitted to control the Congress or the executive when acting in their legislative capacities, but to have only such influence as the force of their reasoning may deserve.

(Jackson 1832)

Recognizing, like Hamilton before him, that executives held the power of the sword, and courts "merely judgment," Jackson happily observed that the Supreme Court's ruling in *Worcester v. Georgia* (1832) fell "stillborn" when it was not enforced (R. Ellis 2007).

In sum, the period between 1790 and 1836 was a time when the two major parties held stable positions with regard to judicial power and intervention because party control of the Supreme Court remained stable. The Federalists, National Republicans, and Whigs advocated judicial independence, judicial review, and judicial supremacy. The Jeffersonian Republicans and Democrats, on the other hand, criticized an undemocratic Court for opposing popularly elected majorities, and for violating states' rights. Since Jeffersonian Republicans and Democrats controlled the national government between 1801 and 1836, this period was characterized by congressional and presidential attacks on the Marshall Court, in particular, and the Federalist judiciary in general.

3.3 Other Factors that Explain Party Ideology Development

Party control of the Supreme Court is not, of course, the only factor that helps us understand party theories of governance and judicial intervention espoused in the early American republic. The two parties' different attitudes toward judicial authority were also a product of their different views on popular rule. According to Tocqueville, political parties are always divided between democrats who want to extend popular power and aristocrats who want to restrict popular power (Tocqueville 1835, 170). In the portion of American history Tocqueville had seen, the parties wanting to extend popular power were the Jeffersonian Republicans and Jacksonian Democrats, while the parties wanting to restrict popular power were the Hamiltonian Federalists,

National Republicans, and Whigs. Given this understanding of party ideologies, it is easy to understand the parties' theories of governance and theories of judicial intervention. As the least democratic of the three institutions of government, the judiciary was celebrated or scorned based on these foundational ideas about who should rule. While this theoretical insight can explain the positions of the two parties, with respect to judicial power, up until the time of Tocqueville's writing in 1835, it cannot explain the following four decades of American history.

4 JACKSONIAN ERA, CIVIL WAR, THE TANEY COURT, AND THE CHASE COURT, 1836–1874

By 1836, President Jackson had been able to appoint enough justices to the Supreme Court to reverse the Federalist majority on the Court, and he also replaced John Marshall with Roger Taney as Chief Justice. This represented a change in party control of the Supreme Court by the Democrats that lasted until 1874. During this time, the ideologies of the two parties, with respect to the judiciary, evolved as predicted. As Robert McCloskey pointed out: "Now the Chief and a majority of his associates were Jackson-approved, and this meant that the anti-judicial tradition of the Democrats lost much of its edge" (2000, 55). The two major political issues that entangled the Supreme Court in party politics, and brought these ideological changes to the fore, were the extension of slavery into the federal territories and Reconstruction. Most notably, the Taney Court's *Dred Scott* (1857) decision got the two parties talking about the Supreme Court again.

4.1 Historical Context

The years between 1836 and 1874 were characterized by American westward expansion, the slavery crisis, the Civil War, and Reconstruction. The debates between Whigs and Democrats, and later between Republicans and Democrats, over national versus state power were bound up with the question of whether the national government could regulate slavery in the states and territories. With the Democratic Party now in control of the Supreme Court, as the two parties debated these issues, they began to change their theories of governance and theories of judicial intervention accordingly.

4.2 Party Control of the Supreme Court and Party Ideology Development

In 1835, during the Jackson administration, political observers noticed that the Supreme Court might finally change partisan hands. As discussions over who should fill vacancies on the Court captured national attention, the staunch Democratic Republican organ, the *Richmond Enquirer*, bemoaned the Court's Federalist history but celebrated the idea that a Democratic Republican appointment like Taney as Chief Justice would change the Court's jurisprudence:

The Court has done more to change the character of that instrument and to shape, as it were, a new Constitution for us, than all the other departments of the Government put together. The President will nominate a Democratic Chief Justice, and thus, we hope, give some opportunity for the good old State-Rights doctrines of Virginia of '98 –'99 to be heard and weighed on the Federal Bench. The very profound and brilliant abilities, with which they have been hitherto opposed in the Supreme Court, have only contributed to make us more anxious to bring back the ship to the Republican tack. We believe that Taney is a strong State-Rights man.

(Warren 1922, 283)

The National Republicans and Whigs, for their part, feared the end of the Federalist judiciary: Daniel Webster wrote to his wife, Caroline, in 1836: "Judge Story arrived last Evening, in good health, but bad spirits. He thinks the Supreme Court gone, & I think so too" (Webster 1836, 198).

4.2.1 Party Ideology Change under the Taney Court, 1836–1864

Although the Taney Court discontinued the Marshall Court's practice of favoring national government power over state power, the Democrats did not destroy the Supreme Court, or allow the national judiciary to wither away into weakness (Stephenson 1999, 79). Once in power, Democrats on the bench of the Supreme Court did not entirely follow the calls for judicial deference that had become a hallmark of Jeffersonian Republican and Democratic Party ideology over the preceding half century. Instead, true to Jefferson's insight, the Democratic justices on the Supreme Court faced the same incentives to expand their powers, and intervene in political life, that the Federalist justices had faced. Although they started out, because of their previous party ideology, less interventionist than the Marshall Court, they still ended up intervening more than we would expect given the party's previous rhetoric concerning the judiciary (but as predicted by the political institutional theory). Seeking to correct the myth of a weak Taney Court, Robert McCloskey has observed:

> The legend of Taney and his brethren as radical democrats, hostile to property rights, nationalism, and Marshall's memory, was stronger than the facts ... The old jurisprudence had not been broken down after all, or even greatly altered ... Judicial power was not surrendered. In fact, the position of the Supreme Court as the final arbiter of constitutional questions had become, within a few years of Taney's accession, more secure than ever before. The concept of judicial sovereignty, which Marshall had nurtured so lovingly and defended against so many challenges, was by 1840 an almost unquestioned premise of American government.
>
> (McCloskey 1960, 54)

After Democrats took control of the Supreme Court in 1836, they faced incentives to intervene in political life, but because Democratic justices had a different theory of ends than Federalist justices, they exercised their powers in pursuit of different objectives.

Under Democratic control, reversing the jurisprudence of Marshall, the Court now ruled in favor of state, rather than national, sovereignty. In *Charles River Bridge v. Warren Bridge* (1837), the Taney Court upheld a Massachusetts State charter given in 1828 to construct a bridge. In *Mayor of New York v. Miln* (1837), the Court upheld a New York State regulation on ships entering the port of New York. Similarly, in *Cooley v. Board of Wardens* (1852), the Court upheld a Pennsylvania law regulating shipping in Philadelphia.

The Democratic Court particularly enlarged the place of the Supreme Court through overturning antislavery legislation. In *Prigg v. Pennsylvania* (1842), the Court struck down a Pennsylvania law that outlawed taking African Americans out of the state's borders for the purpose of placing them under slavery.[15] In *Dred Scott v. Sandford* (1857), the Taney Court ruled that the Missouri Compromise's prohibition of slavery in northern US territories was unconstitutional. This decision proved that the Court was willing to expand its power, and intervene in American social and political life, if there were a piece of congressional legislation that the Democratic Party did not like.

---

[15] While it is true that the Taney Court rarely struck down national legislation as unconstitutional, this has more to do with the kind of legislation being passed than the timidity of Democratic justices (Graber 2000, 34). The Whig Party never had control of unified government, and so the legislation passed by Congress and the president was not typically the kind of legislation to which Democratic justices would have been opposed.

Although the Republican Party emerged in the 1850s as a successor to the Whig Party,[16] the Republicans were founded in opposition to a Supreme Court dominated by the Democratic Party. Thus, these former Whigs, opposed to the westward expansion of slavery, had to finesse their ideological evolution in the aftermath of the *Dred Scott* decision. One of these former Whigs, Abraham Lincoln, became the leading spokesperson for Republican Party ideology in the late 1850s, and he challenged the doctrine of judicial supremacy while still maintaining the old Whig respect for the rule of law and judicial institutions:

We oppose the Dred Scott decision in a certain way ... We do not propose that when Dred Scott has been decided to be a slave by the court, we, as a mob, will decide him to be free. We do not propose that, when any other one, or one thousand, shall be decided by that court to be slaves, we will in any violent way disturb the rights of property thus settled; but we nevertheless do oppose that decision as a political rule which shall be binding on the voter, to vote for nobody who thinks it wrong, which shall be binding on the members of Congress or the President to favor no measure that does not actually concur with the principles of that decision. We do not propose to be bound by it as a political rule in that way, because we think it lays the foundation not merely of enlarging and spreading out what we consider an evil, but it lays the foundation for spreading that evil into the States themselves. We propose so resisting it as to have it reversed if we can, and a new judicial rule established upon this subject.

(Lincoln 1858, 255)

The Republican Party's opposition to the Court in 1858 represented an important change in Whig Party ideology. However, in its moderation and respect for order and the rule of law, we see a layering of new party ideology on top of, rather than discarding, old party ideology. In this way, the old Whig Party ideology, with its defense of judicial power and intervention, continued to constrain and structure the ideas expressed by Whigs and Republicans even after the parties switched control of the Court.

No major party platform had ever discussed the role of the judiciary until after the *Dred Scott* decision, but starting in 1860, party platforms reveal how the Democratic and Republican parties developed divergent theories of governance and judicial intervention in response to the Taney Court's ruling. The 1860 Republican Party platform criticized the Court's interpretation "that the Constitution, of its own force, carries slavery into any or all of the territories of the United States" as a

---

[16] "At least three quarters of the Republican electorate were former Whigs" (Graber 2000, 32).

"dangerous political heresy," and argued that "perversions of judicial power" had reopened "the African slave trade," which was "a crime against humanity and a burning shame to our country and age" (RNC 1860).

The Democratic Party, for its part, justified its support of slavery in the territories by pointing to the decision of the Supreme Court. The party did not take an explicit stand in favor or against slavery, but instead made a claim for judicial supremacy, including acceptance of the Court's decision to overturn any legislation outlawing slavery in the territories. Departing from their Jeffersonian departmentalist past, and borrowing language from the Federalists and Whigs who they previously opposed, Democrats now argued that the meaning of the Constitution is "determined by the Supreme Court of the United States," and that decisions by the Supreme Court "should be respected by all good citizens, and enforced with promptness and fidelity by every branch of the general government" (DNC 1860). In his description of American party ideology development, Charles Beard wrote:

> From its Jeffersonian forerunner, the Democratic party, with its theory of majority rule, had inherited a tradition of criticism with respect to the federal judiciary. In the middle period, however, after all the old Federalist judges had died or resigned and good Democrats had been appointed to the bench, the tradition faded. When the Supreme Court, in the Dred Scott case (1857) upheld slavery in the territories, Democrats demanded unqualified loyalty and obedience to the decision of the great tribunal. It was the Republican party, whose anti-slavery plank had been splintered by the decision, that now criticized the Court and talked about 'reconstructing' it.
>
> (Beard 1928, 87–88)

Although Democrats lost control of the government in 1860, they still had many holdover Democratic-appointed justices on the Supreme Court during and after the Civil War, and so the party division between pro-judiciary Democrats and anti-judiciary Republicans remained.

4.2.2 Party Ideology Maintenance under the Chase Court, 1864–1874

The Republican Party had several opportunities to replace Jacksonian Democrats on the Supreme Court in the early 1860s, but Lincoln's practice of appointing former and future Democrats to fill these vacancies during the Civil War kept Democrats in the majority on the Court until 1874. When Lincoln took the oath of office, there was already one vacancy on the Court. Before he could fill that vacancy during the secession crisis, two more vacancies opened up when John Campbell resigned from the Court to join the Confederacy and John McLean died. Lincoln's first two appointments in 1862 – Noah Haynes Swayne and Samuel Miller – were nationalists who supported the Union and expanded powers of the national government. Lincoln's next three appointments to the Court, however, frequently sided with the anti-nationalist Democrats on the Court (Graber 2000).[17]

The Chase Court defied the Republican Party's expansion of national government power. In the seventy-four years of the Marshall and Taney Courts, between 1790 and 1864, the Supreme Court had only twice ruled that a federal law was unconstitutional: in *Marbury v. Madison* (1803) and *Dred Scott* (1857). In the ten years of the Chase Court, however, the Supreme Court ruled almost a dozen federal policies as unconstitutional (Kutler 1968). For example, in *ex parte Milligan* (1866), the Supreme Court ruled that Lincoln's military tribunals and suspension of habeas corpus were unconstitutional. In *Hepburn v. Griswold* (1870), the Court ruled that the national government's issuance of greenbacks as currency was unconstitutional. The Chase Court's use of judicial review was unprecedented in the number of federal laws it ruled unconstitutional, but, as Mark Graber (2000) points out, the Chase Court's judicial activism had Jacksonian origins, and was a product of the Court's Democratic Party ideology opposed to the nationalist measures of the Republican Party.

Given the temporal extension of Democratic Party entrenchment on the Supreme Court, the two parties maintained their theories of judicial intervention throughout the Civil War and Reconstruction. Notably, Republicans engaged in another era of court-curbing. In 1866, Congress redrew the boundaries of the circuit courts to decrease the influence of Southern Democratic judges and passed a Judiciary Act that prevented Democratic President Andrew Johnson from making several appointments to the federal judiciary. In 1867, Congress passed a law that prevented the Court from hearing a habeas petition from William McCardle, a Democratic newspaper editor in Mississippi who had been jailed under the Military Reconstruction Act (Clark 2011, 35). Furthermore, the House passed a bill, which failed in the Senate, that

---

[17] David Davis, a native of Maryland and a close friend of Lincoln, generally ruled against Republican Party preferences while on the Court. He was nominated for president by the Labor Reform Party in 1872, and was elected to the Senate by the Democratic state legislature of Illinois in 1876. Stephen Field, a Democrat from California, was the first Supreme Court justice in American history to be nominated by a president from the opposing party. Salmon P. Chase was one of the few founders of the Republican Party who had previously identified with the Democratic Party more than the Whig Party.

would require a two-thirds majority in order for the Supreme Court to rule a federal law unconstitutional (Engel 2011, 206). Ultimately, though, Republicans settled on jurisdiction stripping to curb the court. The Jeffersonian Republicans' zeal for judicial impeachments in the early nineteenth century was only matched by the Radical Republicans' zeal for jurisdiction stripping in the mid-nineteenth century (Engel 2011).

The Democratic Party, of course, criticized these attacks and continued to argue for a strong and independent judiciary throughout the 1860s. "The Radical party ... has abolished the right of appeal, on important constitutional questions, to the Supreme Judicial tribunal, and threatens to curtail, or destroy, its original jurisdiction, which is irrevocably vested by the Constitution" (DNC 1868). The pro-judicial ideology of the Democrats, and the anti-judicial ideology of the Republicans, would change, however, at the turn of the twentieth century.

5 GILDED AGE AND THE LOCHNER ERA, 1874–1937

In the 1870s, the Republican Party took long-term control of the Supreme Court from the Democrats, and over the course of the Progressive Era, the two parties' ideologies evolved on judicial power and intervention as expected. This time, the political issue that entangled the Courts in politics was social democratic reform legislation. Although the two parties' theories of economic intervention were in flux at the turn of the twentieth century, in the aftermath of the New Deal, the Democratic Party moved decisively in favor of government intervention in the economy, while the GOP resisted it. Thus, Lochner Era decisions that overturned social reform legislation as unconstitutional were celebrated by Republicans during the 1930s and criticized by Democrats. Republican theories of governance and judicial intervention evolved in a way that defended judicial power, independence, and intervention. Democratic ideology, on the other hand, evolved in a way that attacked these things.

5.1 Historical Context of the Gilded Age and Lochner Era

After the Civil War, reform movements emerged in American politics that called for social democratic policies to ameliorate the new conditions brought on by industrial capitalism. As explained in Chapter 4, these movements were first advocated by third parties in the 1870s, then adopted piecemeal by the Republican Party beginning in the 1880s, and by the Democratic Party beginning in the 1890s. In the 1870s–1880s, when the GOP was clearly more in favor of these policies than the Democrats, the Republican Supreme Court was more tolerant of this kind of legislation. For example, in *Munn v. Illinois* (1877), the Court ruled 7–2 that the State of Illinois could fix maximum rates charged by railroad and grain elevator companies. Republican Chief Justice Morrison Waite, using communitarian ideas typical in the Republican Party, explained that when a businessperson "devotes his property to a use in which the public has an interest, he, in effect, grants to the public an interest in that use, and must submit to be controlled by the public for the common good" (Waite 1876). Democratic Justice Stephen Field, and former Democrat William Strong, dissented from Waite using traditional Democratic ideas about individualism and limited government.

However, once the Democratic Party adopted the Populist Party in the 1890s and began advocating for some of these reforms, the Republican Supreme Court, for the first time, began overturning some legislation regulating the market economy. Although the progressive wing of the Republican Party, and the populist and progressive wings of the Democratic Party, managed to pass limited social democratic reforms in the 1890s–1930s, the Supreme Court struck down much of this legislation in what became known as the Lochner Era. Like other eras of Supreme Court history, the federal judiciary grew in power during this time as part of the continual secular shift toward greater judicial power and intervention (Clark 2011, 35).

Given the two parties' ideological heterogeneity at the turn of the twentieth century, presidents from both parties nominated justices who took a variety of positions on the constitutionality of state and national government regulations of the economy. For example, although we might view Republican Presidents Grant, Hayes, Garfield, Harrison, and McKinley as ideologically similar, they nominated an ideologically diverse group of justices: Grant nominated Bradley and Waite, who supported government regulation of business; Garfield and Harrison nominated Matthews and Brewer, who opposed government regulation of business; and McKinley nominated Sanford, who supported government regulation. Even within one administration, we can see diversity: Taft nominated a pro-regulation Democrat (Lurton), a pro-regulation Republican (Hughes), an anti-regulation Democrat (Lamar), and an anti-regulation Republican (Van Devanter). Given that Republican presidents appointed a majority of the justices between 1874 and 1896, I code this period as one of Republican Party control of the Supreme Court but without significant party debate over the role of the Court.

5.2 Party Control of the Supreme Court and Party Ideology Development

Between 1870 and 1882, four different Republican presidents made a total of nine appointments to the Supreme Court, and by 1874 the party had established long-term control of the Supreme Court. Between 1874 and 1895, the two parties' platforms do not mention the federal judiciary, but an analysis of Court-curbing bills introduced into Congress can still give us insight into the ideological developments of this period.[18] During this era of Republican Party control of the Supreme Court, members of Congress introduced sixty-one different court-curbing bills, but only seventeen of these bills were introduced by Republican congressmen. This indicates that the Republican Party was less opposed to judicial intervention than the Democratic Party.

5.2.1 Party Ideologies during the Progressive Era

In 1894, Congress lowered tariffs while instituting a small income tax impacting a very small portion of the population. In *Pollock v. Farmers' Loan Trust Co.* (1895), the Supreme Court ruled that this income tax violated the Constitution's prescription that direct taxes must be apportioned among the states. In addition, in *United States v. E. C. Knight* (1895), the Court again angered populists and progressives when it interpreted the Sherman Act much more narrowly than reformers who crafted the legislation had hoped.[19] These rulings drew the ire of Democrats opposed to the Republican Court (Westin 1953).

Like the Jeffersonian Republicans at the beginning of the nineteenth century, Populist Democrats at the end of the nineteenth century began calling for impeachment of federal judges. Even though the Democratic Party had supported the practice of judicial review during the Taney and

---

[18] This data was gathered from a list of "all Court-curbing bills introduced in Congress from 1877 through 2010" provided by Tom Clark (2013).

[19] The justices, themselves, did not divide between Republicans and Democrats on the Court. In *Pollock*, of the two justices appointed by Democratic President Cleveland, Chief Justice Fuller wrote the majority opinion and Associate Justice Edward White wrote the dissenting opinion. The seven justices appointed by Republicans split four in favor and three dissenting. The four in favor included Democrat Stephen Field. In *E. C. Knight*, Democratic Chief Justice Fuller once again wrote the majority opinion, and only Republican justice John Marshall Harlan dissented.

Chase Courts, some party members now claimed that no such power existed:

> If the Supreme Court has a right to declare a law of Congress void for lack of conformity to the Constitution, it obtains it outside of that instrument itself; for in no single one of its provision is there any warrant for it, either expressed or implied ... Under the Constitution, the Supreme Court can no more nullify a law of Congress, by a decision, than can Congress nullify a decision of the court by an enactment, or than can the president nullify both by an executive order ... The power claimed by the Supreme Court, to nullify a law of Congress, is entirely a self-assumed power ... Our constitutional government has been supplanted by a judicial oligarchy. The time has now arrived when the government should be restored to its constitutional basis ... with all of its faultless outlines and harmonious proportions.
>
> (Pennoyer 1895)

A quarter century before he became Chief Justice, Republican William Taft responded to Governor Pennoyer's discourse in *The American Law Review* by defending the authority of federal courts to overturn unconstitutional state legislation under the Fourteenth Amendment's guarantee to the right of property (Taft 1895).

As the Democratic Party incorporated the populist movement, the Democratic Party began articulating that faction's critique of the courts. In 1896, the "Bryan Democrats," which included the Populist Party, criticized the Court's behavior, while the National Democratic platform of the "Cleveland Democrats" insisted on the traditional Democratic position defending judicial independence.

Former Republican President Benjamin Harrison argued that this plank in the Populist Democratic Party platform was the most important issue of the 1896 election.[20] Republican politician Chauncy Depew warned in the *Literary Digest* that "Bryan proposes to abolish the Supreme Court and make it the creature of the party caucus whenever a new Congress comes in" (Depew 1896). In the four years from 1896 through 1899, MCs introduced eighteen court-curbing bills, but only four of these bills were introduced by Republicans. Once again, this

---

[20] "In my opinion there is no issue presented by the Chicago convention more important or vital than the question they have raised of prostituting the power and duty of the national courts ... I cannot exaggerate the gravity and the importance and the danger of this assault upon our constitutional form of government; [upon] the high-minded, independent judiciary that will hold to the line on questions between wealth and labor, the rich and poor" (Harrison, 1896).

indicates that Democrats were more concerned about weakening the power of the federal courts than Republicans.

The partisan debate over the role of the Court died down after 1899 but was revived again when the GOP nominated for president former Solicitor General, and future Supreme Court Chief Justice, William Taft in 1908 and 1912. "The Republican party will uphold at all times the authority and integrity of the courts, State and Federal, and will ever insist that their powers to enforce their process and to protect life, liberty and property shall be preserved inviolate" (RNC 1908). In contrast, the Democratic Party's 1908 platform sounded like the Jeffersonian Republicans from a century earlier. "Believing, with Jefferson, in 'the support of the State governments in all their rights as the most competent administrations for our domestic concerns, and the surest bulwarks against anti-republican tendencies' ... we are opposed to the centralization implied in the suggestion, now frequently made, that the powers of the General Government should be extended by judicial construction (DNC 1908).

Just as populist insurgents had officially split the Democratic Party in 1896, progressive insurgents officially split the Republican Party in 1912. In a challenge to both the Democratic Party and the Progressive Party, the Taft-supporting platform of 1912 defended the judiciary against reformers who called for less judicial intervention and more direct democracy: "The Republican party ... will ever insist that ... life, liberty and property shall be preserved inviolate ... Until these constitutional provisions are so altered or amended, in orderly fashion, it is the duty of the courts to see to it that when challenged they are enforced." Eight years later, in the aftermath of the Wilson administration, the 1920 platform complained of an "executive usurpation" of the "judicial function." In 1924 Republicans expressed their desire to pass Progressive legislation banning child labor, but their judicial ideology, and support of the Court's decisions, made them insist in the party platform that the Constitution must be amended before the law could be passed (RNC 1924).

5.2.2 Party Ideologies during the New Deal

The clashes between Republicans and Democrats over the role of the Supreme Court in American politics during the New Deal are well documented. Under the leadership of President Franklin D. Roosevelt, the Democratic Party eschewed its mostly limited government past and durably changed its ideology concerning government intervention in the economy. In a series of cases the Supreme Court struck down several New Deal laws. The "four horsemen" who voted to overturn the legislation included two Democrats (Pierce Butler, a Cleveland Democrat appointed by Warren Harding, and James McReynolds, a Southern Democrat appointed by Woodrow Wilson), and two Republicans (Harding-appointee George Sutherland and Taft-appointee Willis Van Devanter). The "three musketeers" who typically voted to let the legislation stand included two Republicans (Louis Brandeis, a Progressive Republican nominated by Wilson, and Coolidge-appointee Harlan Fiske Stone) and one Democrat (Benjamin Cardozo, who was nominated by Republican President Herbert Hoover). The swing voters on this Court were two Hoover appointees: Chief Justice Charles Evans Hughes and Owen Roberts.

In response to these Lochner Era judicial interventions, the Democratic Congress and president set a record for court-curbing legislation in 1935–1937 (Nagel 1965). In these three years, MCs introduced fifty-two court-curbing bills, but less than a quarter were introduced by Republicans. The GOP voiced its support for the Supreme Court's actions and resisted "all attempts to impair the authority of the Supreme Court of the United States, the final protector of the rights of our citizens against the arbitrary encroachments of the legislative and executive branches of government. There can be no individual liberty without an independent judiciary" (RNC 1936). During the 1936 campaign, the Republican presidential challenger attacked President Roosevelt's views of the judiciary: "He has publicly belittled the Supreme Court of the United States ... If changes in our civilization make amendment to the Constitution desirable it should be amended ... Will an amendment be submitted to the people or will he attempt to get around the Constitution by tampering with the Supreme Court?" (Landon 1936).

Most famously, on February 5, 1937, FDR unveiled his plan to put more judges sympathetic to his administration's legislation on the Supreme Court. It is during this time that we have the first surveys available to measure party attitudes toward the Court. Gallup surveys conducted between February and May 1937 showed that, by a slight margin, more Americans opposed the proposal than supported it. However, this opposition and support was strictly partisan. In one survey, Gallup found that 73 percent of Democrats supported FDR's court-packing plan while just 6 percent of Republicans supported it (Dolbeare 1967).

Thus, between 1874 and 1937 the two parties had switched positions with regard to their theories of judicial intervention. At the time of the

Civil War, Lincoln's Republican Party criticized the Democratic Supreme Court's "perversions of judicial power" while the Democratic Party insisted that Supreme Court decisions "should be respected by all good citizens, and enforced with promptness and fidelity by every branch of the general government." After the Republican Party took control of the Supreme Court, Democrats began complaining of "judicial oligarchy" while Republicans began defending the authority of the courts.

5.3 Other Factors that Explain Party Ideology Development

The evolution of Democratic and Republican Party theories of judicial intervention was not, of course, only about change in control of the Supreme Court. These developments were also the product of changes in party coalitions. The Democratic Party, whose base of membership had always been in the South and West, responded to the emerging Granger and Populist movements in the 1860s–1890s. The adoption of the Populist Party in 1896 represented a significant evolution in party ideology: The Democratic Party now advocated for national government regulation of the railroads and an inflationary monetary policy, and the party revived its anti-elitist rhetoric from the past. Just as the Jeffersonian Republicans' anti-elitist language fit with anti-judiciary sentiment at the turn of the nineteenth century, the Bryan Democrats' anti-elitist language fit with anti-judiciary sentiment at the turn of the twentieth century.

The Republican Party's coalition also changed during this period. An insurgent Progressive faction emerged within the party in the 1880s that eventually led to a split from the party in the presidential nomination battle of 1912. This Progressive movement not only wanted to expand national government administrative power to regulate the economy and redistribute economic outcomes, but it also wanted to promote direct, or "pure," democracy, which included a critique of judicial independence (Milkis 2009). Thus, between 1874 and 1912 the Republican Party was ambivalent about judicial power, but after the party split in 1912 the GOP remnant took a strong stand in favor of judicial independence, judicial review, and judicial supremacy that lasted through the New Deal.

6 LIBERAL CONSENSUS AND CONSERVATIVE RESPONSE, 1937–1991

Around the time of the court-packing controversy, the Supreme Court ceased striking down FDR's New Deal legislation (the famous, and arguably mythical, "switch in time that saved nine"). From that point forward, the American government undertook many social democratic reforms that have increased the power and scope of the national government among all three branches. Since 1937, the two parties have been consistently divided over the question of "big government": Democrats typically calling for more government intervention in society and the economy to overcome social and economic inequalities, and Republicans typically calling for less government intervention in the name of individual liberty.

By the time FDR died in office in 1945, he had appointed nine justices to the Supreme Court – with eight of them still serving alongside Hoover appointee Owen Roberts (the one whose switch saved nine). FDR's successor, Truman, appointed four more. Democrats kept control of the Supreme Court for the next half-century, and during that time the two parties' ideologies evolved as expected.

6.1 Historical Context of the Mid-Twentieth Century

In the postwar era, the Supreme Court became entangled in politics through the emergence of social issues like racial desegregation, criminal law reform, and abortion. The two parties debated the role of the judiciary more in the context of social legislation than economic legislation. As in previous periods, the Court once again expanded its power and reach into American social and political life. In the mid-nineteenth century, the Republican Party advocated the use of national government power to abolish slavery and end racial discrimination conducted by state governments, while the Democratic Party opposed the expansion of national government power to pursue these Reconstruction measures. By the mid-twentieth century, the Democrats now advocated for the use of national government power to end racial discrimination and segregation conducted by both governments and citizens, while the Republican Party opposed the expansion of national government power to pursue school busing and affirmative action. These developments in party ideology had implications for the parties' evolving theories of judicial intervention.

6.2 Party Control of the Supreme Court and Party Ideology Development

Even though Democrats took control of the Court in 1937, the path dependence of party ideologies meant that these ideologies would continue into the future until political entrepreneurs could use a political issue, over which the parties disagreed, to bring about party ideology change. Thus, the 1940 GOP platform continued to support the judiciary against the elected branches. "Instead of the Establishment of Justice the Administration has sought the subjection of the Judiciary to Executive discipline and domination ... Our greatest protection against totalitarian government is the American system of checks and balances" (RNC 1940). Similarly, after twenty straight years of opposition to the White House, the party called for "the protection of independent judicial review against administrative invasions" (RNC 1952). By the 1950s, civil rights legislation and judicial decisions no longer divided the parties, and, thus, the Court's decision in *Brown v. Board* (1954) did not change the Republicans' continuing commitment to judicial power and intervention.

The Republican Party points to an impressive record of accomplishment in the field of civil rights and commits itself anew to advancing the rights of all our people regardless of race, creed, color or national origin. In the area of exclusive Federal jurisdiction, more progress has been made in this field under the present Republican Administration than in any similar period in the last 80 years ... We support the enactment of the civil rights program already presented by the President to the Second Session of the 84th Congress ... The Republican Party has unequivocally recognized that the supreme law of the land is embodied in the Constitution, which guarantees to all people the blessings of liberty, due process and equal protection of the laws. It confers upon all native-born and naturalized citizens not only citizenship in the State where the individual resides but citizenship of the United States as well. This is an unqualified right, regardless of race, creed or color. The Republican Party accepts the decision of the U.S. Supreme Court that racial discrimination in publicly supported schools must be progressively eliminated. We concur in the conclusion of the Supreme Court that its decision directing school desegregation should be accomplished with "all deliberate speed" locally through Federal District Courts.

(RNC 1956)

The 1960 platform included a similar civil rights plank that again expressed support for the actions and authority of the federal judiciary in desegregation.[21]

---

[21] "The Department of Justice will continue its vigorous support of court orders for school desegregation ... It will use the new authority provided by the Civil Rights Act of 1960 to prevent obstruction of court orders. We will propose legislation to authorize the Attorney General to bring actions for school desegregation in the name of the United States in appropriate cases, as when economic coercion or threat of physical harm is used to deter persons from going to court to establish their rights. We oppose the pretense of fixing a

Even though the Democratic Party was quicker to switch to an ideology of judicial supremacy than the GOP was to switch to an ideology of judicial deference, some veterans of the New Deal Era continued to worry about a "counter-majoritarian problem" with the Supreme Court. Felix Frankfurter, a social democratic Progressive appointed to the Court by FDR, often dissented from his Democratic colleagues who used the activist tradition of the Court to pursue liberal causes in civil rights. Frankfurter's dissents from his liberal colleagues show the constraining power of previously developed judicial ideologies (Keck 2004). By the 1950s, however, Frankfurter was increasingly in the minority in the Democratic Party. The 1956 Democratic Party platform, the first to comment on the Supreme Court since the 1912 platform's denunciation of it, proclaimed:

The Democratic Party emphatically reaffirms its support of the historic principle that ours is a government of laws and not of men; it recognizes the Supreme Court of the United States as one of the three Constitutional and coordinate branches of the Federal Government, superior to and separate from any political party, the decisions of which are part of the law of the land. We condemn the efforts of the Republican Party to make it appear that this tribunal is a part of the Republican Party.

(DNC 1956)

The DNC felt the need to address the party's views about judicial power and intervention because of the Southern Manifesto signed by ninety-six Southern Democrats in Congress. The manifesto criticized judicial supremacy and called for judicial deference to the elected representatives in Congress: "We regard the decision of the Supreme Court in the school cases as a clear abuse of judicial power. It climaxes a trend in the Federal judiciary undertaking to legislate, in derogation of the authority of Congress, and to encroach upon the reserved rights of the States and the people" (George 1956). Even though the Democratic Party was split on this issue between its Northern and Southern membership, the Northerners became the dominant party faction during the New Deal. The 1960 platform again expressed its commitment to judicial authority. By the early 1960s, "the Democratic Party abandoned its traditional unease

---

target date 3 years from now for the mere submission of plans for school desegregation. Slow-moving school districts would construe it as a three-year moratorium during which progress would cease, postponing until 1963 the legal process to enforce compliance. We believe that each of the pending court actions should proceed as the Supreme Court has directed and that in no district should there be any such delay" (RNC 1960).

with the judiciary and instead concluded that a Great Society needed a great Court" (Powe 2009, 255).

Three decades after the change in party control of the Supreme Court, judicial issues finally began dividing the two parties and provided the incentive Republicans needed to change their party's theory of judicial intervention. In *Mapp v. Ohio* (1961), the Court ruled that evidence for a case obtained in violation of the Fourth Amendment may not be included in a criminal trial. In *Escobido v. Illinois* (1964), the Court ruled that confessions given in violation of the Sixth Amendment may not be included. In *Miranda v. Arizona* (1966), the Court ruled that evidence obtained by law enforcement without the suspect being given four warnings, including the right to remain silent, may not be used in a criminal trial. *Miranda* "nationalized opposition to the Warren Court in the Republican Party. All of a sudden the Republicans had a winning issue —law and order" (Powe 2009, 265). In his 1968 RNC nomination acceptance speech, Nixon explained: "Let us always respect, as I do, our courts and those who serve on them. But let us also recognize that some of our courts in their decisions have gone too far in weakening the peace forces as against the criminal forces in this country and we must act to restore the balance" (Nixon 1968). Nixon's prefatory remarks indicate that the Republican Party's pro-judicial ideology, built up over six decades of control of the Court, continued to constrain the rhetoric and attitudes of party members. However, in the 1960s, the Republican Party began layering a new anti-judicial ideology on top of their older pro-judicial sentiments.

The Court's entanglement in the presidential election of 1968 coincided "with widespread debate over the legitimacy of judicial review and the Court's role in the political system" (Stephenson 1999, 15). In addition to the Court's criminal law rulings, the Court's rulings in desegregation busing cases were also unpopular. When Nixon received the party nomination in August, a reporter asked him about school busing and federal judges, to which he "replied that he preferred those who attempted to interpret rather than make the law and that he did not think it proper for judges to act as local school boards" (New York Times 1968). Two days before the general election, Nixon made his judicial ideology clear, claiming that his appointments to the Supreme Court "would be strict constructionists who saw their duty as interpreting law and not making law. They would see themselves as caretakers of the Constitution and servants of the people, not super-legislators with a free hand to impose their social forces and political viewpoints on the American people"

(Kenworthy 1968). In response, Democratic presidential candidate Hubert Humphrey argued that Nixon's attacks on the Court were irresponsible and would lead to "civil explosions" (Semple 1968).

Almost every major party platform since 1968 has made reference to the Supreme Court and its role in the political system: Republicans typically warning about judicial activism and Democrats typically defending the Court's actions. The 1972 GOP platform supported the Student Transportation Moratorium Act, as a way to halt "court-ordered busing" and give Congress time to determine a solution to desegregated schools, and supported the Equal Employment Opportunity Commission as a way to have Congress ensure the protection of civil rights "rather than leaving this task to judges appointed for life." The 1972 Democratic Party platform voiced support for "Court decisions holding unconstitutional the disparities in school expenditures produced by dependence on local property taxes." The 1976 and 1980 GOP platforms took issue with what they perceived as the Court's overreach in *Roe v. Wade*. In contrast, the 1980 Democratic Party platform maintained support for "the 1973 Supreme Court decision on abortion rights as the law of the land and oppose[d] any constitutional amendment to restrict or overturn that decision."

The Republican Party campaigned in opposition to *Roe v. Wade* with success. "The enlarged Republican presence on Capitol Hill and a sympathetic president begot the most Court-curbing bills in over a decade: twenty-three in the House and four in the Senate, all by late spring 1981" (Stephenson 1999). In response, the 1984 Democratic Party platform opposed "efforts to strip the federal courts of their historic jurisdiction to adjudicate cases involving questions of federal law and constitutional right ... The hard truth is that if Mr. Reagan is reelected our most vigorous defender of the rule of law—the United States Supreme Court —could be lost to the cause of equal justice for another generation."

By 1984, the Republican Party had developed a new theory of jurisprudence to accompany their ideological opposition to judicial activism and judicial supremacy: "originalism." Since 1984, GOP platforms have typically included a long critique of judicial activism and a defense of strict construction like the one articulated here:

Our Constitution, now almost 200 years old, provides for a federal system, with a separation of powers among the three branches of the national government. In that system, judicial power must be exercised with deference toward State and local officials; it must not expand at the expense of our representative institutions. It is not a judicial function to reorder the economic, political, and social priorities of our nation. The intrusion of the courts into such areas undermines the stature of the judiciary and erodes respect for the rule of law. Where appropriate, we support congressional efforts to restrict the jurisdiction of federal courts ... We share the public's dissatisfaction with an elitist and unresponsive federal judiciary ... In his second term, President Reagan will continue to appoint Supreme Court and other federal judges who share our commitment to judicial restraint.

(RNC 1984)

The Republican Party of 1984, with its call for deference to democratically elected branches of government, sounded like the Republican Party of 1804. In 1986, Republican Attorney General Edwin Meese challenged the postwar liberal consensus on the role of the federal courts with a speech at Tulane University. Writing in the *Chicago Tribune*, Professor Richard Labunski argued that Meese "made some of the most reckless, dangerous and irresponsible statements ever uttered by an attorney general when he said the Supreme Court's interpretations of the Constitution were not 'the supreme law of the land' ... It is strange that Meese would choose now to attack the Supreme Court. President Reagan has appointed two very conservative jurists, and picked the even more conservative William Rehnquist to be the chief justice" (Labunski 1986). While puzzling to Labunski, this call for a noninterventionist Court, just as Republicans were about to control it, can be understood in light of our understanding of path dependency: It takes several years (not days) for party ideologies to change in accordance with party control of government institutions.

Between 1937 and 1991, the rhetoric of the two parties concerning judicial intervention evolved in the expected way. The Democrats, who had railed against judicial oligarchy at the turn of the twentieth century, stood for judicial authority and integrity in the second half of that century. The Republicans, who held up the Supreme Court as a bulwark against majority tyranny during the New Deal, now argued for judicial deference to majority will.

These developments in party theories of intervention had implications for changes in party theories of ends. The anti-judicial sentiment that emerged in the Republican Party beginning in the 1960s coincided with that party's embrace of a New Right that was more populist in orientation than the GOP's Old Right. The Republican Party's theory of ends during this time came to include calls for liberty, equality, and limited government that resembled Jefferson's Republican Party. The Democratic Party's embrace of judicial power and intervention, on the other hand, aided the party's change in ideological foundations from populism to universalism in the postwar era (Gerring 1998).

7 REHNQUIST AND ROBERTS COURTS, 1991–PRESENT

After winning five of six presidential elections between 1968 and 1988, the Republican Party took control of the Supreme Court in 1991, but our current period marks the first era in American history in which the two parties have not changed their theories of judicial intervention as predicted by the political institutional theory. The Republican Party has continued to develop its ideology in opposition to judicial activism and judicial supremacy. The 1992 GOP platform represented this high watermark for GOP anti-judicial sentiment:

The American people have lost faith in their courts, and for good reason. Some members of the federal judiciary threaten the safety, the values, and the freedom of law-abiding citizens. They make up laws and invent new rights as they go along, arrogating to themselves powers King George III never dared to exercise. They free vicious criminals, pamper felons in prison, frivolously overturn State laws enacted by citizen referenda, and abdicate the responsibility of providing meaningful review of administrative decisions. The delicate balance of power between the respective branches of our national government and the governments of the 50 states has been eroded. The notion of judicial review has in some cases come to resemble judicial supremacy, affecting all segments of public and private endeavor ... The federal judiciary, including the U.S. Supreme Court, has overstepped its authority under the Constitution. It has usurped the right of citizen legislators and popularly elected executives to make law by declaring duly enacted laws to be "unconstitutional" through the misapplication of the principle of judicial review. Any other role for the judiciary, especially when personal preferences masquerade as interpreting the law, is fundamentally at odds with our system of government in which the people and their representatives decide issues great and small.

(RNC 1992)

Of the 138 court-curbing bills introduced in Congress since 1991, 80 percent of them have been introduced by Republicans MCs.

In response, Democrats have reaffirmed their opposition to "efforts to strip the federal courts of jurisdiction to decide critical issues affecting workers, immigrants, veterans and others of access to justice" (DNC 2000). The path dependence of the ideologies that developed in the 1960s–1980s has not yet been overcome by party entrepreneurs acting in response to emerging judicial issues.

This may be due to the fact that the Republican Party has not actually taken decisive control of the Supreme Court, which means that the Court does not clearly and consistently favor the preferences of the Republican Party over the Democratic Party. In the past three decades, many

Republican-appointed justices have joined with the Democratic-appointed justices on a variety of issues, including hot-button cultural issues, to hand down decisions in line with Democratic Party preferences.

7.1 Party Control of the Supreme Court and Party Ideology Development

Similar to Republican presidents in the early nineteenth century, Republican presidents in the late twentieth century, over a twenty-four-year period, made every appointment to the Supreme Court, but in both cases the party failed to take control of the Court. Just as Republican appointees Livingstone, Todd, Duvall, and Story ended up siding with the Federalists on the Court, Republican appointees Warren, Brennan, Blackmun, and Stevens ended up siding with the Democrats on the Court. Not until George H. W. Bush appointed Clarence Thomas to join Rehnquist, O'Connor, Scalia, and Kennedy did the Republican Party have a majority of justices on the Supreme Court who favored their policies.

However, to claim that the Supreme Court has been controlled by a 5–4 Republican majority since 1991 requires two contestable assumptions: that both O'Connor and Kennedy should be counted as generally supporting the Republican Party's jurisprudential preferences – in the way that Rehnquist, Scalia, Thomas, Alito, Roberts, Gorsuch, and Kavanaugh are counted – rather than as swing voters. If either of them is coded as a swing voter, then the Court cannot be coded as Republican from 1991–2019. If either of them is coded as Democratic voters, then the Democrats have, in fact, kept control of the Court from 1937 to 2019.

Given the tenuous nature of this Republican "majority" on the bench, upon closer examination it is not actually that surprising that the two parties' theories of judicial intervention have not changed much since 1991. Perhaps we should not expect the bare Republican majority, and the uncertainty about which way swing justices will cast their votes, to provide enough of an incentive for the parties to completely overcome the path dependence of ideological inertia. Since 1991, the Court has not consistently favored one party's policies over the other, and so there are no long-term tensions that have caused party ideologies to durably switch.

Having said that, to the extent that the Court has, since 1991, favored the Republicans, then we do see the parties make some marginal movements away from the more static and strident division over the role of the Court seen in the 1970s and 1980s. After all, Democratic rhetoric becomes relatively more anti-Court, and Republican rhetoric becomes relatively more pro-Court after decisions like *Bush v. Gore* (2000) and *Citizens United v. Federal Election Commission* (2010). Recent scholarship has noted that conservative theories of jurisprudence became more contradictory and nuanced under the Rehnquist Court than they were under the Warren and Burger Courts (Keck 2004). It seems that the two parties have moderated their theories of judicial intervention since control of the Court has been up for grabs. However, the layers of past ideological changes cannot simply be peeled away from the parties, and it will take a much more decisive and long-term change in party control of the Supreme Court to effect a more decisive change in party attitudes toward the judiciary like we have witnessed in earlier periods of American political history.

8 CONCLUSION

Party control of the Supreme Court has changed five times in American history, and in four of those instances the parties' theories of judicial intervention clearly developed as predicted by the political institutional theory (see Table 5.2). In one case, our current era, the parties have not clearly changed as predicted. That the five instances of change in long-term party control of the Supreme Court resulted in four instances of expected change in party ideologies is worth noting.

These empirical results demonstrate the importance of all the necessary ingredients coming together for party ideology change. While changes in party control of the Supreme Court provide the structural tensions and incentives needed for party ideologies to evolve, they do not change unless entrepreneurial political actors use historically contingent political issues to entangle the Court in electoral politics, and thus focus party leaders and members on the issue of judicial intervention. In each historical era, the parties changed their ideologies when a political issue emerged that caused the two parties to divide and debate over the role of the Courts, when justices on the Supreme Court intervened in ways contrary to the preferences of one of the two major parties, when party entrepreneurs acted to change their party's ideology, when party factions rose and fell, when the new rhetorical structures and ideological frameworks were adopted by partisans, and when these new narratives and ideas became instantiated in partisan discourse. Jacksonian Democratic control of the Supreme Court only resulted in party ideology change through Republican opposition to

Ideas of Power

TABLE 5.2 *Party control of the Supreme Court and party theories of judicial intervention (results)*

Time period	Independent variable: Change in long-term party control of the Supreme Court	Dependent variable: Change in relative party ideologies as expected?
1 Federalist Era and Marshall Court 1790–1836	Federalist Supreme Court	Yes: Federalists moved more toward intervention than Republicans
2 Taney Court and Chase Court 1836–1874	Democratic Supreme Court	Yes: Democrats moved more toward intervention than Whigs and Republicans
3 Gilded Age and the Lochner Era 1874–1937	Republican Supreme Court	Yes: Republicans moved more toward intervention than Democrats
4 Postwar liberal consensus and conservative response 1937–1991	Democratic Supreme Court	Yes: Democrats moved more toward intervention than Republicans
5 Rehnquist Court and Roberts Court 1991–present	Republican Supreme Court	No: Republicans did not clearly move more toward intervention than Democrats

the *Dred Scott* decision. GOP control of the Supreme Court at the turn of the twentieth century only resulted in party ideology change through the successes of the populist and progressive movements passing social democratic reforms like the income tax and the New Deal. Postwar Democratic control of the Supreme Court only resulted in party ideology change through New Right Republican opposition to cases like *Miranda* and *Roe*. The foregoing empirical tests lend credence to the idea that a political factor – party control of political institutions – can help explain party ideology dynamics in addition to the sociological factors and historical contingencies focused on by previous scholarship.

6

Politics, History, and American Party Ideology Development

Any body of men who enjoy the powers and profits of public employments, will unavoidably wish to have those profits and powers increased ... The effect seems to be universal. It has ever been the case that government has had an universal tendency, to increase its own powers, revenues, and influence. No people ought to expect that things will have a different tendency among them.

–Samuel Williams (1794)

I THE POLITICS OF AMERICAN PARTY IDEOLOGY DEVELOPMENT

The three preceding chapters of this book have tested three hypotheses derived from my political institutional theory of American party ideology development. Overall, I identified twenty instances of long-term change in party control of government institutions, and in seventeen of those cases, party ideologies developed as predicted by the theory. These empirical findings lend credence to the theoretical idea that exercising government power influences how party ideologies evolve. It turns out that George Mason, James Madison, and Samuel Williams were right about human nature. Furthermore, their insight – that politicians almost universally exercise and expand the powers at their disposal – has important implications for American party ideology development. The society-centered factors focused on by previous scholars are, of course, important, but to neglect the influence of party control of government institutions would be to ignore one of the most important causes of change in party ideologies.

The political institutional theory presented in this book will remain relevant going forward because it provides testable hypotheses for the future. For example, I began writing the chapter on party control of the presidency and party theories of foreign intervention when Republicans were still defending the Iraq War and Democrats were calling for a "Come Home, America" foreign policy. President Obama's two terms as president provided another test case for the theory: Given that Democrats took long-term control of the presidency between 2009 and 2017, my theory predicted that Republican ideology would change in ways that called for less foreign intervention. Sure enough, during Obama's second term, the paleoconservative and isolationist strands of GOP ideology – dormant during most of the Bush administration – regained the dominant position they held in the 1990s. In 2016, Republicans nominated Pat Buchanan's favored presidential candidate, who campaigned on promises of isolationism and "America First."

2 AMERICAN POLITICAL DEVELOPMENT AND AMERICAN POLITICAL THOUGHT

In addition to providing testable hypotheses for theory-building, this book contributes to our understanding of American political development and American political thought. One theme that emerged in the foregoing historical narrative is that recurrent cycles of change in party ideologies have long-term consequences for the secular development of the American "public philosophy." Using Orren and Skowronek's concept of "intercurrence" we can understand the historical development of American political thought as, in part, the product of "political," or "recurrent," changes in party ideology interacting with "secular," or "linear," changes in party ideology (Orren and Skowronek 2004). In this book, the recurrent pattern in "political time" (cyclical change in party ideologies) contributes to the linear pattern in "secular time" (party ideologies that call for ever increasing presidential power and foreign intervention, national government power and economic intervention, and judicial power and judicial intervention). As a result, Americans today generally accept more foreign, economic, and judicial intervention than Americans in previous generations. While the party ideologies cycle back and forth between calling for more and less government power, the long-term impact is that American public opinion becomes more interventionist because the party in power is, more often than not, the party that wants more intervention.

For example, when a party controls the presidency, that party's ideology is placed in political time in such a way that party actors have incentives to change their party's ideology to be more interventionist on foreign policy. When a party opposes the presidency, that party's ideology is placed in political time in such a way that party actors have incentives to change their party's ideology to be less interventionist. Thus, over time and on average, the party that controls the presidency is more likely to favor a more interventionist foreign policy than the party out of power. Since the party in control of the presidency has more influence in determining American foreign policy and setting the new baseline of cultural expectations about the role of the United States in foreign affairs, the trend over time is for the consensus on American foreign policy to become more interventionist. This pattern in secular time moves in the same direction as, rather than in opposition to, other important historical developments – like increasing military and economic power – that have also pushed American public ideology to become more interventionist on foreign policy.

3 IDEAS OF POWER

As explained in the preface, this book is entitled *Ideas of Power* for three reasons. First, it demonstrates that party ideologies are powerful ideas. Although they are subject to change over time by political entrepreneurs, they also have tremendous constraining power on political leaders and the American citizenry. Party ideologies provide the mental frameworks and linguistic structures in which most Americans operate – for better or for worse – and those who wish to change party ideologies must do so in ways that maintain continuity with the past. To understand the American political system, we must understand the ideas that animate the individuals who participate in it.

Second, this book illustrates how ideas about power are some of the most compelling and interesting ideas over which the public debates. The US Constitution peculiarly divides sovereignty between US states and the national government, and between the different branches of the federal government. As a result, American political history has been characterized by arguments over what should be the relative power of these various governmental institutions. Furthermore, the American republic was founded by Federalists and Anti-Federalists who were deeply suspicious of governmental power. As a result, political discourse has always involved competing claims about how much government should intervene in society and in the world. By chronicling the two major parties' theories of governance and theories of intervention, this book has described the political ideas that Americans are uniquely designed by their political founding to care about.

Third, the political institutional theory articulated in this book demonstrates that exercising power in government leads to change in party ideologies. In this way, it brings the study of politics back into political science. As indicated in Chapter 1, in recent years the political science discipline has become preoccupied with the concept of ideology (Lee 2009, 29–30). Unfortunately, most scholars who have sought to explain ideology have focused almost exclusively on theories from psychology, sociology, and economics (Gerring 1998, 257–275). While these other theoretical approaches are useful, this book has sought to add to that literature by showing how a political factor can help explain ideology.

4 POLITICAL SCIENCE AND INTELLECTUAL HISTORY

The two main findings in this book (that ideologies change and that the experience of holding power changes them) have been overlooked in the political science literature because the value of intellectual history and (ironically) politics have generally been underappreciated in the discipline. The scholarly contributions of this book are the result of trying to bring both politics and intellectual history back into political science research. Thus, the two key insights are the result of what Karl Popper described as a "culture clash, a clash between ideas, or frameworks of ideas. Such a clash may help us break through the ordinary bounds of imagination" (Popper 1974, 47).

First, bringing in the insights of intellectual historians shows us that ideologies are created and transformed by political actors (Forcey 1961, H. Lewis 2012). This helps us recognize the Liberal Conservative Myth, and helps us realize that we cannot measure party ideology change using static spatial spectra. By combining this insight with the very important conceptual, theoretical, and methodological work done by political scientists of the "new institutional" variety (Ceaser 1979, Shepsle and Weingast 1981, Moe 1985, Aldrich 1995, R. Smith 1995, Skowronek 1997, Orren and Skowronek 2004, Pierson 2004, Katznelson and Weingast 2005, Skowronek and Glassman 2008), I have found a useful conceptual tool kit (institutional development) to talk about ideological development that was previously unused by both political scientists and intellectual historians.

Second, focusing on politics and institutions helps us see how party control of government institutions helps drive party ideology change. Although political scientists have long focused on "society-centered" sources of party ideology development, they have failed to focus on how exercising political power also influences party ideology evolution. Historians of eighteenth and nineteenth-century liberal political thought, on the other hand, are constantly studying arguments about how exercising power in government can change the way people think and act. This idea, a central preoccupation of the American Founders, seemed readily applicable to a modern concern of political scientists: party ideology. Thus, the contributions of this book emerged from a fruitful cross-fertilization of political science and intellectual history.

5 IDEOLOGY AND POLITICAL SCIENCE IN THE FUTURE

I began this book, in Chapter 1, by demonstrating the severe problems caused by the Liberal Conservative Myth. As we come to realize that the meanings of "left" and "right," and "liberal" and "conservative," are constantly changing, then we can stop making incoherent claims about politicians, groups, and parties moving "left" and "right" or becoming more or less "liberal" and "conservative" over time. This problem currently plagues the political science discipline and political commentary more generally. We would be much better off if scholars operating within the currently dominant "master theory" of American political science abandoned the Liberal Conservative Myth upon which so much of their scholarship rests.

As we give up on making incoherent claims about movement through static ideological space over time, we may even give up on the left-right, liberal-conservative, ideological spectrum altogether. This potential change in language and modes of thinking could make our society a more civil, less extreme, less combative, and less "polarized" place to live. Such a change could help preserve liberal democracy in America by tempering the identity politics, Left and Right, that currently threaten the stability of the American republic (Ceaser 1992, Fukuyama 2018, L. Mason 2018).

If people stop thinking in terms of ideological camps, then they will be less willing to demonize the "other." Our society already has enough "tribal" groupings – ethnic, partisan, class-based, racial, regional, etc. – that facilitate people thinking in an "us" vs. "them" mentality. The salience of these various mental modes of group solidarity and warfare rise and fall throughout world history. In American politics, ideology has emerged as another salient form of group thinking in the past half-century. During this time, American politics and society have witnessed increasing acrimony and incivility as ideology was added to the preexisting tribal divisions. If people stop thinking in terms of "our" ideological group vs. "their" ideological group, they are more likely to evaluate political issues, candidates, and positions on an issue-by-issue and person-by-person basis. When we do this, we are more likely to recognize commonalities we have with people who identify with the opposite party and differences we have with people within our own party. This could help us to think less about what divides us, and more about what unites us, as a political community.

Appendix 1: Percentage of Respondents Expressing a More Interventionist Attitude on Foreign Policy, 1948–2016

Year	President (independent variable)	Democrats	Independents	Republicans	Party difference (dependent variable)
1948	D	48		44	−5
1952	D	38		25	−13
1956	R	57	56	61	4
1958	R	57	58	61	4
1960	R	64	69	72	8
1968	D	74	71	76	2
1972	R	77	67	83	6
1976	R	62	68	73	11
1980	D	78	67	81	3
1984	R	67	71	80	13
1986	R	62	63	74	12
1988	R	61	62	75	14
1990	R	62	51	78	16
1992	R	67	62	81	14
1994	D	65	58	71	6
1996	D	72	64	74	2
1998	D	82	74	81	−1
2000	D	69	61	73	4
2002	R	72	61	86	14
2004	R	75	65	86	11
2008	R	65	55	75	10
2012	D	63	60	65	2
2016	D	73	53	69	−4
Average		65.66	62.67	71.46	5.85

Note: These data were compiled from the ANES dataset variables VAR 480040, VAR 520051, and VCF0823. The percentages and party difference for 1948 are rounded to the nearest whole number.

Appendix 2: Level of Economic Interventionism in Major Party Platforms, 1920–2016

Year	Democratic Party score	Republican Party score	Party difference
1920	8.68	6.57	2.11
1924	18.38	4.20	14.18
1928	14.55	16.06	−1.51
1932	9.68	12.05	−2.37
1936	14.97	10.88	4.09
1940	20.54	−3.61	24.15
1944	10.09	3.21	6.88
1948	20.40	3.71	16.69
1952	33.60	−10.00	43.60
1956	30.50	11.80	18.70
1960	24.40	17.10	7.30
1964	23.80	−5.50	29.30
1968	22.40	14.00	8.40
1972	18.50	14.90	3.60
1976	24.80	1.80	23.00
1980	36.20	2.60	33.60
1984	29.00	−3.80	32.80
1988	26.10	6.60	19.50
1992	24.74	4.99	19.75
1996	26.69	14.51	12.18
2000	34.56	10.72	23.84
2004	23.65	7.89	15.76
2008	20.12	11.72	8.40
2012	20.87	1.31	19.56
2016	48.02	6.11	41.91

Note: Party intervention scores were derived from the issue category coding of Democratic and Republican Party platforms retrieved from the Manifesto Project Dataset (Volkens et al. 2018). Scores were calculated by adding together the values from variables 403, 404, 405, 406, 409, 410, 411, 412, 413, 501, 502, 503, 504, and 506, and subtracting the values from variables 401, 402, 407, 414, 505, and 507 for each party's platform.

Appendix 3: Partisan Composition of the US Supreme Court, 1789–2019

	Justice	Nominating President	President's party	Date of oath	Prior party affiliation	Operational party affiliation on the court	Operational court composition
1	Wilson	Washington	Federalist	1789	Federalist	Federalist	Federalist 1–0
2	Jay	Washington	Federalist	1789	Federalist	Federalist	Federalist 2–0
3	Cushing	Washington	Federalist	1790	Federalist	Federalist	Federalist 3–0
4	Blair	Washington	Federalist	1790	Federalist	Federalist	Federalist 4–0
5	J. Rutledge	Washington	Federalist	1790	Federalist	Federalist	Federalist 5–0
6	Iredell	Washington	Federalist	1790	Federalist	Federalist	Federalist 6–0
7	T. Johnson	Washington	Federalist	1792	Federalist	Federalist	Federalist 6–0
8	Paterson	Washington	Federalist	1793	Federalist	Federalist	Federalist 6–0
9	J. Rutledge	Washington	Federalist	1795	Federalist	Federalist	Federalist 6–0
9	S. Chase	Washington	Federalist	1796	Federalist	Federalist	Federalist 5–0
10	Ellsworth	Washington	Federalist	1796	Federalist	Federalist	Federalist 6–0
11	Washington	J. Adams	Federalist	1799	Federalist	Federalist	Federalist 6–0
12	Moore	J. Adams	Federalist	1800	Federalist	Federalist	Federalist 6–0
13	J. Marshall	J. Adams	Federalist	1801	Federalist	Federalist	Federalist 6–0
14	W. Johnson	Jefferson	Dem-Rep	1804	Dem-Rep	Dem-Rep	Fed 5 – Dem 1
15	Livingston	Jefferson	Dem-Rep	1807	Dem-Rep	*Federalist*	Fed 5 – Dem 1
16	Todd	Jefferson	Dem-Rep	1807	Dem-Rep	*Federalist*	Fed 6 – Dem 1
17	Duvall	Madison	Dem-Rep	1811	Dem-Rep	*Federalist*	Fed 6 – Dem 1
18	Story	Madison	Dem-Rep	1812	Dem-Rep	*Federalist*	Fed 6 – Dem 1
19	Thompson	Monroe	Dem-Rep	1823	Dem-Rep	Dem-Rep	Fed 5 – Dem 2

(continued)

(continued)

	Justice	Nominating President	President's party	Date of oath	Prior party affiliation	Operational party affiliation on the court	Operational court composition
20	Trimble	J.Q. Adams	Nat'l Repub	1826	Dem-Rep	Federalist	Fed 5 – Dem 2
21	McLean	Jackson	Democrat	1830	Democrat	Federalist	Fed 5 – Dem 2
22	Baldwin	Jackson	Democrat	1830	Democrat	Democrat	Fed 4 – Dem 3
23	Wayne	Jackson	Democrat	1835	Democrat	Democrat	Fed 4 – Dem 3
24	Taney	Jackson	Democrat	1836	Democrat	Democrat	Dem 4 – Fed 3
25	Barbour	Jackson	Democrat	1836	Democrat	Democrat	Dem 5 – Fed 2
26	Catron	Jackson	Democrat	1837	Democrat	Democrat	Dem 6 – Fed 2
27	McKinley	Van Buren	Democrat	1838	Democrat	Democrat	Dem 7 – Fed 2
28	Daniel	Van Buren	Democrat	1842	Democrat	Democrat	Dem 7 – Fed 2
29	Nelson	Tyler	Democrat	1845	Democrat	Democrat	Dem 7 – Fed 2
30	Woodbury	Polk	Democrat	1845	Democrat	Democrat	Dem 8 – Fed 1
31	Grier	Polk	Democrat	1846	Democrat	Democrat	Dem 8 – Fed 1
32	Curtis	Fillmore	Whig	1851	Whig	Whig	Dem 7 – Fed 1 - Whig 1
33	Campbell	Pierce	Democrat	1853	Democrat	Democrat	Dem 7 – Fed 1 - Whig 1
34	Clifford	Buchanan	Democrat	1858	Democrat	Democrat	Dem 8 – Fed 1
35	Swayne	Lincoln	Republican	1862	Republican	Republican	Dem 6 – GOP 1
36	Miller	Lincoln	Republican	1862	Republican	Republican	Dem 6 – GOP 2
37	Davis	Lincoln	Republican	1862	Republican	Democrat	Dem 7 – GOP 2
38	Field	Lincoln	Republican	1863	Democrat	Democrat	Dem 8 – GOP 2
39	S. P. Chase	Lincoln	Republican	1864	Republican	Democrat	Dem 8 – GOP 2
40	Strong	Grant	Republican	1870	Republican	Republican	Dem 5 – GOP 3
41	Bradley	Grant	Republican	1870	Republican	Republican	Dem 5 – GOP 4
42	Hunt	Grant	Republican	1873	Republican	Democrat	Dem 5 – GOP 4
43	Waite	Grant	Republican	1874	Republican	Republican	GOP 5 – Dem 4
44	Harlan, I	Hayes	Republican	1877	Republican	Republican	GOP 6 – Dem 3

45	Woods	Hayes	Republican	1881	Republican	Republican	GOP 6 – Dem 3
46	Matthews	Garfield	Republican	1881	Republican	Republican	GOP 6 – Dem 3
47	Gray	Arthur	Republican	1882	Republican	Republican	GOP 7 – Dem 2
48	Blatchford	Arthur	Republican	1882	Republican	Republican	GOP 8 – Dem 1
49	L. Lamar	Cleveland	Democrat	1888	Democrat	Democrat	GOP 7 – Dem 2
50	**Fuller**	Cleveland	Democrat	1888	Democrat	Democrat	GOP 6 – Dem 3
51	Brewer	Harrison	Republican	1890	Republican	Republican	GOP 6 – Dem 3
52	Brown	Harrison	Republican	1891	Republican	Republican	GOP 6 – Dem 3
53	Shiras	Harrison	Republican	1892	Republican	Republican	GOP 6 – Dem 3
54	H. Jackson	Harrison	Republican	1893	*Democrat*	Republican	GOP 7 – Dem 2
55	E. White	Cleveland	Democrat	1894	Democrat	Democrat	GOP 6 – Dem 3
56	Peckham	Cleveland	Democrat	1896	Democrat	Democrat	GOP 5 – Dem 4
57	McKenna	McKinley	Republican	1898	Republican	Republican	GOP 6 – Dem 3
58	Holmes	T. Roosevelt	Republican	1902	Republican	Republican	GOP 6 – Dem 3
59	Day	T. Roosevelt	Republican	1903	Republican	Republican	GOP 6 – Dem 3
60	Moody	T. Roosevelt	Republican	1906	Republican	Republican	GOP 6 – Dem 3
61	Lurton	Taft	Republican	1910	*Democrat*	Republican	GOP 7 – Dem 2
62	Hughes	Taft	Republican	1910	Republican	Republican	GOP 7 – Dem 2
	E. White	Taft	Republican	1910	Democrat	Democrat	GOP 7 – Dem 2
63	Van Devanter	Taft	Republican	1911	Republican	Republican	GOP 8 – Dem 1
64	J. Lamar	Taft	Republican	1911	*Democrat*	Republican	GOP 8 – Dem 1
65	Pitney	Taft	Republican	1912	Republican	Republican	GOP 8 – Dem 1
66	McReynolds	Wilson	Democrat	1914	Democrat	Democrat	GOP 7 – Dem 2
67	Brandeis	Wilson	Democrat	1916	*Republican*	Democrat	GOP 7 – Dem 2
68	Clarke	Wilson	Democrat	1916	Democrat	Democrat	GOP 6 – Dem 3

(*continued*)

(*continued*)

	Justice	Nominating President	President's party	Date of oath	Prior party affiliation	Operational party affiliation on the court	Operational court composition
69	**Taft**	Harding	Republican	1921	Republican	Republican	GOP 6 – Dem 3
70	Sutherland	Harding	Republican	1922	Republican	Republican	GOP 7 – Dem 2
71	Butler	Harding	Republican	1923	*Democrat*	Republican	GOP 7 – Dem 2
72	Sanford	Harding	Republican	1923	Republican	Republican	GOP 7 – Dem 2
73	Stone	Coolidge	Republican	1925	Republican	*Democrat*	GOP 6 – Dem 3
	Hughes	Hoover	Republican	1930	Republican	Republican	GOP 6 – Dem 3
74	O. Roberts	Hoover	Republican	1930	Republican	Republican	GOP 6 – Dem 3
75	Cardozo	Hoover	Republican	1932	*Democrat*	*Democrat*	GOP 5 – Dem 4
76	Black	F.D. Roosevelt	Democrat	1937	Democrat	Democrat	Dem 5 – GOP 4
77	Reed	F.D. Roosevelt	Democrat	1938	Democrat	Democrat	Dem 6 – GOP 3
78	Frankfurter	F.D. Roosevelt	Democrat	1939	*Republican*	Democrat	Dem 6 – GOP 3
79	Douglas	F.D. Roosevelt	Democrat	1939	Democrat	Democrat	Dem 6 – GOP 3
80	Murphy	F.D. Roosevelt	Democrat	1940	Democrat	Democrat	Dem 6 – GOP 3
	Stone	F.D. Roosevelt	Democrat	1941	*Republican*	Democrat	Dem 6 – GOP 2
81	Byrnes	F.D. Roosevelt	Democrat	1941	Democrat	Democrat	Dem 7 – GOP 2
82	R. Jackson	F.D. Roosevelt	Democrat	1941	Democrat	Democrat	Dem 7 – GOP 2
83	W. Rutledge	F.D. Roosevelt	Democrat	1943	Democrat	Democrat	Dem 7 – GOP 2
84	Burton	Truman	Democrat	1945	*Republican*	Democrat	Dem 8 – GOP 1
85	**Vinson**	Truman	Democrat	1946	Democrat	Democrat	Dem 9 – GOP 0
86	Clark	Truman	Democrat	1949	Democrat	Democrat	Dem 9 – GOP 0
87	Minton	Truman	Democrat	1949	Democrat	Democrat	Dem 9 – GOP 0
88	**Warren**	Eisenhower	Republican	1953	Republican	*Democrat*	Dem 9 – GOP 0
89	Harlan, II	Eisenhower	Republican	1955	Republican	Republican	Dem 8 – GOP 1
90	Brennan	Eisenhower	Republican	1956	*Democrat*	*Democrat*	Dem 8 – GOP 1
91	Whittaker	Eisenhower	Republican	1957	Republican	Republican	Dem 7 – GOP 2
92	Stewart	Eisenhower	Republican	1958	Republican	Republican	Dem 6 – GOP 3

#	Justice	President		Year			Composition
93	B. White	Kennedy	Democrat	1962	Democrat	Democrat	Dem 7 – GOP 2
94	Goldberg	Kennedy	Democrat	1962	Democrat	Democrat	Dem 7 – GOP 2
95	Fortas	L.B. Johnson	Democrat	1965	Democrat	Democrat	Dem 7 – GOP 2
96	T. Marshall	L.B. Johnson	Democrat	1967	Democrat	Democrat	Dem 7 – GOP 2
97	**Burger**	Nixon	Republican	1969	Republican	Republican	Dem 6 – GOP 3
98	Blackmun	Nixon	Republican	1970	Republican	*Democrat*	Dem 6 – GOP 3
99	Powell	Nixon	Republican	1972	*Democrat*	Republican	Dem 5 – GOP 4
100	**Rehnquist**	Nixon	Republican	1972	Republican	Republican	Dem 5 – GOP 4
101	Stevens	Ford	Republican	1975	Republican	*Democrat*	Dem 5 – GOP 4
102	O'Connor	Reagan	Republican	1981	Republican	Republican	Dem 5 – GOP 4
	Rehnquist	Reagan	Republican	1986	Republican	Republican	Dem 5 – GOP 3
103	Scalia	Reagan	Republican	1986	Republican	Republican	Dem 5 – GOP 4
104	Kennedy	Reagan	Republican	1988	Republican	Republican	Dem 5 – GOP 4
105	Souter	G.H.W. Bush	Republican	1990	Republican	*Democrat*	Dem 5 – GOP 4
106	Thomas	G.H.W. Bush	Republican	1991	Republican	Republican	GOP 5 – Dem 4
107	Ginsburg	Clinton	Democrat	1993	Democrat	Democrat	GOP 5 – Dem 4
108	Breyer	Clinton	Democrat	1994	Democrat	Democrat	GOP 5 – Dem 4
109	**J. Roberts**	G.W. Bush	Republican	2005	Republican	Republican	GOP 5 – Dem 4
110	Alito	G.W. Bush	Republican	2006	Republican	Republican	GOP 5 – Dem 4
111	Sotomayor	Obama	Democrat	2009	Democrat	Democrat	GOP 5 – Dem 4
112	Kagan	Obama	Democrat	2010	Democrat	Democrat	GOP 5 – Dem 4
113	Gorsuch	Trump	Republican	2017	Republican	Republican	GOP 5 – Dem 4
114	Kavanaugh	Trump	Republican	2018	Republican	Republican	GOP 5 – Dem 4

[a] The names of chief justices are printed in boldface type.

[b] Chief justices who previously served as associate justices on the Court are italicized.

[c] The prior party affiliations of justices that differ from that of the nominating president are italicized.

[d] The operational party affiliations of justices that differ from that of the nominating president are italicized.

[e] Supreme Court appointments that lead to long-term changes in partisan composition of the Court are highlighted in gray.

Bibliography

Abraham, Henry. 2008. *Justices, Presidents, and Senators: A History of the U.S. Supreme Court Appointments from Washington to Bush II.* 5th edn. Lanham, MD: Rowman & Littlefield Publishers, Inc.

Abramowitz, Alan. 2010. *The Disappearing Center: Engaged Citizens, Polarization, and American Democracy.* New Haven, CT: Yale University Press.

Adams, Greg. 1997. "Abortion: Evidence of an Issue Evolution." *American Journal of Political Science* 41 (3): 718–737.

Adams, Henry. 1891. *History of the United States of America during the First Administration of Thomas Jefferson.* Vol. 2. 9 vols. New York: Scribner.

Aldrich, John. 1980. *Before the Convention.* Chicago: University of Chicago Press.

1995. *Why Parties? The Origin and Transformation of Political Parties in America.* Chicago: University of Chicago Press.

2011. *Why Parties?: A Second Look.* Chicago: University of Chicago Press.

Aldrich, John, and Ruth Grant. 1993. "The Antifederalists, the First Congress, and the First Parties." *Journal of Politics* 55 (2): 295–326.

Aldrich, John, Jacob Montgomery, and David Sparks. 2014. "Polarization and Ideology: Partisan Sources of Low Dimensionality in Scaled Roll Call Analyses." *Political Analysis* 22 (4): 1–22.

Aldrich, John, John L. Sullivan, and Eugene Borgida. 1989. "Foreign Affairs and Issue Voting: Do Presidential Candidates 'Waltz Before a Blind Audience?'" *American Political Science Review* 83 (1): 123–141.

American Political Science Association. 1950. "Toward a More Responsible Two-Party System: A Report of the Committee on Political Parties." *American Political Science Review* 44 (3): Part 2, Supplement.

Anzia, Sarah F., and Terry M. Moe. 2016. "Do Politicians Use Policy to Make Politics? The Case of Public-Sector Labor Laws." *American Political Science Review* 110 (4): 763–777.

Balkin, Jack M., and Sanford Levinson. 2001. "Understanding the Constitutional Revolution." *Virginia Law Review* 87 (6): 1045–1104.

Banning, Lance. 1978. *The Jeffersonian Persuasion: Evolution of a Party Ideology*. Ithaca, NY: Cornell University Press.

Barber, Michael, and Nolan McCarty. 2013. "Causes and Consequences of Polarization." In *Negotiating Agreement in Politics*, edited by Jane Mansbridge and Cathie Jo Martin, 19–53. Washington, DC: American Political Science Association.

Beard, Charles A. 1928. *The American Party Battle*. New York: Workers Education Bureau Press, Inc.

Beer, Samuel H. 1978. "In Search of a New Public Philosophy." In *The New American Political System*, edited by Anthony King, 5–44. Washington, DC: American Enterprise Institute for Public Policy Research.

Bensel, Richard. 2005. "A Cross of Gold, a Crown of Thorns: Preferences and Decisions in the 1896 Democratic National Convention." In *Preferences and Situations: Points of Intersection between Historical and Rational Choice Institutionalism*, edited by Ira Katznelson and Barry R. Weingast, 27–61. New York: Russell Sage Foundation.

   2016. "Political Economy and American Political Development." In *The Oxford Handbook of American Political Development*, edited by Richard M. Vallelly, Suzanne Mettler, and Robert C. Lieberman, 69–95. New York: Oxford University Press.

Benson, Allan. 1911. *The Usurped Power of the Courts*. Chicago: Socialist Party National Office.

Berkman, Michael. 1993. *The State Roots of National Politics: Congress and the Tax Agenda, 1978–1986*. Pittsburgh, PA: Pittsburgh University Press.

Binkley, Wilfred. 1943. *American Political Parties: Their Natural History*. New York: Alfred A. Knopf.

Boorstin, Daniel. 1953. *The Genius of American Politics*. Chicago: University of Chicago Press.

Borosage, Robert L. 1994. "The Nation: Despite GOP Attacks, Clinton Foreign Policy Echos Bush's." *The Los Angeles Times*, June 26. Accessed February 15, 2014. http://articles.latimes.com/1994-06-26/opinion/op-8579_1_foreign-policy.

Breckenridge, John. 1802. "Proceedings February 2, 1801." *Annals of Congress*. Washington, DC: Library of Congress, February 2. 178–180.

Brewer, Mark, and Jeffrey Stonecash. 2009. *Dynamics of American Political Parties*. New York: Cambridge University Press.

Brutus. 1787/2014. "The Antifederalist, No. 1." In *Readings in American Politics: Analysis and Perspectives*, 3rd edn, edited by Ken Kollman. New York: W. W. Norton & Company, Inc.

   1788/1981. "Essays of Brutus XV." In *The Complete Anti-Federalist*. Vol. 2, edited by Herbert J. Storing, 360–452. Chicago: University of Chicago Press.

Bryce, James. 1888. *The American Commonwealth*. Vol. 2. 3 vols. London: Macmillan and Co.

Burke, Edmund. 1770/1981. "Thoughts on the Cause of the Present Discontents." In *The Writings and Speeches of Edmund Burke*. Vol 2, edited by Paul Langford. New York: Oxford University Press.

Burnham, Walter Dean. 1970. *Critical Elections and the Mainsprings of American Politics*. New York: W. W. Norton & Company, Inc.

Burnham, Walter Dean, and William Nisbet Chambers (eds.). 1967. *The American Party Systems: Stages of Political Development*. New York: Oxford University Press.

Burns, Jennifer. 2017. "Objectively Speaking, Rand Is History." *Hoover Digest* 3: 170–174.

Burns, John W. 1997. "Party Policy Change: The Case of the Democrats and Taxes, 1956–68." *Party Politics* 3 (4): 513–532.

Busby, Joshua W., Jonathan Monten, and William Inboden. 2012. "American Foreign Policy Is Already Post-Partisan." *Foreign Affairs*. May 30. Accessed February 14, 2019. www.foreignaffairs.com/articles/united-states/2012-05-30/american-foreign-policy-already-post-partisan.

Bush, George Walker. 2000. "Presidential Candidates Debates: 'Presidential Debate in Winston-Salem, North Carolina.'" *The American Presidency Project*. October 11. Accessed February 21, 2014. www.presidency.ucsb.edu/ws/?pid=29419.

Campbell, Angus, Philip Converse, Warren Miller, and Donald Stokes. 1960. *The American Voter*. Chicago: University of Chicago Press.

Campbell, Angus, Gerald Gurin, and Warren Miller. 1999. *American National Election Studies, 1952: Time Series Study*. Ann Arbor: University of Michigan, Center for Political Studies.

Carmines, Edward, and James Stimson. 1989. *Issue Evolution: Race and the Transformation of American Politics*. Princeton, NJ: Princeton University Press.

Caro, Robert. 2003. *Master of the Senate: The Years of Lyndon Johnson*. New York: First Vintage Books.

Carroll, Royce, Jeff Lewis, James Lo, Nolan McCarty, Keith Poole, and Howard Rosenthal. 2015. "DW-NOMINATE Scores with Bootstrapped Standard Errors." May 25. Accessed August 26, 2016. voteview.com/dwnomin.htm.

Carsey, Thomas, and Geoffrey Layman. 2006. "Changing Sides or Changing Minds? Party Identification and Policy Preferences in the American Electorate." *American Journal of Political Science* 50 (2): 464–477.

Ceaser, James. 1979. *Presidential Selection: Theory and Development*. Princeton, NJ: Princeton University Press.

　1984. "The Theory of Governance of the Reagan Administration." In *The Reagan Presidency and the Governing of America*, edited by Lester M. Salamon and Michael S. Lund, 57–87. Washington, DC: The Urban Institute.

　1992. *Liberal Democracy and Political Science*. Baltimore: Johns Hopkins University Press.

　2000. *What Is the Public Philosophy?* Oxford: Oxford University Press.

　2006. *Nature and History in American Political Development*. Cambridge, MA: Harvard University Press.

Chicago Tribune. 1952. "The New Eisenhower." *The Chicago Tribune*. September 27: 10.

Clark, Tom S. 2011. *The Limits of Judicial Independence*. New York: Cambridge University Press.

2013. "Data." Accessed July 1, 2015. www.tomclarkphd/data.html.

Cogan, John F. 2017. *The High Cost of Good Intentions: A History of U.S. Federal Entitlement Programs*. Stanford, CA: Stanford University Press.

Congressional Quarterly. 1950. "Description of Key Votes, 1944–1919." In *CQ Almanac 1949*. Washington, DC: Congressional Quarterly.

Converse, Philip. 1964. "The Nature of Belief Systems in Mass Publics." In *Ideology and Discontent*, edited by David Apter. New York: The Free Press.

Crawford, Sue E. S., and Elinor Ostrom. 1995. "A Grammar of Institutions." *The American Political Science Review* 89 (3): 582–600.

Croly, Herbert. 1909. *The Promise of American Life*. Norwood, MA: Norwood Press.

Dahl, Robert. 1957. "Decision-Making in a Democracy: The Supreme Court as a National Policy Maker." *Journal of Public Law* 6 (1): 279–295.

Democratic National Convention (DNC). 1840–2016. "National Political Party Platforms." *The American Presidency Project*. Accessed January 24, 2019. https://www.presidency.ucsb.edu/documents/presidential-documents-archive-guidebook/national-political-party-platforms.

Depew, Chauncey. 1896. "Depew on 'Popocracy.'" *The Literary Digest* 13 (25): 776–777.

Diermeier, Daniel, and Keith Krehbiel. 2003. "Institutionalism as Methodology." *Journal of Theoretical Politics* 15 (2): 123–144.

DiSalvo, Daniel. 2012. *Engines of Change: Party Factions in American Politics, 1868–2010*. New York: Oxford University Press.

Dolbeare, Kenneth M. 1967. "The Public Views the Supreme Court." In *Law, Politics, and the Federal Courts*, edited by Herbert Jacob. Boston: Little Brown.

Donovan, Hedley. 1964. "The Difficulty of 'Being Fair' to Goldwater." *Life*, September 18: 93–112.

Downs, Anthony. 1957. *An Economic Theory of Democracy*. New York: Harper.

Dueck, Colin. 2010. *Hard Line: The Republican Party and U.S. Foreign Policy since World War II*. Princeton, NJ: Princeton University Press.

Edling, Max. 2014. *A Hercules in the Cradle: War, Money, and the American State, 1783–1867*. Chicago: University of Chicago Press.

Eisenhower, Dwight. 1952. "I Shall Go to Korea Speech, October 25, 1952." Dwight D. Eisenhower Presidential Library. October 25. Accessed May 2, 2017. www.eisenhower.archives.gov/education/bsa/citizenship_merit_badge/speeches_national_historical_importance/i_shall_go_to_korea.pdf.

Elkins, Stanley M., and Eric L. McKitrick. 1993. *The Age of Federalism*. New York: Oxford University Press.

Ellis, Christopher, and James Stimson. 2012. *Ideology in America*. New York: Cambridge University Press.

Ellis, Richard. 1971. *The Jeffersonian Crisis: Courts and Politics in the Young Republic*. New York: Oxford University Press.

2007. *Aggressive Nationalism: McCulloch v. Maryland and the Foundation of Federal Authority in the Young Republic*. New York: Oxford University Press.

Engel, Stephen. 2011. *American Politicians Confront the Court: Opposition Politics and Changing Responses to Judicial Power*. New York: Cambridge University Press.

Erikson, Robert S., Michael B. MacKuen, and James A. Stimson. 2002. *The Macro Polity*. New York: Cambridge University Press.

Farrand, Max. 1911. *The Records of the Federal Convention of 1787*. Edited by Max Farrand. Vol. 1. 3 vols. New Haven, CT: Yale University Press.

Fiorina, Morris. 2013. "Party Homogeneity and Contentious Politics." In *Can We Talk? The Rise of Rude, Nasty, Stubborn Politics*, edited by Daniel M. Shea and Morris P. Fiorina, 142–153. New York: Pearson.

Forcey, Charles B. 1961. *The Crossroads of Liberalism: Croly, Weyl, Lippmann, and the Progressive Era, 1900–1925*. New York: Oxford University Press.

Fordham, Benjamin O. 2007. "The Evolution of Republican and Democratic Positions on Cold War Military Spending: A Historical Puzzle." *Social Science History* 31 (4): 603–636.

Fukuyama, Francis. 2018. *Identity: The Demand for Dignity and the Politics of Resentment*. New York: Farrar, Straus and Giroux.

George, Walter F. 1956. "The Southern Manifesto." *Federal Judicial Center*. March 12. Accessed June 1, 2015. www.fjc.gov/history/home.nsf/page/tu_bush_doc_6.html.

Gerring, John. 1998. *Party Ideologies in America, 1828–1996*. New York: Cambridge University Press.

Gillman, Howard. 1993. *The Constitution Besieged*. Durham, NC: Duke University Press.

   2006. "Party Politics and Constitutional Change: The Political Origins of Liberal Judicial Activism." In *The Supreme Court and American Political Development*, edited by Ronald Kahn and Ken I. Kersch. Lawrence: University Press of Kansas.

Goldstein, Judith, and Robert Keohane. 1993. *Ideas and Foreign Policy: Beliefs, Institutions, and Political Change*. Ithaca, NY: Cornell University Press.

Graber, Mark. 2000. "The Jacksonian Origins of Chase Court Activism." *Journal of Supreme Court History* 25 (1): 17–39.

Grassmuck, George. 1951. *Sectional Biases in Congress on Foreign Policy*. Baltimore: Johns Hopkins University Press.

Gries, Peter. 2014. *The Politics of American Foreign Policy: How Ideology Divides Liberals and Conservatives*. Palo Alto, CA: Stanford University Press.

Hacker, Jacob S., and Paul Pierson. 2005. *Off Center: The Republican Revolution and the Erosion of American Democracy*. New Haven, CT: Yale University Press.

   2014. "After the 'Master Theory': Downs, Schattschneider, and the Rebirth of Policy-Focused Analysis." *Perspectives on Politics* 12 (3): 643–662.

Hall, Peter A., and Rosemary C. R. Taylor. 1996. "Political Science and the Three New Institutionalisms." *Political Studies* XLIV: 936–957.

Hall, Stuart. 1986. "The Problem of Ideology: Marxism Without Guarantees." *Journal of Communication Inquiry* 10 (2): 28–44.

Hall, Timothy L. 2001. *Supreme Court Justices: A Biographical Dictionary*. New York: Facts on File, Inc.

Hare, Christopher, and Keith T. Poole. 2014. "The Polarization of Contemporary American Politics." *Polity* 46: 411–429.

Harrison, Benjamin. 1896. "Ex-President Harrison's Speech at New York." In *Public Opinion: A Comprehensive Summary of the Press throughout the World on All Important Current Topics*, Vol. 21. 297–298. New York: The Public Opinion Company.

Hartz, Louis. 1955. *The Liberal Tradition in America*. New York: Harcourt Brace Jovanovich.

Hattam, Victoria, and Joseph Lowndes. 2007. "The Ground Beneath our Feet: Language, Culture, and Political Change." In *Formative Acts: American Politics in the Making*, edited by Stephen Skowronek and Matthew Glassman, 199–222. Philadelphia: University of Pennsylvania Press.

Hayek, F. A. 1949. "The Intellectuals and Socialism." *The University of Chicago Law Review* 16 (3): 417–433.

Herring, Pendleton. 1940. *The Politics of Democracy: American Parties in Action*. New York: W. W. Norton & Co.

Hetherington, Marc. 2001. "Resurgent Mass Partisanship: The Role of Elite Polarization." *American Political Science Review* 95 (3): 619–631.

Hinich, Melvin, and Michael Munger. 1994. *Ideology and the Theory of Political Choice*. Ann Arbor: University of Michigan Press.

Hofstadter, Richard. 1948. *The American Political Tradition and the Men Who Made It*. New York: A. A. Knopf.

1969. *The Idea of a Party System*. Berkeley: University of California Press.

Holcombe, Arthur N. 1924. *The Political Parties of To-Day*. New York: Harper & Bros.

Holsti, Ole. 2006. *Making American Foreign Policy*. New York: Routledge.

Holt, Michael F. 1999. *The Rise and Fall of the American Whig Party: Jacksonian Politics and the Onset of the Civil War*. New York: Oxford University Press.

Howell, William. 2013. *Thinking about the Presidency: The Primacy of Power*. Princeton, NJ: Princeton University Press.

Howell, William, and Jon C. Pevehouse. 2007. *While Dangers Gather: Congressional Checks on Presidential War Powers*. Princeton, NJ: Princeton University Press.

Hurwitz, Jon, and Mark Peffley. 1987. "How Are Foreign Policy Attitudes Structured? A Hierarchical Model." *American Political Science Review* 81 (4): 1099–1120.

Jackson, Andrew. 1832. "Bank Veto (July 10, 1832)." *Miller Center*. Accessed December 21, 2018. www.millercenter.org/thepresidency/presidential-speeches/july-10-1832-bank-veto

James, Scott C. 2000. *Presidents, Parties, and the State: A Party System Perspective on Democratic Regulatory Choice, 1884–1936*. Cambridge: Cambridge University Press.

Jefferson, Thomas. 1795/1904. "Notes on Prof. Ebeling's Letter of July 30, 95." In *The Works of Thomas Jefferson*. Vol. 8, edited by Paul Leicester Ford, 205–211. New York: G. P. Putnam's Sons.

1801a/2019. "Inaugural Address." *The American Presidency Project.* Gerhard Peters and John T. Woolley. March 4. Accessed February 12, 2019. www .presidency.ucsb.edu/ws/index.php?pid=25803.

1801b/1905. "To John Dickinson." In *The Works of Thomas Jefferson.* Vol. 9, edited by Paul Leicester Ford, 280–282. New York and London: G. P. Putnam's Sons.

1801c/1905. "First Annual Message." In *The Works of Thomas Jefferson.* Vol. 9, 321–346. New York and London: G. P. Putnam's Sons.

1807/1999. "To Thomas Cooper." In *Jefferson: Political Writings,* edited by Joyce Appleby and Terrence Ball, 424–425. Cambridge: Cambridge University Press.

1813/2019. "Thomas Jefferson to John Melish, January 13, 1813." *The Library of Congress.* Accessed January 1, 2019. https://www.loc.gov/item/mtjbib021292/.

1820/1905. "To William Charles Jarvis." In *The Works of Thomas Jefferson.* Vol. 12, edited by Paul Leicester Ford, 161–163. New York and London: G. P. Putnam's Sons.

1821/1905. "To James Pleasants." In *The Works of Thomas Jefferson.* Vol. 12, edited by Paul Leicester Ford, 213–217. New York and London: G. P. Putnam's Sons.

1822a/1905. "Letter to Henry Dearborn." In *The Works of Thomas Jefferson.* Vol. 12, edited by Paul Leicester Ford, 396. New York and London: G. P. Putnam's Sons.

1822b/1905. "To William Johnson." In *The Works of Thomas Jefferson.* Vol 12, edited by Paul Leicester Ford, 213–217. New York and London: G. P. Putnam's Sons.

1823/2019. "Thomas Jefferson to Marie Joseph Paul Yves Roch Gilbert du Motier, Marquis de Lafayette, November 4, 1823." *The Library of Congress.* https://www.loc.gov/resource/mtj1.054_0067_0069/?st=gallery. Accessed January 1, 2019.

John, Richard R. 2003. "Affairs of Office: The Executive Departments, the Election of 1828, and the Making of the Democratic Party." In *The Democratic Experiment: New Directions in American Political History,* edited by Meg Jacobs, William J. Novak, and Julian E. Zelizer, 50–84. Princeton, NJ: Princeton University Press.

Kahn, Ronald, and Ken Kersch. 2006. "Introduction." In *The Supreme Court and American Political Development,* edited by Ronald Kahn and Ken Kersch, 1–30. Lawrence: University Press of Kansas.

Karol, David. 2009. *Party Position Change in American Politics: Coalition Management.* New York: Cambridge University Press.

Katznelson, Ira, and Barry Weingast. 2005. "Intersections between Historical and Rational Choice Institutionalism." In *Preferences and Situations: Intersections between Historical and Rational Choice Institutionalism,* edited by Ira Katznelson and Barry Weingast, 1–26. New York: Russell Sage Foundation.

Keck, Thomas. 2004. *The Most Activist Supreme Court in History: The Road to Modern Judicial Conservatism.* Chicago: University of Chicago Press.

2007. "Party, Policy, or Duty: Why Does the Supreme Court Invalidate Federal Statutes?" *American Political Science Review* 101 (2): 321–338.

Kelley, Robert. 1977. "Ideology and Political Culture from Jefferson to Nixon." *American Historical Review* 82 (3): 531–562.

Kendall, Willmoore, and Austin Ranney. 1956. *Democracy and the American Party System.* New York: Harcourt, Brace and Company.

Kennedy, David M. 1999. *Freedom from Fear: The American People in Depression and War, 1929–1945.* New York: Oxford University Press.

Kenworthy, Edwin W. 1968. "Nixon Scores 'Indulgence'." *New York Times*, November 3: 79.

Key, Vladimir O., Jr. 1955. "A Theory of Critical Elections." *Journal of Politics* 17 (1): 3–18.

1964. *Politics, Parties, and Pressure Groups.* New York: Crowell.

Keynes, J. M. 1936. *A General Theory of Employment, Interest, and Money.* London: Macmillan.

Kleppner, Paul. 1979. *The Third Electoral System, 1853–92: Parties, Voters, and Political Cultures.* Chapel Hill: University of North Carolina Press.

Knight, Kathleen. 2006. "Transformations of the Concept of Ideology in the Twentieth Century." *American Political Science Review* 100 (4): 619–626.

Kolodny, Robin. 1996. "The Several Elections of 1824." *Congress & The Presidency* 23: 139–164.

Kramer, Larry. 2007. "'The Interest of the Man': James Madison, Popular Constitutionalism, and the Theory of Deliberative Democracy." *Valparaiso University Law Review* 41 (2): 697–754.

Krehbiel, Keith. 1991. *Information and Legislative Organization.* Ann Arbor: University of Michigan Press.

Kriner, Douglas. 2014. "Obama's Authorization Paradox: Syria and Congress's Continued Relevance in Military Affairs." *Presidential Studies Quarterly* 44 (2): 309–327.

Kutler, Stanley. 1968. *Judicial Power and Reconstruction Politics.* Chicago: University of Chicago Press.

Labunski, Richard. 1986. "The 'Dangerous' Views of Ed Meese." *Chicago Tribune*, November 6: C27.

Ladd, Everett C., Jr. 1970. *American Political Parties: Social Change and Political Response.* New York: Norton.

Landon, Alf. 1936. "The Texts of Governor Landon's Addresses at Madison Square Garden and Over the Radio." *New York Times.* October 30: 16.

Layman, Geoffrey, and Thomas Carsey. 2002. "Party Polarization and 'Conflict Extension' in the American Electorate." *American Journal of Political Science* 46 (4): 786–802.

Lee, Frances. 2009. *Beyond Ideology: Politics, Principles, and Partisanship in the U.S. Senate.* Chicago: University Of Chicago Press.

2016. "Patronage, Logrolls and 'Polarization': Congressional Parties of the Gilded Age, 1876–1896." *Studies in American Political Development* 30 (2): 116–127.

Leighton, Wayne A., and Edward J. Lopez. 2013. *Madmen, Intellectuals, and Academic Scribblers*. Stanford, CA: Stanford University Press.

Levendusky, Matthew. 2009. *The Partisan Sort: How Liberals Became Democrats and Conservatives Became Republicans*. Chicago: University of Chicago Press.

Lewis, Hyrum. 2012. "Historians and the Myth of American Conservatism." *Journal of the Historical Society* 12 (1): 27–45.

　　2017. "It's Time to Retire the Political Spectrum." *Quillette*. May 3. Accessed July 12, 2017. http://quillette.com/2017/05/03/time-retire-political-spectrum/.

Lewis, Verlan. 2017. "Why Presidential Candidates (Like Trump) Campaign as Isolationists but (Like Trump) Govern as Hawks." *The Washington Post*. April 18. Accessed December 30, 2017. https://wapo.st/2pwxvMa?tid=ss_mail&utm_term=.de357248609d.

Lieber, Robert J. 2014. "Politics Stops at the Water's Edge? Not Recently." *The Washington Post*. February 10. https://wapo.st/1f9hiix?tid=ss_mail&utm_term=.0b4a2669a2cf. Accessed June 6, 2015.

Lieberman, Robert C. 2002. "Ideas, Institutions, and Political Order: Explaining Political Change." *American Political Science Review* 96 (4): 697–712.

Lincoln, Abraham. 1858/1953. "Sixth Debate with Stephen A. Douglas, at Quincy, Illinois." In The *Collected Works of Abraham Lincoln*. Vol. 3, edited by Roy P. Basler. New Brunswick, NJ: Rutgers University Press, 245–283.

　　1859/1953. "Letter to Henry L. Pierce and Others." In The *Collected Works of Abraham Lincoln*. Vol. 3, edited by Roy P. Basler. New Brunswick, NJ: Rutgers University Press, 374–375.

Lippmann, Walter. 1932. *Interpretations, 1931–1932*. New York: The Macmillan Company.

　　1955. *Essays in the Public Philosophy*. Boston: Little Brown.

Lowi, Theodore. 1969. *The End of Liberalism: Ideology, Policy, and the Crisis of Public Authority*. New York: W. W. Norton & Company, Inc.

Madison, James. 1792. "A Candid State of the Parties." *National Gazette* 1 (95).

　　1817/2018. "Veto Message on the Internal Improvements Bill." Miller Center of Public Affairs. millercenter.org/the-presidency/presidential-speeches/march-3-1817-veto-message-internal-improvements-bill. Accessed December 31, 2018.

Mann, Thomas, and Norman Ornstein. 2012. *It's Even Worse than It Looks: How the American Constitutional System Collided with the New Politics of Extremism*. New York: Basic Books.

Mansfield, Harvey. 2006. "The Law and the President." *Weekly Standard* 11 (17).

Mason, Lilliana. 2018. *Uncivil Agreement: How Politics Became Our Identity*. Chicago: University of Chicago Press.

Mason, Matthew. 2002. "'Nothing Is Better Calculated to Excite Divisions': Federalist Agitation against Slave Representation during the War of 1812." *The New England Quarterly* 75 (4): 531–561.

Mayhew, David. 2002. *Electoral Realignments: A Critique of an American Genre.* New Haven, CT: Yale University Press.

2005. *Divided We Govern: Party Control, Lawmaking and Investigations, 1946–2002.* New Haven, CT: Yale University Press.

McCarty, Nolan, Keith Poole, and Howard Rosenthal. 2006. *Polarized America: The Dance of Ideology and Unequal Riches.* Cambridge, MA: MIT Press.

McCloskey, Robert. 1960/2016. *The American Supreme Court.* 6th edn, edited by Sanford Levinson. Chicago: University of Chicago Press.

2000. *The American Supreme Court.* 4th edn, edited by Sanford Levinson. Chicago: University of Chicago Press.

McPherson, Alan. 2014. "Herbert Hoover, Occupation Withdrawal, and the Good Neighbor Policy." *Presidential Studies Quarterly* 44 (4): 623–639.

Merriam, Charles. 1922. *The American Party System: An Introduction to the Study of Political Parties in the United States.* New York: Macmillan.

Mettler, Suzanne. 1996. "Review of Political Parties and the State: The American Historical Experience by Martin Shefter." *The Journal of Interdisciplinary History* 27 (2): 338–340.

Milkis, Sidney M. 1992. "Programmatic Liberalism and Party Politics: The New Deal Legacy and the Doctrine of Responsible Party Government." In *Challenges to Party Government*, edited by John Kenneth White and Jerome M. Mileur, 104–132. Carbondale: Southern Illinois University Press.

1993. *The President and the Parties.* New York: Oxford University Press.

2009. *Theodore Roosevelt, the Progressive Party, and the Transformation of American Democracy.* Lawrence, KS: Kansas University Press.

Milkis, Sidney M., and Michael Nelson. 2008. *The American Presidency: Origins and Development, 1776–2007.* 5th edn. Washington, DC: CQ Press.

Minicucci, Stephen. 2004. "Internal Improvements and the Union, 1790–1860." *Studies in American Political Development* 18 (2): 160–185.

Moe, Terry. 1985. "The Politicized Presidency." In *The New Direction in American Politics*, edited by John E. Chubb and Paul E. Peterson. Washington, DC: Brookings Institution Press.

2009. "The Revolution in Presidential Studies." *Presidential Studies Quarterly* 39 (4): 701–724.

Moe, Terry, and William Howell. 1999. "Unilateral Action and Presidential Power: A Theory." *Presidential Studies Quarterly* 29 (4): 850–873.

Morris, Gouverneur. 1801/1888. *The Diary and Letters of Gouverneur Morris.* Vol. 2, edited by Anne Cary Morris. New York: Charles Scribner's Sons.

Nagel, Stuart. 1965. "Court-Curbing Periods in American History." *Vanderbilt Law Review* 18: 925–44.

Nash, George. 2006. *The Conservative Intellectual Movement in America since 1945.* Wilmington, DE: ISI Books.

Nau, Henry. 2013. *Conservative Internationalism: Armed Diplomacy under Jefferson, Polk, Truman, and Reagan.* Princeton, NJ: Princeton University Press.

Neustadt, Richard E. 1960. *Presidential Power: The Politics of Leadership*. New York: Wiley.

New York Times. 1968. "Nixon Said to Bar Southerners' Bid: Shuns Pledge on Choosing Conservative for Ticket." *New York Times*, August 7: 30.

Nixon, Richard. 1968. "Address Accepting the Presidential Nomination at the Republican National Convention in Miami Beach, Florida." *The American Presidency Project*. Gerhard Peters and John T. Woolley. August 8. Accessed May 30, 2015. www.presidency.ucsb.edu/ws/?pid=25968.

Noel, Hans. 2013. *Political Ideologies and Political Parties in America*. New York: Cambridge University Press.

——— 2016. "Separating Ideology from Party in Roll Call Data." *hansnoel.com*. August 10. Accessed July 16, 2017. http://faculty.georgetown.edu/hcn4/Downloads/Noel_Rollcalls.pdf.

North, Douglass. 1981. *Structure and Change in Economic History*. New York: Norton.

Orren, Karen, and Stephen Skowronek. 2004. *The Search for American Political Development*. Cambridge: Cambridge University Press.

Ostrogorski, Moisey. 1902. *Democracy and the Organization of Political Parties*. London: Macmillan & Co.

Ostrom, Elinor. 1986. "An Agenda for the Study of Institutions." *Public Choice* 4 (1): 3–25.

Page, Benjamin I., and Marshall M. Bouton. 2006. *The Foreign Policy Disconnect: What Americans Want from Our Leaders but Don't Get*. Chicago: University of Chicago Press.

Peffley, Mark A., and Jon Hurwitz. 1985. "A Hierarchical Model of Attitude Constraint." *American Journal of Political Science* 29 (4): 871–890.

Pennoyer, Slvester. 1895. *American Law Review* 29: 550–558.

Perry, H. W., Jr., and L. A. Powe. 2004. "The Political Battle for the Constitution." *Constitutional Commentary* 21 (3): 641–696.

Pierson, Paul. 2004. *Politics in Time*. Princeton, NJ: Princeton University Press.

Pierson, Paul, and Theda Skocpol. 2007. *The Transformation of American Politics: Activist Government and the Rise of Conservatism*. Princeton, NJ: Princeton University Press.

Pomper, Gerald M. 1968. *Elections in America: Control and Influence in American Politics*. New York: Dodd, Mead and Company.

Poole, Keith, and Howard Rosenthal. 1997. *Congress: A Political-Economic History of Roll-Call Voting*. New York: Oxford University Press.

——— 2007. *Ideology and Congress*. New Brunswick, NJ: Transaction Publishers.

——— 2015. "Democrat and Republican Party Voting Splits Congresses 35–113." May 31. Accessed July 1, 2015. voteview.org/partycount.htm.

——— 2015. "The Polarization of Congressional Parties." March 21. Accessed June 27, 2015. voteview.org/political_polarization_2014.htm.

Popper, Karl. 1974/1992. *Unended Quest: An Intellectual Biography*. London: Routledge.

Powe, Lucas A. 2009. *The Supreme Court and the American Elite, 1789–2008*. Cambridge, MA: Harvard University Press.

Publius. 1787/2003. *The Federalist Papers*. New York: Signet Classic.

Reichley, James. 2000. *The Life of the Parties*. Lanham, MD: Rowman and Littlefield.

Reiter, Howard L., and Jeffrey Stonecash. 2011. *Counter Realignment: Political Change in the Northeastern United States*. New York: Cambridge University Press.

Remini, Robert. 1959. *Martin Van Buren and the Democratic Party*. New York: Columbia University Press.

1963. *The Election of Andrew Jackson*. Philadelphia: Lipincott.

1972. *The Age of Jackson*. Columbia: University of South Carolina Press.

Republican National Convention (RNC). 1856–2016. "National Political Party Platforms." *The American Presidency Project*. Edited by Gerhard Peters and John T. Woolley. Accessed January 24, 2019. https://www.presidency .ucsb.edu/documents/presidential-documents-archive-guidebook/national-political-party-platforms.

Risjord, Norma K. 1965. *The Old Republicans: Southern Conservatism in the Age of Jefferson*. New York: Columbia University Press.

Rodrik, Dani. 2014. "When Ideas Trump Interests." *Journal of Economic Perspectives* 28 (1): 189–208.

Rodrik, Dani, and Sharun W. Mukand. 2016. "Ideas versus Interests: A Unified Political Economy Framework." April 10. Accessed July 12, 2017. https:// drodrik.scholar.harvard.edu/files/dani-rodrik/files/ideasinterestsapri0sm_dr.pdf.

Roosevelt, Franklin D. 1928. "Our Foreign Policy: A Democratic View." *Foreign Affairs* 6 (4): 573–586.

1932a. "Address Accepting the Presidential Nomination at the Democratic National Convention in Chicago (July 2, 1932)." *The American Presidency Project*, edited by Gerhard Peters and John T. Woolley. Accessed December 22, 2017. www.presidency.ucsb.edu/ws/?pid=75174.

1932b. "Campaign Address on the Federal Budget at Pittsburgh, Pennsylvania (October 19, 1932)." *The American Presidency Project*, edited by John T. Wooley and Gerhard Peters. Accessed January 29, 2014. www.presidency .ucsb.edu/ws/?pid=88399.

1932c. "Radio Address from Albany, New York (April 7, 1932)." The American Presidency Project, edited by John T. Wooley and Gerhard Peters. Accessed February 1, 2018. www.presidency.ucsb.edu/ws/?pid=88408.

Roosevelt, Theodore. 1904a. "Fourth Annual Message (December 6, 1904)." *The American Presidency Project*, edited by Gerhard Peters and John T. Wooley. Accessed June 4, 2015. www.presidency.ucsb.edu/ws/?pid=29545.

1904b. "Letter to George Otto Trevelyan." In *The Letters of Theodore Roosevelt: The Square Deal, 1901–1903*, edited by Elting E. Morison. Cambridge, MA: Harvard University Press.

1907. "President a Guest: Makes a Rousing Speech at Commerce Banquet. Stands for Fast Vessels. Says American Merchant Flag Should Fly in South America. Mr. Roosevelt Enthuses Delegates to Trade Extension Convention with a Ringing Speech–Praises Secretary Root's Work for Nation–Says Monroe Doctrine Is in Interests of Peace and Big Navy Is Insurance Against War." *Washington Post*, January 17: 1.

1912. "Letter to Gifford Pinchot." *The Letters of Theodore Roosevelt*. Vol. 7, edited by Elting Elmore Morison. Cambridge, MA: Harvard University Press.

1913. *An Autobiography*. New York: Charles Scribner's Sons.

Salisbury, Robert. 1986. "The Republican Party and Positive Government, 1860–1890." *Mid-America: An Historical Review* 68: 15–34.

Sandel, Michael. 1996. *Democracy's Discontent: America in Search of a Public Philosophy*. Cambridge, MA: Harvard University Press.

Schattschneider, E. E. 1942. *Party Government*. New York: Rinehart & Co.

Schickler, Eric. 2013. "New Deal Liberalism and Racial Liberalism in the Mass Public, 1937–1968." *Perspectives on Politics* 11: 75–98.

Schlesinger, Arthur, Jr. 1945. *The Age of Jackson*. Boston: Little, Brown, and Co.

1995. "Back to the Womb? Isolationism's Renewed Threat." *Foreign Affairs* 74 (4): 2–8.

Segal, Jeffrey A., and Harold J. Spaeth. 1993. *The Supreme Court and the Attitudinal Model*. New York: Cambridge University Press.

Semple, Robert. 1968. "Humphrey Links Wallace to Fear." *New York Times*, October 2: 1, 27.

Shafer, Byron E. 1991. "The Notion of an Electoral Order: The Structure of Electoral Politics at the Accession of George Bush." In *The End of Realignment? Interpreting American Electoral Eras*, edited by Byron E. Shafer, 37–84. Madison: University of Wisconsin Press.

Sheingate, Adam. 2003. "Political Entrepreneurship, Institutional Change, and American Political Development." *Studies in American Political Development* 17 (2): 185–203.

Shepsle, Kenneth A., and Barry R. Weingast. 1981. "Structure-Induced Equilibrium and Legislative Choice." *Public Choice* 37 (3): 503–519.

Skocpol, Theda. 1992. *Protecting Soldiers and Mothers: The Political Origins of Social Policy in the United States*. Cambridge, MA: Harvard University Press.

Skocpol, Theda, and Vanessa Williamson. 2012. *The Tea Party and the Remaking of Republican Conservatism*. New York: Oxford University Press.

Skowronek, Stephen. 1997. *The Politics Presidents Make: Leadership from John Adams to Bill Clinton*. Cambridge, MA: Harvard University Press.

2009. "The Conservative Insurgency and Presidential Power: A Developmental Perspective." *Harvard Law Review* 122 (8): 2071–2103.

Smith, Al. 1936. "The Facts in the Case." American Liberty League Pamphlets. No. 97. Washington, DC: American Liberty League.

Smith, Rogers. 1993. "Beyond Tocqueville, Myrdal, and Hartz: The Multiple Traditions in America." *American Political Science Review* 87 (3): 549–566.

1995. "Ideas, Institutions, and Strategic Choice." *Polity* 28 (1): 135–140.

1997. *Civic Ideals*. New Haven, CT: Yale University Press.

Sollenberger, Mitchel A. 2014. "Presidential Studies, Behavioralism, and Public Law." *Presidential Studies Quarterly* 44 (4): 758–778.

Stathis, Stephen. 2014. *Landmark Legislation 1774–2012: Major U.S. Acts and Treaties*. Washington, DC: CQ Press.

Stephenson, Donald Grier. 1999. *Campaigns and the Court: The U.S. Supreme Court in Presidential Elections*. New York: Columbia University Press.

Stevenson, Adlai. 1952. "Text of Stevenson's Talk at Rochester." *New York Times*, October 25: 10.

Stonecash, Jeffrey. 2010. *New Directions in American Political Parties*. New York: Routledge.

Sundquist, James. 1973. *Dynamics of the American Party System*. Washington, DC: Brookings Institution.

Taft, William. 1895. "Criticisms of the Federal Judiciary." *The American Law Review* 29: 641–674.

Teles, Steven, and David Dagan. 2015. "The Social Construction of Policy Feedback: Incarceration, Conservatism, and Ideological Change." *Studies in American Political Development* 29 (2): 127–153.

Tocqueville, Alexis de. 1835/2000. *Democracy in America*. Edited by Harvey Mansfield and Delba Winthrop. Translated by Harvey Mansfield and Delba Winthrop. Vol. 1. 2 vols. Chicago: University of Chicago Press.

Treanor, William Michael. 2005. "Judicial Review before 'Marbury.'" *Stanford Law Review* 58 (2): 455–562.

Tulis, Jeffrey. 1987. *The Rhetorical Presidency*. Princeton, NJ: Princeton University Press.

Tullock, Gordon. 1981. "Why So Much Stability." *Public Choice* 37 (2): 189–205.

Turner, Frederick Jackson. 1911. "Social Forces in American History." *American Historical Review* 16 (2): 217–33.

Urofsky, Melvin. 2006. *Biographical Encyclopedia of the Supreme Court: The Lives and Legal Philosophies of the Justices*. Washington, DC: CQ Press.

Van Buren, Martin. 1822/1875. "Letter to Charles Dudley." In *Legacy of Historical Gleanings*. Vol. 1, edited by Catharina V. R. Bonney. 382. Albany, NY: J. Munsell.

Vandenberg, Arthur H. 1952. *The Private Papers of Senator Vandenberg*, edited by Arthur H. Vandenberg, Jr. Boston: Houghton Mifflin.

Volkens, Andrea, Pola Lehmann, Theres Matthieß, Nicolas Merz, Sven Regel, and Annika Werner. 2015. "The Manifesto Data Collection." *Manifesto Project (MRG/CMP/MARPOR)*. Berlin: Wissenschaftszentrum Berlin für Sozialforschung (WZB).

Waite, Morrison. 1876. "Munn v. State of Illinois, 84 U.S. 113 (1876)." *FindLaw*. October. Accessed November 17, 2018. http://laws.findlaw.com/us/94/113.html.

Ware, Alan. 2006. *The Democratic Party Heads North*. New York: Cambridge University Press.

Warren, Charles. 1922. *The Supreme Court in United States History*. Vol. 1. 3 vols. New York: Little, Brown, and Company.

　1922. *The Supreme Court in United States History*. Vol. 2. 3 vols. Boston: Little, Brown, and Company.

Webster, Daniel. 1836/1902. "To Mrs. Caroline Webster." In *The Letters of Daniel Webster*, edited by C. H. Van Tyne 198–199. New York: McClure, Phillips & Co.

Westin, Alan. 1953. "The Supreme Court, the Populist Movement, and the Campaign of 1896." *Journal of Politics* 15 (1): 3–41.

Whig National Convention. 1844. "Whig Party Platform of 1844." *The American Presidency Project*. Edited by Gerhard Peters and John T. Woolley. May 1. Accessed May 20, 2015. www.presidency.ucsb.edu/ws/index.php?pid=25852.

Whig National Convention. 1856. "Whig Party Platform of 1856." *The American Presidency Project*. Edited by Gerhard Peters and John T. Woolley. September 17. Accessed February 14, 2019. www.presidency.ucsb.edu/documents/whig-party-platform-1856.

Whittington, Keith E. 2007. *The Political Foundations of Judicial Supremacy: The Presidency, the Supreme Court, and Constitutional Leadership in U.S. History*. Princeton, NJ: Princeton University Press.

Wilentz, Sean. 2005. *The Rise of American Democracy: Jefferson to Lincoln*. New York: W. W. Norton & Company, Inc.

Williams, Samuel. 1794. *The Natural and Civil History of Vermont*. Walpole, New Hampshire: Isaiah Thomas and David Carlisle, Jun.

Wilson, Woodrow. 1879. "Cabinet Government in the United States." *International Review* 7: 146–163.

1885. *Congressional Government: A Study in American Politics*. Baltimore: Johns Hopkins University Press.

1901. *Congressional Government: A Study in American Politics*. 15th edn. Boston: Houghton, Mifflin and Company.

1913. "Address before the Southern Commercial Congress in Mobile, Alabama." *The American Presidency Project*, edited by Gerhard Peters and John T. Woolley. Accessed June 4, 2015. www.presidency.ucsb.edu/ws/?pid=65373.

Wolbrecht, Christina. 2000. *The Politics of Women's Rights: Parties, Positions, and Change*. Princeton, NJ: Princeton University Press.

Wood, Gordon S. 2009. *Empire of Liberty: A History of the Early Republic, 1789–1815*. New York: Oxford University Press.

Yarbrough, Jean. 2012. *Theodore Roosevelt and the American Political Tradition*. Lawrence: University Press of Kansas.

Index

CPSIA information can be obtained
at www.ICGtesting.com
Printed in the USA
LVHW091911260221
680050LV00004B/51